SRIMAD BHAGAVAD GITA

SRIMAD BHAGAVAD GITA

with
text in Sanskrit,
transliteration,
English translation
and brief introduction
to each chapter

by Swami Jyotirmayananda

Published by
Yoga Research Foundation

Printed by:
Yoga Research Foundation
6111 SW 74th Avenue
Miami, Florida 33143

ISBN 0-934664-44-7

Library of Congress Catalog Card Number 86-50858

Publisher's Note

There is no scripture in the world as profound, practical and lucid as the *Srimad Bhagavad Gita*. It is one of the most sacred religious works of the Hindus, and yet, it is not confined to the realm of the Hindu Faith alone. It is universal in its exposition of man's mystical movement towards God. Great men and women all over the world have derived immense inspiration from this great teaching.

Srimad Bhagavad Gita is a portion from the great epic work the *Mahabharata*, composed by Sage Vyasa many centuries before Christ. It contains the essence of the *Vedas* and the *Upanishads*. The term *Gita* means "Song." The teachings of the *Gita* are presented in most elegant Sanskrit verses which are recited and sung in melodious notes. Apart from its unique literary beauty, the *Gita* turns the confusion of the mind into a song of spiritual devotion; therefore it is befittingly called "The Song." The Hindus add reverential terms to glorify the *Gita*, thus calling it *"Srimad Bhagavad Gita,"* implying "The Song of the Supreme Divinity."

There are three basic texts of Vedanta philosophy: The *Upanishads*, the *Brahma-Sutras* (aphorisms of Vedanta), and the *Gita*. All great teachers of India commence their teachings by presenting their commentaries on these three great texts, of which the *Gita* is the crest-jewel. Over centuries there have been numerous traditional commentaries written on the *Gita* by great *Acharyas* and Sages of India. The *Gita* has thus become surrounded by a vast literature rich with spiritual insight and wisdom.

The *Gita* presents a dynamic picture of spiritual life. It does not advocate a passive withdrawal from the world in search of spiritual peace and perfection; rather it beckons the soul of a person to fight the battle of life heroically in order to attain victory in the form of Self-realization.

A great warrior of antiquity, Arjuna was confounded and confused in the midst of two contending armies. Divine Krishna, who was acting as his charioteer, gave his sublime teachings to the grief-stricken Arjuna. However, these teachings became universal in their implications. The very setting of the *Gita* presents a symbolic picture of life's incessant battle. The soul must face the contending forces of darkness and light, of virtue and vice, in the battlefield of life. Being guided by the intuitive vision represented by Divine Krishna, the soul is led to join the forces of light in order to destroy the forces of darkness and attain victory in the form of Self-realization.

Without a doubt, there is no book so inspiring, so elevating, so sublime and soul-stirring as the *Gita*. No matter what problem you confront, the *Gita* has a solution for you. This work is not just for advanced *Sanyasins* (monks) or for erudite scholars, but is for all sincere seekers after perfection, peace and bliss.

In this present edition, our revered Guru Sri Swami Jyotirmayananda has given a brief introduction to each chapter, and transliteration of each verse along with its English rendering. The style is simple and direct and yet profound in conveying the lofty wisdom contained in the teachings. This edition is specially made for those who would like to practise *Swadhyaya* (repeated study of the scripture); and even those who possess little or no knowledge of Sanskrit literature may learn to chant the verses in original Sanskrit and enjoy their sweetness and sublimity.

We express our deep appreciation to our Ashram staff members who have given their assistance in the publication of this magnificent work.

May the readers of this book, the *Srimad Bhagavad Gita*, receive the blessings of Bhagavan Krishna to overcome the multiple obstacles of life and reach the highest summit of perfection—the blessed Goal of Self-realization!

Swami Lalitananda.
August 1986

YOGA RESEARCH FOUNDATION

(Non-profit Organization)

President: Swami Jyotirmayananda
Vice-President: Swami Lalitananda

6111 SW 74th Avenue
Miami, Florida, 33143
(305) 666-2006

Aims and Objects

1. To spread the laws of spiritual life.

2. To promote understanding of the unity of life among all people, regardless of race, sect, creed and sex, and also to promote harmony among all religions by emphasizing the fundamental unity of all prophets, saints, sages and teachers.

3. To help suffering humanity by teaching the higher moral standards, prayers and meditation.

4. To give regular classes in the teachings of Yoga, Vedanta and Indian Philosophy.

5. To promote Universal Peace and Universal Love.

6. To promote the cultural growth of humanity on the basis of everlasting spiritual values of life.

7. To guide students and devotees all over the world.

8. To print and publish spiritual literature.

9. Anyone devoted to the ideals of truth, non-violence and purity can be a member of this Foundation.

मन्मनां भव मद्भक्तो मद्याजी मां नमस्कुरु ।
मामेवैष्यसि सत्यं ते प्रतिजाने प्रियोऽसि मे ॥

Fix your mind on Me, be devoted to Me, sacrifice to Me, offer adorations to Me; you will indeed attain Me—this I truly promise you, because you are my dearly beloved.

Gita XVIII-65

Gita Dhyanam

(Invocatory Meditaiton on the Gita)

ॐ पार्थाय प्रतिबोधितां भगवता नारायणेन स्वयं
व्यासेन ग्रथितां पुराण मुनिना मध्ये महाभारतम् ।
अद्वैतामृतवर्षिणीं भगवतीमष्टादशाध्यायिनी-
मंब त्वामनुसंदधामि भगवद्गीते भवद्वेषिणीम् ॥१॥

Om Paarthaaya pratibhodhitam bhagavataa naaraayanena swayam
Vyaasena grathitaam puraanamuninaa madhye mahaabhaaratam
Adwaitaamritavarshineem bhagavateem ashtaadashaadhyayineem
Amba twaamanusandadhaami bhagavadgeete bhavadweshineem.

1. Om. O Mother Bhagavad Gita, with which Partha (Arjuna) was illumined by Lord Narayana Himself and which was composed within the Mahabharata by the ancient Sage Vyasa, the showerer of the nectar of Non-duality, the destroyer of the world-process, consisting of eighteen chapters—upon Thee O Mother Bhagavad Gita! I meditate!

नमोऽस्तु ते व्यास विशालबुद्धे फुल्लारविंदायतपत्रनेत्र ।
येन त्वया भारततैलपूर्णः प्रज्वालितो ज्ञानमयः प्रदीपः ॥२॥

Namostute vyaasa vishaala buddhe phullaaravindaayatapatra netra.
Yena twayaa bhaaratatailapoornah prajwaalito jnaanamayah
pardeepah.

2. Salutations unto thee, O Vyasa of broad intellect, whose eyes are like the petals of full blown lotuses, by whom was lighted the lamp of wisdom, filled with the oil of the Mahabharata.

प्रपन्नपारिजाताय तोत्रवेत्रैकपाणये ।
ज्ञानमुद्राय कृष्णाय गीतामृतदुहे नमः ॥३॥

Prapanna paarijaataaya totravetraikapaanaye
Jnaanamudraaya krishnaaya geetaamritaduhe namah.

3. Salutations to Krishna, who is the Parijata or the Tree of fulfillment to all those who take refuge in Him, who holds the whip (symbol of power) in one hand and Jnanamudra (symbol of knowledge) on the other, who is the milker of the Gita Nectar.

सर्वोपनिषदो गावो दोग्धा गोपालनन्दन: ।
पार्थो वत्स: सुधीर्भोक्ता दुग्धं गीतामृतं महत् ॥४॥

Sarvopanishado gaavo dogdhaa gopalanandanah;
Paartho vatsah sudheerbhokta dugdham geetaamritam mahat.

4. All the Upanishads are the cows, while Krishna—the
cowherd boy is their milker. Arjuna is the calf, the men of
purified intellect are the drinkers of the milk, and the
milk is the great nectar of the Gita.

वसुदेवसुतं देवं कंसचाणूरमर्दनम् ।
देवकीपरमानन्दं कृष्णं वंदे जगद्गुरुम् ॥५॥

Vasudevasutam devam kamsachaanoormardanam;
Devakee paramaanandam krishnam vande jagadgurum.

5. I offer adorations to Lord Krishna, the preceptor of the
universe, the son of Vasudeva, the destroyer of Kamsa
and Chanura (the forces of darkness), the supreme bliss
of Devaki.

भीष्मद्रोणतटा जयद्रथजला गांधारनीलोत्पला
शल्यग्राहवती कृपेण वहनी कर्णेन वेलाकुला ।

अश्वत्थामविकर्णघोर मकरा दुर्योधनावर्तिनी
सोत्तीर्णा खलु पांडवैं रणनदी कैवर्तकः केशवः ॥६॥

Bheeshmadronatataa jayadrathajalaa gandhaareeneelotpalaa,
Shalyagraahavatee kripena vahanee karnena velaakulaa;
Ashwatthaama vikarnaghoramakaraa duryodhanaavartinee-
Sotteernaa khalu pandavairananadee kaivartakah keshavah.

6. With Lord Krishna as the ferry-man, indeed was crossed over by the Pandavas the battle-river whose banks were Bhishma and Drona, whose water was Jayadratha, whose blue-lotus was the King of Gandhara, whose shark was Shalya, whose current was Kripacharya, whose billow was Karna, whose terrible crocodiles were Ashwatthama and Vikarna, whose whirlpool was Duryodhana.

पाराशर्यवचः सरोजममलं गीतार्थगन्धोत्कटं
नानाख्यानककेसरं हरिकथा संबोधनाबोधितम् ।
लोके सज्जनषट्पदैरहरहः पेपीयमानं मुदा
भूयाद्भारतपंकजं कलिमलप्रध्वंसि नः श्रेयसे ॥७॥

Paaraasharyavachah sarojamamalam geetaarthagandhotkaram,
Naanaakhyaanakakesaram harikathaasambodhanaabodhitam;
Loke sajjanshatpadairaharahah pepeeyamaanam mudaa,
Bhooyaadbhaaratapankajam kalimalapradhwamsinah sreyase.

7. May this spotless lotus of the Mahabharata, born in the lake of the words of Sri Parashara's son (Sage Vyasa), sweet with the fragrance of the import of the Gita, with many narratives as its filaments, fully opened by the discourses on Hari, the destroyer of the sins of Kali Yuga and drunk joyously day after day by the bees of good and pure men, become the bestower of good to us!

मूकं करोति वाचालं पंगुं लंघयते गिरिम् ।
यत्कृपा तमहं वंदे परमानन्द माधवम् ॥८॥

Mookam karoti vaachaalam pangum langhayate girim;
Yatkripaa tamaham vande paramaanandamaadhavam.

8. I salute that Madhava (Krishna), the embodiment of Supreme Bliss, whose grace turns the mute eloquent, and makes the lame scale mountains.

यं ब्रह्मा वरुणेन्द्ररुद्रमरुतः स्तुन्वंति दिव्यैः स्तवै-
र्वेदैः सांगपदक्रमोपनिषदैर्गायंति यं सामगाः ।
ध्यानावस्थिततद्गतेन मनसा पश्यंति यं योगिनो
यस्यांतं न विदुःसुरासुरगणा देवाय तस्मै नमः ॥९॥

Yam brahmaavarunendrarudramarutah stunwanti divyaih stavair,
Vedaih sangpadakramopanishadaih gaayanti yam saamagaah;
Dhyaanaavasthitatadgatenamanasaa pashyanti yam yogino,
Yasyaantam na viduh suraasuraganaah devaaya tasmai namah.

9. Adorations to that God whom Brahma, Varuna, Indra, Rudra and the Maruts praise with divine hymns, whom the singers of the Sama hymns invoke by the Vedas and their branches, in the Pada and Krama methods, and by the Upanishads, whom the Yogis behold with their minds absorbed in Him through meditation, and whose limit the hosts of Devas and Asuras know not!

श्रीमद्भगवद्गीता

SRIMAD BHAGAVAD GITA

अथ प्रथमोऽध्यायः

Atha Prathamo'dhyaayah

Chapter 1

Arjun Vishad Yogah

The Yoga of the Despondency of Arjuna

The ancient battle of the virtuous Pandavas and their evil-minded cousins, the Kauravas have become symbolic of the battle between the forces of light (virtue) and the forces of darkness (vice). It is the battle that is being fought constantly in the mind of every individual.

The intention of the first chapter is to show that grief and confusion are the results of ignorance which gives rise to egoism, attachment, likes and dislikes, and manifold impurities of the mind. The teachings of Lord Krishna are meant to lead the soul to the state of spiritual victory—God-realization, where sorrow is terminated forever.

धृतराष्ट्र उवाच

धर्मक्षेत्रे कुरुक्षेत्रे समवेता युयुत्सवः ।
मामकाः पाण्डवाश्चैव किमकुर्वत संजय ॥१॥

Dhritaraashtra uvaacha
Dharmakshetre kurukshetre samavetaa yuyutsavah;
Maamakaah paandavaaschaiva kim akurvata sanjaya.

1. Dhritarashtra asked: O Sanjaya, what did my sons and the sons of (my brother) Pandu (the Pandavas) do, assembled in the holy place of Kurukshetra, eager to fight?

संजय उवाच

दृष्ट्वा तु पाण्डवानीकं व्यूढं दुर्योधनस्तदा ।
आचार्यमुपसङ्गम्य राजा वचनमब्रवीत् ॥२॥

Sanjaya uvaacha
Drishtwaa tu paandavaaneekam vyudham duryodhanastadaa;
Aachaaryam upasamgamya raajaaa vachanam abraveet.

2. Sanjaya said: Then, seeing the army of the Pandavas arrayed in battle formations, King Duryodhana approached his teacher Dronacharya, and spoke thus:

पश्यैतां पाण्डुपुत्राणामाचार्य महतीं चमूम् ।
व्यूढां द्रुपदपुत्रेण तव शिष्येण धीमता ॥३॥

Pasyaitaam paanduputraanaam aachaarya mahateem chamoom;
Vyudhaam drupadaputrena tava sishyena dheemataa.

3. Behold, O Teacher, the mighty army of the Pandavas arrayed for battle under the command of the son of Drupada (Dhrishtadyumna), your wise disciple.

अत्र शूरा महेष्वासा भीमार्जुनसमा युधि ।
युयुधानो विराटश्च द्रुपदश्च महारथः ॥४॥

Atra sooraa maheshwaasaa bheemaarjuna samaa yudhi;
Yuyudhano viraatascha drupadascha mahaarthah.

4. In this army there have gathered great chariot-warriors who hold mighty bows, such as Bhima and Arjuna; those mighty heroes, the great chariot-warrior Satyaki, the powerful King Virata, and the heroic Drupada.

धृष्टकेतुश्चेकितानः काशिराजश्च वीर्यवान् ।
पुरुजित्कुन्तिभोजश्च शैब्यश्च नरपुङ्गवः ॥५॥

Drishtaketus chekitaanah kaasiraajascha veeryavaan;
Purujit kunti-bhojascha saibhascha narapungavah.

5. There are those great heroes, the valiant Dhrishtaketu, Chekitan and Kashiraj, as well as those best among men, Purujit, Kuntibhoja and Shaivya.

युधामन्युश्च विक्रान्त उत्तमौजाश्च वीर्यवान् ।
सौभद्रो द्रौपदेयाश्च सर्व एव महारथाः ॥६॥

Yudhaamanyuscha vikraanta uttamaujaaschaveeryavaan;
Soubhadro draupadeyaascha sarva eva mahaarathaah.

6. The powerful hero Yudhamanyu, the valiant Uttamauja, as well as the son of Subhadra (Abhimanyu), and sons of Draupadi—all these are great Maharathas (chariot-drivers).

अस्माकं तु विशिष्टा ये तान्निबोध द्विजोत्तम ।
नायका मम सैन्यस्य संज्ञार्थं तान्ब्रवीमि ते ॥७॥

Asmaakam tu visishtaa ye taan nibodha dwijjottama;
Naayakaah mama sainyasya samjnaartham taan braveemi te.

7. O best among the Brahmins, now I will introduce you
to the highly qualified leaders of our army, for your
information, so that you may know them well.

भवान्भीष्मश्च कर्णश्च कृपश्च समितिंजयः ।
अश्वत्थामा विकर्णश्च सौमदत्तिस्तथैव च ॥८॥

Bhavaan bheeshmascha karnascha kripascha samitinjayah;
Aswaththaamaa vikarnascha saumadattis tathaiva cha.

8. You (Dronacharya), Bhishma, and the victorious Kripa
are the best of the heroes, as well as Ashwatthama,
Vikarna, Saumadatti, who are the valiant chiefs of (our)
army.

अन्ये च बहवः शूरा मदर्थे त्यक्तजीविताः ।
नानाशस्त्रप्रहरणाः सर्वे युद्धविशारदाः ॥९॥

Anye cha bahavah sooraa madarthe tyaktajeevitaah;
Naanaasastrapraharanaah sarve yuddhavisaaradaah.

9. In addition to this, there are many heroes in the army who are ready to give up their lives for my sake. They are endowed with numerous weapons and are well skilled in the art of fighting.

अपर्याप्तं तदस्माकं बलं भीष्माभिरक्षितम् ।
पर्याप्तं त्विदमेतेषां बलं भीमाभिरक्षितम् ॥१०॥

Aparyaaptam tad asmaakam balam bheeshmabhirakshitam;
Paryaaptam twidam etesham balam bheemaabhirakshitam.

10. Protected by Bhishma our army is boundless, while under the protection of Bhima the army of the Pandavas is indeed limited.

अयनेषु च सर्वेषु यथाभागमवस्थिताः ।
भीष्ममेवाभिरक्षन्तु भवन्तः सर्व एव हि ॥११॥

Ayaneshu cha sarveshu yathaabhaagam avasthitaah;
Bheeshmam evaabhirakshantu bhavantah sarva eva hi.

11. May you and all others protect Bhishma from all sides by remaining stationed in the proper places according to the divisions of the army.

तस्य संजनयन्हर्षं कुरुवृद्ध: पितामह: ।
सिंहनादं विनद्योच्चै: शङ्खं दध्मौ प्रतापवान्।१२।

Tasya sanjanayan harsham kuruvriddhah pitaamahah;
Simhanaadam vinadyocchaih sankham dadhmau prataapavaan.

12. Then the oldest among the Kauravas, Grandfather Bhishma, roared like a lion and blew his conch, augmenting joy in the heart of Duryodhana.

तत: शङ्खाश्च भेर्यश्च पणवानकगोमुखा: ।
सहसैवाभ्यहन्यन्त स शब्दस्तुमुलोऽभवत् ॥

Tatah sankhaascha bheryascha panavaanakagomukhaah;
Sahasaivabhyahanyanta sa sabdastumulo'bhavat.

13. Then there sounded conches, kettledrums, tabors, drums and cow-horns, and a great tumult was caused all of a sudden by the blaring forth of all these sounds.

ततः श्वेतैर्हयैर्युक्ते महति स्यन्दने स्थितौ ।
माधवः पाण्डवश्चैव दिव्यौ शङ्खौ प्रदध्मतुः ॥

Tatah svetair hayair yukte mahati syandane sthitau;
Maadhavah paandavaschaiva divyau sankhau pradadhmatuh.

14. This was followed by Sri Krishna and Arjuna who blew their divine conches while seated in a mighty chariot to which white horses were yoked.

पाञ्चजन्यं हृषीकेशो देवदत्तं धनंजयः ।
पौण्ड्रं दध्मौ महाशङ्खं भीमकर्मा वृकोदरः ॥

Paanchajanyam hrishikeso devadattam dhananjayah;
Paundramdadhmau mahaasankham bheemakarmaa vrikodharah.

15. Hrishikesha (Lord Krishna) blew his conch known as Panchajanya, and the conqueror of wealth, Arjuna, blew his called Devadatta. The doer of terrible deeds, the valiant Bhima, who had the belly of a wolf, blew his conch, Paundram.

अनन्तविजयं राजा कुन्तीपुत्रो युधिष्ठिरः ।
नकुलः सहदेवश्च सुघोषमणिपुष्पकौ ॥१६॥

Anantavijayam raajaa kuntee-putro yudhishthirah;
Nakulah sahadevascha sughoshamanipushpakau.

16. The son of Kunti, King Yudhishthira, blew his conch called Ananta Vijaya, and Nakula and Sahadeva blew their conches known as Sughosha and Manipushpaka respectively.

काश्यश्च परमेष्वास: शिखण्डी च महारथ: ।
धृष्टद्युम्नो विराटश्च सात्यकिश्चापराजित: ॥

Kaasyascha parameshwasah sikhandee cha mahaarathah;
Drishtadyumno viraatascha saatyakischaaparaajitah.

17. The great archer Kashi Raja, the great chariot-warrior Shikhandi, and other valiant warriors such as Dhristadyumna, Virata and the unvanquishable Satyaki (blew their conches).

द्रुपदो द्रौपदेयाश्च सर्वश: पृथिवीपते ।
सौभद्रश्च महाबाहु: शङ्खान्दध्मु: पृथक्पृथक् ॥

Drupado draupadeyaascha saravasah prithiveepate;
Saubhadrascha mahaabaahuh sankhaan dadhmuh prithakprithak.

18. Drupada and the sons of Draupadi, as well as the great armed Abhimanyu, all blew their conches, O Lord of Earth.

स घोषो धार्तराष्ट्राणां हृदयानि व्यदारयत् ।
नभश्च पृथिवीं चैव तुमुलो व्यनुनादयन् ।।१९।।

Sa ghosho dhaartaraashtraanaam hridayaani vyadaarayat
Nabhascha prithiveem chaiva tumulo vyanunaadayan.

19. The terrible noise reverberating in the sky and the earth rent, as it were, the hearts of the sons of Dhritarashtra.

अथ व्यवस्थितान्दृष्ट्वा धार्तराष्ट्रान् कपिध्वजः ।
प्रवृत्ते शस्त्रसंपाते धनुरुद्यम्य पाण्डवः ।।२०।।

Atha vyavasthithaan drishtwaa dhaartharaashtraan kapidhwajah;
Pravritte sastrasampaate dhanur udyamya paandavah.

20. Then, O King, seeing the sons of Dhritarashtra well marshalled and ready to discharge their weapons, Arjuna, whose ensign was the monkey, Hanuman, raised his bow, and said to Krishna:

हृषीकेशं तदा वाक्यमिदमाह महीपते ।
अर्जुन उवाच
सेनयोरुभयोर्मध्ये रथं स्थापय मेऽच्युत ।२१।

Hrisheekesam tadaa vaakyamidamaaha maheepate;
Arjuna uvaacha
Senyor ubhayormadhye ratham sthaapaya me Achyuta.

21. Arjuna said: O Immutable Krishna, do drive my chariot and place it between the two armies,

यावदेतान्निरीक्षेऽहं योद्धुकामानवस्थितान् ।
कैर्मया सह योद्धव्यमस्मिन्रणसमुद्यमे ॥२२॥

Yaavad etaan nireeksheham yoddhukaamaan avasthitaan,
Kair mayaa saha yodhavyam asmin ranasamudyame.

22. So that I can behold these warriors who stand here ready for battle, and thus, determine with whom I should fight at the commencement of the battle.

योत्स्यमानानवेक्षेऽहं य एतेऽत्र समागताः ।
धार्तराष्ट्रस्य दुर्बुद्धेर्युद्धे प्रियचिकीर्षवः ॥२३॥

Yotsyamaanaan avekshe'ham ya ete'tra samaagataah;
Dhataraashtrasya durbuddher yuddhe priyachikeershavah.

23. For, I desire to observe those heroes who have assembled here and who are eager to please the evil-minded sons of Dhritarashtra in this battle.

संजय उवाच
एवमुक्तो हृषीकेशो गुडाकेशेन भारत ।
सेनयोरुभयोर्मध्ये स्थापयित्वा रथोत्तमम् ॥

Sanjaya uvaacha
Evamukto hrishikeso gudaakesena bharata;
Senayor ubhayormadhye sthaapayitwa rathottamam.

24. Sanjaya continued: O Bharata (Dhritarashtra), having been thus addressed by Arjuna, known as the conqueror of sleep, Lord Krishna stationed the best of the chariots in between the two armies.

भीष्मद्रोणप्रमुखतः सर्वेषां च महीक्षिताम् ।
उवाच पार्थ पश्यैतान्समवेतान्कुरूनिति ॥२५॥

Bheeshmadronapramukhatah sarveshaam cha maheekshitaam;
Uvaacha paartha pasyaitaan samavetaan kuroon iti.

25. Then facing Bhishma and Drona, and all the rulers of the earth, Sri Krishna spoke: O Son of Kunti (Arjuna), behold these Kurus, the army of Duryodhana, gathered together before us.

तत्रापश्यत्स्थितान्पार्थः पितॄनथ पितामहान् ।
आचार्यान्मातुलान्भ्रातॄन्पुत्रान्पौत्रान्सखींस्तथा ।

Tatraapasyat sthitaan paarthah pitrin atha pitaamahaan;
Aachaaryaan maatulaan bhraatreen putraan pautraan sakhimstatha.

26. Then Partha (Arjuna) beheld in both armies that were stationed to fight his grandfathers, uncles, cousins, teachers, maternal uncles, brothers, sons, grandsons,

श्वशुरान्सुहृदश्चैव   सेनयोरुभयोरपि ।
तान्समीक्ष्य स कौन्तेयः सर्वान्बन्धूनवस्थितान्

Svasuraan suhridaschaiva senayor ubhayor api;
Taan sameekshya sa kaunteyah sarvaan bandhoon avasthitaan.

27. And fathers-in-law, and friends; then seeing all his dear relatives prepared to fight, Arjuna, the son of Kunti,

कृपया परयाविष्टो विषीदन्निदमब्रवीत् ।
अर्जुन उवाच
दृष्ट्वेमं स्वजनं कृष्ण युयुत्सुं समुपस्थितम् ।।२८।।

Kripayaa parayaavishto visheedannidam abraveet;
Arjuna uvaacha
Drishtwemam swajanam krishna yuyutsum samupasthitaam.

28. Spoke sorrowfully with his head overwhelmed with pity: Now that I see my dear relatives stationed in the battlefield eager to fight, O Krishna,

सीदन्ति मम गात्राणि मुखं च परिशुष्यति ।
वेपथुश्च शरीरे मे रोमहर्षश्च जायते ।।२९।।

Seedanti mama gaatraani mukham cha parisushyati;
Vepathuscha shareere me romaharshascha jaayate.

29. I experience pain in every limb of my body. My mouth feels dry, my body is trembling, and the hairs of my body stand on their end.

गाण्डीवं स्रंसते हस्तात्त्वक्चैव परिदह्यते ।
न च शक्नोम्यवस्थातुं भ्रमतीव च मे मनः ।।

Gaandeeva sramsate hastaat twak chaiva paridahyate;
Na cha saknomyavasthaatum bhramateeva cha me manah.

30. The mighty bow Gandiva is falling from my hands, and there is an immense burning sensation all over my body. I cannot keep my body steady; my mind is wandering.

निमित्तानि च पश्यामि विपरीतानि केशव ।
न च श्रेयोऽनुपश्यामि हत्वा स्वजनमाहवे ॥

Nimittaani cha pasyaami vipareetaani kesava;
Na cha sreyo'nupasyaami hatwaa swajanam aahave.

31. I see inauspicious omens foreboding adverse developments, O Keshava (krishna). I do not see any good in destroying my own kinsmen.

न काङ्क्षे विजयं कृष्ण न च राज्यं सुखानि च ।
किं नो राज्येन गोविन्द किं भोगैर्जीवितेन वा

Na kangkshe vijayam krishna na cha raajyam sukhaani cha;
Kim no raajyena govinda kim bhogair jeevitena vaa.

32. O Krishna, I do not desire victory, nor do I wish for kingdom and prosperity. O Govinda, what have I to do with kingdom? What have I to gain from the pleasures of the senses or from life itself?

येषामर्थे काङ्क्षितं नो राज्यं भोगाः सुखानि च ।
त इमेऽवस्थिता युद्धे प्राणांस्त्यक्त्वा धनानि च

Yeshaam arthe kaangkshitam no raajyam bhogaah sukhaani cha;
Ta ime avasthitaa yuddhe praanaamstyaktwaa dhanaani cha.

33. People for whom I would have desired to gain kingdom, enjoyments and prosperity, are here assembled having given up their concern for their life and wealth.

आचार्याः पितरः पुत्रास्तथैव च पितामहाः ।
मातुलाःश्वशुराःपौत्राःश्यालाःसम्बन्धिनस्तथा॥

Aachaaryah pitarah putraasthaiva cha pitaamahaah;
Matulaah swasuraah pautraah syaalaah sambandhinas tathaa.

34. Teachers, fathers, sons, grandfathers, maternal uncles, fathers-in-law, grandsons, brothers-in-law and other relatives (are prepared to give up their lives).

एतान्न हन्तुमिच्छामि घ्नतोऽपि मधुसूदन ।
अपि त्रैलोक्यराज्यस्य हेतोः किं नु महीकृते ॥

Etaan na hantum icchaami ghnato'pi madhusoodhana;
Api trailokyaraajyasya hetoh kim nu maheekrite.

35. O Madhusudana (destroyer of the demon Madhu), even if they kill me, I do not want to kill them even if I were to gain control over the three worlds by doing so, what to speak of gaining this little earth.

निहत्य धार्तराष्ट्रान्नः का प्रीतिः स्याज्जनार्दन ।
पापमेवाश्रयेदस्मान्हत्वैतानाततायिनः ॥३६॥

Nihatya dhaartaraashtraan nah preetih syaaj janaardana;
Paapam evaa srayed asmaan hatwaitaan aatataayinah.

36. O Janardana (destroyer of the demon Jana), what joy could it give me to kill the sons of Dhritarashtra? Sin alone will be on our hands for killing these felons.

तस्मान्नार्हा वयं हन्तुं धार्तराष्ट्रान्स्वबान्धवान् ।
स्वजनं हि कथं हत्वा सुखिनः स्याम माधव ॥

Tasman naarhaa vayam hantum dhaartraashtraan swabaandhavaan;
Swajanam hi katham hatwaa sukhinah syaama maadhava.

37. Therefore, it is not proper for us to destroy the sons of Dhritarashtra, because, O Madhava, how can we become happy by killing our kinsmen?

यद्यप्येते न पश्यन्ति लोभोपहतचेतसः ।
कुलक्षयकृतं दोषं मित्रद्रोहे च पातकम् ॥३८॥

Yadyapyete na pasyanti lobhopahatachetasah;
Kulakshayakritam dosham mitradrohe cha paatakam.

38. Their minds are overcome by greed, and they do not see the defects that arise due to the destructions of families, nor do they see the sin of developing animosity towards friends.

कथं न ज्ञेयमस्माभिः पापादस्मान्निवर्तितुम् ।
कुलक्षयकृतं दोषं प्रपश्यद्भिर्जनार्दन ॥३९॥

Katham na jneyam asmaabhih paapaad asmaan nivartitum;
Kulakshayakritam dosham prapasyadbhir janaardana.

39. Why shouldn't we who know the defects that arise out of the destruction of families, refrain from this sin (of fighting and killing our kinsmen), O Janardana?

कुलक्षये प्रणश्यन्ति कुलधर्माः सनातनाः ।
धर्मे नष्टे कुलं कृत्स्नमधर्मोऽभिभवत्युत ॥४०॥

Kulakshaye pranasyanti kuladharmaah sanaatanaah;
Dharme nashte kulam kritsnam adharm o'bhibhavatyuta.

40. By the destruction of families, the immemorial religious rites of those families are destroyed. With the destruction of religious rites, the entire family is overcome by unrighteousness.

अधर्माभिभवात्कृष्ण प्रदुष्यन्ति कुलस्त्रियः ।
स्त्रीषु दुष्टासु वार्ष्णेय जायते वर्णसंकरः ॥४१॥

Adharmaabhibhavaat krishna pradushyanti kulastriyah;
Streeshu dushtaasu vaarshneya jaayate varnasankarah.

41. O Krishna, when the family is overcome by unrighteousness, the women of the family become impure, and this leads to intermingling of castes (confusion of castes).

संकरो नरकायैव कुलघ्नानां कुलस्य च ।
पतन्ति पितरो ह्येषां लुप्तपिण्डोदकक्रियाः ॥

Sankaro narakaayaiva kulaghnaanaam kulasya cha;
Patanti pitaro hyeshaam luptapindodakakriyaah.

42. The destroyers of family who cause confusion of castes go to hell, and because the offering of Pinda (rice-ball) and water (meant for libations) are not given to the departed souls, their forefathers fall (from heavenly realms).

दोषैरेतैः कुलघ्नानां वर्णसंकरकारकैः ।
उत्साद्यन्ते जातिधर्माः कुलधर्माश्च शाश्वताः ॥

Doshair etaih kulaghnaanaam varnasankarakaarakaih;
Utsaadyante jaatidharmaah kuladharmaascha saaswataah.

43. By the sinful deeds of these destroyers of family who cause confusion of castes, the eternal religious rites of the family as well as the castes themselves are destroyed.

उत्सन्नकुलधर्माणां मनुष्याणां जनार्दन ।
नरकेऽनियतं वासो भवतीत्यनुशुश्रुम ॥४४॥

Utsanna kuladharmaanaam manushyaanaam janaardna;
Narake niyatam vaaso bhavateetyanususruma.

44. Those persons, O Janardana, whose religious rites pertaining to caste and family are destroyed, abide in hell for an undeterminable period, thus we have heard.

अहो बत महत्पापं कर्तुं व्यवसिता वयम् ।
यद्राज्यसुखलोभेन हन्तुं स्वजनमुद्यताः ।४५।

Aho bata mahat paapam kartum vyavasitaa vayam;
Yadraajya sukha lobhena hantum swajanam udyataah.

45. Alas, it is extremely regretable that for the greed of kingdom we are ready to destroy our dear relatives. We are bent upon performing a very sinful deed.

यदि मामप्रतीकारमशस्त्रं शस्त्रपाणयः ।
धार्तराष्ट्रा रणे हन्युस्तन्मे क्षेमतरं भवेत् ।४६।

Yadi maam aprateekaaram asastram sastrapaanayah;
Dhaartaraashtraa rane hanyus taanme kshemataram bhavet.

46. If the sons of Dhritarashtra who now hold weapons in their hands kill me while I do not resist them, this will be relatively better than my killing them.

संजय उवाच

एवमुक्त्वार्जुनः संख्ये रथोपस्थ उपाविशत् ।

विसृज्य सशरं चापं शोकसंविग्नमानसः ॥४७॥

Sanjaya uvaacha
Evamuktwaarjunah sankhye rathopastha upaavishat;
Visrijya sasaram chaapam sokasamvignamaanasah.

47. Sanjaya continued: Having spoken thus in the battlefield, Arjuna dropped his bow and arrow, and sat down in the chariot with his mind agitated by sorrow.

ॐ तत्सदिति श्रीमद्भगवद्गीतासूपनिषत्सु ब्रह्मविद्यायां

योगशास्त्रे श्रीकृष्णार्जुनसंवादेऽर्जुनविषाद-

योगो नाम प्रथमोऽध्यायः ॥ १ ॥

Om tat sat iti srimad bhagavad gitaasoopanishatsu
brahmavidyaayaam yogashaastre sri krishnaarjunasamvaade
arjunavishaadayogo naama prathamo'dhyaayah.

Om Tat Sat.
Thus, in the Upanishad of the Bhagavad Gita,
the knowledge of Supreme Brahman, the scripture of Yoga,
the dialogue between Sri Krishna and Arjuna,
ends the first chapter entitled,
"The Yoga of the Despondency of Arjuna."

क्लैब्यं मा स्म गमः पार्थ नैतत्त्वय्युपपद्यते ।
क्षुद्रं हृदयदौर्बल्यं त्यक्त्वोत्तिष्ठ परंतप ॥३॥

अथ द्वितीयोऽध्यायः

Atha Dwitiyo'dhyaayah

Chapter 2

Samkhya Yogah

The Yoga of Integral Knowledge

In this chapter Lord Krishna outlines Integral Yoga—the art of blending knowledge, devotion, meditation and action—in order to remove the cause of all misery in life. The highest goal is the attainment of Sthita Prajna or a steady intellect arising out of God-realization. A perfected Yogi is one who is skilled in selfless action, spontaneous in devotion, adept in meditation and lofty in wisdom.

संजय उवाच

तं तथा कृपयाविष्टमश्रुपूर्णाकुलेक्षणम् ।
विषीदन्तमिदं वाक्यमुवाच मधुसूदनः ॥ १ ॥

Sanjaya uvaacha
Tam tatha kripayaavishtam asrupoornaakulekshanam;
Visheedantam idam vaakyam uvaacha madhusoodanah.

1. Sanjaya said: To the sorrowing Arjuna, whose eyes were brimming with tears, and whose heart was laden with a sense of pity and grief, Sri Madhusudana (Lord Krishna) spoke thus:

श्रीभगवानुवाच

कुतस्त्वा कश्मलमिदं विषमे समुपस्थितम् ।
अनार्यजुष्टमस्वर्ग्यमकीर्तिकरमर्जुन   ॥२॥

Sree Bhagavaan uvaacha
Kutastwa kasmalam idam vishame samupasthitam;
Anaaryajushtam aswargyam akeertikaram arjuna.

2. Sri Bhagavan said: Whence, O Arjuna, have you developed this dejection during this crisis? This is unworthy of a Noble Hero, heaven-excluding, and disgraceful!

क्लैब्यं मा स्म गमः पार्थ नैतत्त्वय्युपपद्यते ।
क्षुद्रं हृदयदौर्बल्यं त्यक्त्वोत्तिष्ठ परंतप ॥३॥

Klaibyam ma sma gamah paartha naitat twayyupapadyate;
Kshudram hridaya daurbalyam tyaktwottishtha paramtapa.

3. O Son of Pritha, do not yield to unmanliness. This is not befitting for you. O scorcher of foes, give up this faintheartedness; stand up and fight.

अर्जुन उवाच

कथं भीष्ममहं संख्ये द्रोणं च मधुसूदन ।

इषुभिः प्रति योत्स्यामि पूजाहार्विरिसूदन ।।४।।

Arjuna uvaacha
Katham bheeshmam aham sankhye dronam cha madhusoodana;
Ishubhih pratiyotsyaami poojaarhaavarisoodana.

4. Arjuna said: O Madhusudana, how shall I fight (my grandfather) Bhishma and (my preceptor) Dronacharya on the battlefield with sharp arrows? O destroyer of dark forces, they are worthy of worship.

गुरूनहत्वा हि महानुभावान्
श्रेयो भोक्तुं भैक्ष्यमपीह लोके ।
हत्वार्थकामांस्तु   गुरूनिहैव
भुञ्जीय भोगान्रुधिरप्रदिग्धान् ।।

Guroon ahatwa hi mahaanubhaavaan
Sreyo bhoktum bhaikshyam apeeha loke;
Hatwaarthakaamaamstu guroon ihaiva
Bhunjeeya bhogaan rudhirapradigdhaan.

5. It is better to live on alms in this world than to slay these most reverential elders. If I kill these glorious men, all my enjoyments in this world will be stained with blood.

न चैतद्विद्मः कतरन्नो गरीयो
　　यद्वा जयेम यदि वा नो जयेयुः ।
यानेव हत्वा न जिजीविषाम-
　　स्तेऽवस्थिताः प्रमुखे धार्तराष्ट्राः ॥

Na chaitad vidmah kataran no gareeyo
Yadwaa jayema yadi vaa no jayeyuh.
Yaaneva hatwaa na jijeevishaamas
Te'vasthitaah pramukhe dhaartarashtraah.

6. I do not know which is better—to live on alms or to fight. Further, I do not know for certain who will win in this battle. These men on the side of Dhritarashtra stand arrayed before us; after killing them, we would not even wish to live.

कार्पण्यदोषोपहतस्वभावः
पृच्छामि त्वां धर्मसंमूढचेताः ।
यच्छ्रेयः स्यान्निश्चितं ब्रूहि तन्मे
शिष्यस्तेऽहं शाधि मां त्वां प्रपन्नम् ॥७॥

Kaarpanyadoshopahataswabhaavah
Pricchaami twaam dharmasammoodha chetaah;
Yacchreyah syaan nischitam broohi tanme
Sishyaste'ham saadhi maam twaam prapannam.

7. My very being is afflicted with the talent of sentimental
pity, and my intellect is confused as to my duty. I ask You,
tell me decisively what is good for me. I am Your disciple.
I have taken refuge in you. Please do instruct me.

न हि प्रपश्यामि ममापनुद्याद्-
यच्छोकमुच्छोषणमिन्द्रियाणाम् ।
अवाप्य   भूमावसपत्नमृद्धं
राज्यं सुराणामपि चाधिपत्यम् ॥८॥

Na hi prapasyaami mamaapanudyaad
Yacchokam ucchoshanam indriyaanaam;
Avaapya bhoomaavasapatnam riddham
Raajyam suraanaam api chaadhipatyam.

8. Even if I were to attain undisputed sovereignty over the whole world and conquer even the gods, I do not see how I could remedy this grief that is consuming my senses.

संजय उवाच

एवमुक्त्वा हृषीकेशं गुडाकेश: परंतप ।
न योत्स्य इति गोविन्दमुक्त्वा तूष्णीं बभूव ह

Sanjaya uvaacha
Evam uktwaa hrisheekesam gudaakesah parantapah;
Na yotsya iti govindam uktwaa tooshneem babhoova ha.

9. Sanjaya said: O King, having thus spoken to Bhagavan Hrishikesha, Arjuna, known by the names of Gudakesha and Parantapa, concluded, "O Govinda, I will not fight," and became silent.

तमुवाच हृषीकेश: प्रहसन्निव भारत ।
सेनयोरुभयोर्मध्ये विषीदन्तमिदं वच: ॥१०॥

Tam uvaacha hrisheekesah prahasanniva bhaarata;
Senayor ubhayor madhye visheedantam idam vachah.

10. O King, as if smiling at him there between the two
armies, Lord Krishna spoke to Arjuna who was overcome
by grief.

श्रीभगवानुवाच

अशोच्यानन्वशोचस्त्वं प्रज्ञावादांश्च भाषसे।

गतासूनगतासूंश्च नानुशोचन्ति पण्डिताः ।११।

Sree Bhagavaan uvaacha
Asochyaan anvasochastwam prajnavaadaamscha bhaashase;
Gataasoon agataasoomscha naanusochanti panditaah.

11. The Blessed Lord said: You are grieving over those
who are not fit to be grieved for, yet you speak words like
a great man of wisdom. But the wise do not grieve neither
over the living nor over the dead.

न त्वेवाहं जातु नासं न त्वं नेमे जनाधिपाः।

न चैव न भविष्यामः सर्वे वयमतः परम् ।१२।

Na twevaaham jaatu naasam na twam neme janaadhipaah;
Nachaiva na bhavishyaamah sarve vayam atah param.

12. Never did I not exist, nor did you nor these kings. Nor shall we ever cease to exist in the future.

देहिनोऽस्मिन्यथा देहे कौमारं यौवनं जरा ।
तथा देहान्तरप्राप्तिर्धीरस्तत्र न मुह्यति ।।१३।।

Dehihno'smin yathaa dehe kaumaaram yauvanam jaraa;
Tathaa dehaantara praaptir dheeras tatra na muhyati.

13. Just as an embodied soul attains childhood, youth and old age through the body, so it attains another body after death. Heroic men do not grieve at this.

मात्रास्पर्शास्तु कौन्तेय शीतोष्णसुखदुःखदाः ।
आगमापायिनोऽनित्यास्तांस्तितिक्षस्व भारत १४

Maatraasparsaastu kaunteya seetoshnasukhaduhkhadaah;
Aagamaapaayino'nityaams taamstitikshaswa bhaarata.

14. O Son of Kunti, the objects that are perceived by the senses are subject to birth and death. They give rise to pleasure and pain, to heat and cold; they are transient. Therefore, O Bharata, endure them heroically.

यं हि न व्यथयन्त्येते पुरुषं पुरुषर्षभ ।
समदुःखसुखं धीरं सोऽमृतत्वाय कल्पते ।१५।

Yam hi na vyathayantyete purusham purusharshabhah;
Samaduhkha sukham dheearm soamrititwaaya kalpate.

15. O best among men, anyone who is balanced in
pleasure and pain and who is not agitated by the senses
and their contact with objects, only such a hero is fit to
attain Liberation.

नासतो विद्यते भावो नाभावो विद्यते सतः ।
उभयोरपि दृष्टोऽन्तस्त्वनयोस्तत्त्वदर्शिभिः।१६।

Naasato vidyate bhaavo naabhaavo vidyate satah;
Ubhayorapi drishtontastwanayos tattwadarshibhih.

16. There is no existence for the unreal, and the Real
never ceases to be. Thus, the knowers of Truth have
ascertained the nature of what is real and what is unreal.

अविनाशि तु तद्विद्धि येन सर्वमिदं ततम् ।
विनाशमव्ययस्यास्य न कश्चित्कर्तुमर्हति ।१७।

Avinaasi tu tad viddhi yena sarvam idam tatam;
Vinaasam avyayasyaasya na kaschit kartum arhati.

17. That alone by which all this is pervaded is imperishable, because no one can destroy that Immutable Reality.

अन्तवन्त इमे देहा नित्यस्योक्ताः शरीरिणः।
अनाशिनोऽप्रमेयस्य तस्माद्युध्यस्व भारत ।१८।

Antavanta ime dehaa nityasyoktaah sareerinah;
Anaasino'prameyasya tasmad yudhyaswa bhaarata.

18. O Bharata, the Self is imperishable, but these bodies which inhabit the embodied Self are perishable. Therefore, prepare to fight.

य एनं वेत्ति हन्तारं यश्चैनं मन्यते हतम् ।
उभौ तौ न विजानीतो नायं हन्ति न हन्यते।१९।

Ya enam vetti hantaaram yaschainam manyate hatam;
Ubhau tau na vijaaneeto naayam hanti na hanyate.

19. Those who consider the Self as the killer, and those who think that It is killed, both are ignorant; for the Self neither kills nor is killed.

न जायते म्रियते वा कदाचि-
न्नायं भूत्वा भविता वा न भूयः ।
अजो नित्यः शाश्वतोऽयं पुराणो
न हन्यते हन्यमाने शरीरे ॥२०॥

Na jaayate mriyate vaa kadaachit
   Naayam bhootwaa bhavitaa vaa na bhooyah;
Ajo nityah saaswato'yam puraano
   Na hanyate hanyamaane sareere.

20. This Self is never born, nor does It ever perish; nor having been born before, will It be born in the future. This Self is unborn, eternal, imperishable, and ancient (ageless). Though the body is slain, the Self is not killed.

वेदाविनाशिनं नित्यं य एनमजमव्ययम् ।
कथं स पुरुषः पार्थ कं घातयति हन्ति कम् ॥२१॥

Vedaavinaasinam nityam ya enam ajam avyayam;
Katham sa purushah paartha kam ghaatayati hanti kam.

21. If one knows that the Self is indestructible because It is Immutable, and Unborn because It is Eternal, how can he kill anyone or cause anyone to be killed?

वासांसि जीर्णानि यथा विहाय
नवानि गृह्णाति नरोऽपराणि ।
तथा शरीराणि विहाय जीर्णा-
न्यन्यानि संयाति नवानि देही।।२२।।

Vaasaamsi jeernaani yathaa vihaaya
Navaani grihnaati naro'paraani;
Tathaa sareeraani vihaaya jeernaan
Yanyaani samyaati navaani dehi.

22. Just as a person gives up his old clothes to put on new
ones, so the embodied soul, having discarded the worn-
out bodies, puts on new ones.

नैनं छिन्दन्ति शस्त्राणि नैनं दहति पावकः ।
न चैनं क्लेदयन्त्यापो न शोषयति मारुतः ।२३।

Nainam chhindanti sastraani nainam dahati paavakah;
Na chainam kledayantyaapo na soshyati maarutah.

23. Weapons cannot cut the Self, fire cannot burn It,
water cannot drown It, nor can wind dry It.

अच्छेद्योऽयमदाह्योऽयमक्लेद्योऽशोष्य एव च ।
नित्यः सर्वगतः स्थाणुरचलोऽयं सनातनः ।२४।

Acchedyo'yam adaahyo'yam akledyo'soshya eva cha;
Nityah sarvagatah sthaanur achaloyam sanaatanah.

24. The Self is eternal, all-pervading, immutable, stable, and ancient. Therefore, It cannot be cut, or burnt, or drowned, or dried up.

अव्यक्तोऽयमचिन्त्योऽयमविकार्योऽयमुच्यते ।
तस्मादेवं विदित्वैनं नानुशोचितुमर्हसि ॥२५॥

Avyakto'yam achintyo'yamavikaaryo'yam uchyate;
Tasmaad evam viditwainam naanusochitum arhasi.

25. This Self is said to be nonmanifest, unthinkable, and unchangeable. Therefore, knowing this to be so, you should not grieve.

अथ चैनं नित्यजातं नित्यं वा मन्यसे मृतम् ।
तथापि त्वं महाबाहो नैवं शोचितुमर्हसि॥२६॥

Atha chainam nityajaatam nityam vaa manyase mritam;
Tathaapi twam mahaabaaho naivam sochitum arhasi.

26. O Great-armed Arjuna, even if you consider this Self to be subject to ceaseless birth and death, you should not grieve.

जातस्य हि ध्रुवो मृत्युर्ध्रुवं जन्म मृतस्य च।
तस्मादपरिहार्येऽर्थे न त्वं शोचितुमर्हसि ।।२७।।

Jatasya hi dhruvo mrityur dhruvam janma mritasya cha;
Tasmaad aparihaarye'rthe na twam sochitum arhasi.

27. Death is certain for that which is born, and birth is certain for that which dies. For this unavoidable fact you should not grieve.

अव्यक्तादीनि भूतानि व्यक्तमध्यानि भारत ।
अव्यक्तनिधनान्येव तत्र का परिदेवना ।।२८।।

Avyaktaadeeni bhootaani vyaktamadhyaani bhaarata;
Avyakta nidhanaanyeva tatra kaa paridevanaa.

28. O Bharata, these bodies consisting of the elements were not visible before birth, and they will not be visible after their death. They manifest in the middle. Therefore, why should you grieve?

आश्चर्यवत्पश्यति   कश्चिदेन-
माश्चर्यवद्वदति तथैव चान्यः ।
आश्चर्यवच्चैनमन्यः   श्रृणोति
श्रुत्वाप्येनं वेद न चैव कश्चित् ॥२९॥

Aascharyavat pasyati kaschid enam
Aascharyavad vadati tathaiva chaanyah;
Aascharyavat chainam anyah srinoti
Srutwaapyenam veda na chaiva kàschit.

29. Some behold this Self as a wonder, some talk about
Him as a wonder, and some hear about Him as a wonder:
and yet having heard about Him, none are able to
understand Him.

देही नित्यमवध्योऽयं देहे सर्वस्य भारत ।
तस्मात्सर्वाणि भूतानि न त्वं शोचितुमर्हसि।३०।

Dehee nityam avadhyo'yam dehe sarvasya bhaarata;
Tasmaat sarvaani bhootaani na twam sochitum arhasi.

30. O Bharata, the Eternal Self that indwells the bodies of
all human beings cannot be slain. Therefore, you should
not grieve for any living being.

स्वधर्ममपि चावेक्ष्य न विकम्पितुमर्हसि ।
धर्म्याद्धि युद्धाच्छ्रेयोऽन्यत्क्षत्रियस्य न विद्यते ॥

Swadharmam api chaavekshya na vikampitum arhasi;
Dharmyaddhi yuddhaa cchreyo'nyat kshratriyasya na vidyate.

31. Further, having understood this to be your true duty, you should not waver. There is nothing more blessed for a Kshatriya than a righteous war.

यदृच्छया चोपपन्नं स्वर्गद्वारमपावृतम् ।
सुखिनः क्षत्रियाः पार्थ लभन्ते युद्धमीदृशम् ॥३२॥

Yadricchayaa chopapannam swargadwaaram apaavritam;
Sukhinah kshatriyaah paartha labhante yuddham eedrisam.

32. Fortunate are the Kshatriyas, O Partha, who encounter such an opportunity as this great battle which has come to you of its own accord as an open gate to heaven.

अथ चेत्त्वमिमं धर्म्यं संग्रामं न करिष्यसि ।
ततः स्वधर्मं कीर्तिं च हित्वा पापमवाप्स्यसि ॥

Atha chettwam imam dharmyam samgraamam na karishyasi;
Tatah swadharmam keertim cha hitwaa paapam avaapsyasi.

33. On the other hand, if you do not fight this righteous battle, you will be deprived of both your Swadharma and your fame. Thus, you will incur sin.

अकीर्तिं चापि भूतानि कथयिष्यन्ति तेऽव्ययाम् ।
संभावितस्य चाकीर्तिर्मरणादतिरिच्यते ॥३४॥

Akeertim chaapi bhootaani kathayishyanti te'vyayaam;
Sambhaavitasya chaakeertir maranaad atirichyate.

34. Down through the ages people will talk of your infamy. For one who has earned so much fame, infamy is worse than death.

भयाद्रणादुपरतं मंस्यन्ते त्वां महारथाः ।
येषां च त्वं बहुमतो भूत्वा यास्यसि लाघवम् ॥

Bhayaad ranaad uparatam mamsyante twaam mahaarathaah;
Yeshaam cha twam bahumato bhootwaa yaasyasi laaghavam.

35. The great chariot warriors will think that you turned away from this battle out of fear. Those who hold you in high esteem will look down upon you.

अवाच्यवादांश्च बहून्वदिष्यन्ति तवाहिताः ।
निन्दन्तस्तव सामर्थ्यं ततो दुःखतरं नु किम् ॥

Avaachyavaadamscha bahoon vadishyanti tavaahitaah;
Nindantastava saamarthyam tato duhkhataram nu kim.

36. Your enemies will speak disgraceful words against you. They will ridicule your heroism. What can be more painful than this?

हतो वा प्राप्स्यसि स्वर्गं जित्वा वा भोक्ष्यसे महीम् ।
तस्मादुत्तिष्ठ कौन्तेय युद्धाय कृतनिश्चयः ॥३७॥

Hato vaa praapsyasi swargam jitwaa vaa bhokshyase maheem;
Tasmaad uttishtha kaunteya yuddhaaya kritanischayah.

37. If you are killed, O Son of Kunti, you will attain heaven. If you attain victory, you will enjoy rulership over the earth. Therefore, stand up determined to fight.

सुखदुःखे समे कृत्वा लाभालाभौ जयाजयौ ।
ततो युद्धाय युज्यस्व नैवं पापमवाप्स्यसि ।३८।

Sukhaduhkhe same kritwaa laabhaalaabhau jayaajayau;
Tato yuddhaaya yujyaswa naivam paapamavaapsyasi.

38. Maintaining a balanced mind in pleasure and pain, gain and loss, victory and defeat, engage yourself in battle. Thus, you will not be touched by sin.

एषा तेऽभिहिता सांख्ये बुद्धिर्योगे त्विमां शृणु ।
बुद्ध्या युक्तो यया पार्थ कर्मबन्धं प्रहास्यसि ।।

Eshaa te'bhibhitaa saankhye buddhir yoge twimaam srinu;
Buddhya yukto yayaa paartha karma bandham prahaasyasi.

39. O Partha, this is the wisdom of the Samkhya which I have given to you. Now listen to the wisdom of Yoga. Endowed with this wisdom, you will become free from the fetters of Karma.

नेहाभिक्रमनाशोऽस्ति प्रत्यवायो न विद्यते ।
स्वल्पमप्यस्य धर्मस्य त्रायते महतो भयात् ।४०।

Nehaabhikramanaaso'sti pratyavaayo na vidyate;
Swalpam apyasya dharmasya traayate mahato bhayaat.

40. On this path, no effort is ever rendered void, nor is there a risk of a negative result. Even a small measure of this Dharma (righteousness) protects a person from the great fear (of the world-process).

व्यवसायात्मिका बुद्धिरेकेह कुरुनन्दन ।
बहुशाखा ह्यनन्ताश्च बुद्धयोऽव्यवसायिनाम् ॥

Vyavasaayaatmikaa buddhirekehah karunandana;
Bahusaakhaa hyanantaascha buddhyo'vyavasaayinaam.

41. O Delighter of the race of Kuru (Arjuna), the intellect that ascertains the nature of the Self is one-pointed, but the thoughts of one who desires the fruits of action are many-branched and endless.

यामिमां पुष्पितां वाचं प्रवदन्त्यविपश्चितः ।
वेदवादरताः पार्थ नान्यदस्तीति वादिनः ॥४२॥

Yaam imaam pushpitaam vaacham pravadantyavipaschitah;
Vedavaadarataah paartha naanyad asteeti vaadinah.

42. O Partha, those of perverted intellects speak flowery words and are devoted to the Karma portion of the Vedas, saying that apart from the ritualistic sacrifice, there is nothing else.

कामात्मानः स्वर्गपरा जन्मकर्मफलप्रदाम् ।
क्रियाविशेषबहुलां भोगैश्वर्यगतिं प्रति ।४३।

Kaamaatmaanam swargaparaa janmakarmaphalapradaam;
Kriyaavisesha bahulaam bhogaiswarya gatim prati.

43. Dominated by desires, considering heaven the highest goal, they engage themselves in Karmas only for the sake of prosperity and enjoyment. Thus they create a Karmic basis for future embodiments.

भोगैश्वर्यप्रसक्तानां   तयापहृतचेतसाम् ।
व्यवसायात्मिका बुद्धिः समाधौ न विधीयते ॥

Bhogaiswarya prasaktaanaam tayaapahritachetasaam;
Vyavasaayaatmikaa buddhih samaadhau na vidheeyate.

44. Attached to enjoyment and personal glory, with intellects deprived of discriminative power, they are unable to develop that one-pointed intellect which leads one to Samadhi (superconsciousness).

त्रैगुण्यविषया वेदा निस्त्रैगुण्यो भवार्जुन ।
निर्द्वन्द्वो नित्यसत्त्वस्थो निर्योगक्षेम आत्मवान्

Traigunyavishayaa vedaa nistraigunyo bhavaarjuna;
Nirdwandwo nityasatwastho niryogakshema aatmavaan.

45. O Arjuna, (the Karma portion of) the Vedas deal only with the three Gunas. Therefore, become free from the three Gunas; thus transcending the pairs of opposites, abide in the eternal Sattwa (purity). And having established yourself in the Self, rise above the thoughts of Yoga (objects that have to be acquired) and Kshema (the preservation of objects already acquired).

यावानर्थ उदपाने सर्वतः संप्लुतोदके ।
तावान्सर्वेषु वेदेषु ब्राह्मणस्य विजानतः ।।४६।।

Yaavaanartha udapaane sarvatah samplutodake;
Taavaan sarveshu vedeshu brahmanasya vijaanatah.

46. For the knower of Brahman, the Karma portion of the Vedas serve as much purpose as a small reservoir of water in a place where there is a flood.

कर्मण्येवाधिकारस्ते मा फलेषु कदाचन ।
मा कर्मफलहेतुर्भूर्मा ते सङ्गोऽस्त्वकर्मणि ।४७।

Karmanyevaadhikaraste ma phaleshu kadaachana;
Ma karmaphalahetur bhoor ma te sangostvakarmani.

47. No matter what conditions you encounter in life, your right is only to the works—not to the fruits thereof. You should not be impelled to act for selfish reasons, nor should you be attached to inaction.

योगस्थः कुरु कर्माणि सङ्गं त्यक्त्वा धनंजय ।
सिद्ध्यसिद्ध्योः समो भूत्वा समत्वं योग उच्यते

Yogasthah kuru karmaani sangam tyaktwaa dhananjaya;
Siddhyasiddhyoh samo bhootwaa samatwam yoga uchyate.

48. O Dhananjaya (Conquerer of wealth), be established in Yoga and perform actions devoid of attachment. Be balanced in success and failure, for balance of mind is known as Yoga.

दूरेण ह्यवरं कर्म बुद्धियोगाद्धनंजय ।
बुद्धौ शरणमन्विच्छ कृपणाः फलहेतवः ।४९।

Doorena hyavaram karma buddhiyogaad dhananjaya;
Buddhau sharanamanwiccha kripanaah phalahetavah.

49. O Arjuna, Karma (performed with desire) is far inferior to the practice of Buddhi Yoga (the Yoga of wisdom). Therefore, seeking refuge in the intellect (that flows to Brahman), perform selfless actions; for miserable are those who desire the fruits of action.

बुद्धियुक्तो जहातीह उभे सुकृतदुष्कृते ।
तस्माद्योगाय युज्यस्व योगः कर्मसु कौशलम् ॥

Buddhiyukto jahaateeh ubhe sukrita dushkrite;
Tasmaad yogaaya yujyaswa yogah karmasu kaushalam.

50. If one can maintain a balanced mind, one is able to abandon virtue and vice. Therefore, engage yourself in the practice of Buddhi Yoga. The performance of actions with a balanced mind is indeed the skill in Yoga.

कर्मजं बुद्धियुक्ता हि फलं त्यक्त्वा मनीषिणः ।
जन्मबन्धविनिर्मुक्ताः पदं गच्छन्त्यनामयम् ॥

Karmajam buddhiyuktaa hi phalam tyaktwaa maneeshinah;
Janmabandha vinirmuktaah padam gacchantyanaamayam.

51. Endowed with a balanced mind, renouncing the fruits of action, the Sage breaks the fetters of birth and death, and goes to the diseaseless abode of Brahman.

यदा ते मोहकलिलं बुद्धिर्व्यतितरिष्यति ।
तदा गन्तासि निर्वेदं श्रोतव्यस्य श्रुतस्य च ॥

Yadaa te mohakalilam buddhir vyatitarishyati;
Tadaa gantaasi nirvedam srotavyasya srutasya cha.

52. When your intellect crosses the mire of delusion, you will develop indifference towards whatever you have heard before and whatever you are going to hear in the future.

श्रुतिविप्रतिपन्ना ते यदा स्थास्यति निश्चला ।
समाधावचला बुद्धिस्तदा योगमवाप्स्यसि ॥

Srutivipratipannaa te yadaa sthaasyati nischalaa;
Samaadhaavachalaa buddhistadaa yogam avaapsyasi.

53. When your intellect, which has been distracted by the conflicting statements of the scriptures, becomes steady and abides in the unshakeable state of Samadhi, then you will attain Yoga (Self-realization).

अर्जुन उवाच

स्थितप्रज्ञस्य का भाषा समाधिस्थस्य केशव ।
स्थितधीः किं प्रभाषेत किमासीत व्रजेत किम् ॥

Arjuna uvaacha
Sthitaprajnasya kaa bhaashaa samaadhisthasya keshava;
Sthithadheeh kim prabhaasheta kimaaseeta vrajeta kim.

54. Arjuna said: O Krishna, what are the characteristics of the Sage who is established in Samadhi? How does he of steady wisdom sit, how does he speak, how does he walk?

श्रीभगवानुवाच

प्रजहाति यदा कामान्सर्वान्पार्थ मनोगतान् ।
आत्मन्येवात्मना तुष्टः स्थितप्रज्ञस्तदोच्यते ॥

Sree Bhagavaan uvaacha
Prajahaati yadaa kaamaan sarvaan paartha manogataan;
Aatmanyevatmanaa tushtah stithaprajnasthadochyate.

55. Sri Krishna said: O Arjuna, when a man thoroughly renounces all the desires of the mind and is satisfied in the Self by the Self, he is called a man of steady wisdom.

दुःखेष्वनुद्विग्नमनाः सुखेषु विगतस्पृहः ।
वीतरागभयक्रोधः स्थितधीर्मुनिरुच्यते ।५६।

Dukheshwanudwignamanaah sukheshu vigatasprihah;
Veetaraagabhayakrodhah sthitadheer munir uchyate.

56. He who is not agitated in the the midst of sorrowful conditions and who is devoid of craving in the midst of pleasant circumstances, who is free from attachment, fear, and anger, such a Sage is called a person of steady wisdom.

यः सर्वत्रानभिस्नेहस्तत्तत्प्राप्य शुभाशुभम् ।
नाभिनन्दति न द्वेष्टि तस्य प्रज्ञा प्रतिष्ठिता ।५७।

Yah sarvatraanabhisnehas tattat praapya subhaasubham;
Naabhinandati na dweshti tasya prajnaa pratitishthitaa.

57. He who is without attachment in everything and while meeting with good and evil, neither rejoices nor hates, his wisdom is established.

यदा संहरते चायं कूर्मोऽङ्गानीव सर्वशः ।
इन्द्रियाणीन्द्रियार्थेभ्यस्तस्य प्रज्ञा प्रतिष्ठिता।५८।

Yadaa samharate chaayam koormo'ngaaneeva sarvasah;
Indriyaanindriyaarthebhyas tasya prajnaa pratishthitaa.

58. When he is able to withdraw his senses from the sense-objects, even like a tortoise that withdraws its limbs from all sides, he is then established in wisdom.

विषया विनिवर्तन्ते निराहारस्य देहिनः ।
रसवर्जं रसोऽप्यस्य परं दृष्ट्वा निवर्तते ।५९।

Vishayaa vinivartante niraahaarasya dehinah;
Rasavarjam raso'pyasya param drishtwaa nivartate.

59. When one abstains from sense-enjoyments, the objects turn away from him, but their taste continues to linger in his mind; but, even this taste turns away from him when the Supreme Self is realized.

यततो ह्यपि कौन्तेय पुरुषस्य विपश्चितः ।
इन्द्रियाणि प्रमाथीनि हरन्ति प्रसभं मनः ।६०।

Yatato hyapi kaunteya purushasya vipaschitah;
Indriyaani pramaatheeni haranti prasabham manah.

60. O Son of Kunti, the turbulent senses carry away violently the mind of even a wise man who is striving to control them.

तानि सर्वाणि संयम्य युक्त आसीत मत्परः।
वशे हि यस्येन्द्रियाणि तस्य प्रज्ञा प्रतिष्ठिता।६१

Taani sarvaani samyamya yukta aaseeta matparah;
Vase hi yasyendriyaani tasya prajnaa prathishthitaa.

61. Having controlled his senses and having collected his mind with one-pointed devotion to Me, he should sit steadfast in the Self; for one whose senses are under control, his wisdom becomes steady.

ध्यायतो   विषयान्पुंसः सङ्गस्तेषूपजायते।
सङ्गात्संजायते कामः कामात्क्रोधोऽभिजायते॥

Dhaayato vishayaan pumsah sangas teshoopajaayate;
Sangaat sanjaayate kaamah kaamaat krodhobhijaayate.

62. By constantly dwelling upon objects, one develops attachment to them; from attachment there arises desire, from desire there is born anger.

क्रोधाद्भवति संमोहः संमोहात्स्मृतिविभ्रमः ।
स्मृतिभ्रंशाद्बुद्धिनाशो बुद्धिनाशात्प्रणश्यति॥

Krodhaad bhavati sammohah sammohaat smriti vibhramah;
Smritibhramsaat buddhinaaso buddhinaasaat pranasyati.

63. From anger there arises delusion, from delusion loss of memory, from loss of memory one loses the function of pure reason, and from, the loss of reason one heads towards destruction.

रागद्वेषवियुक्तैस्तु विषयानिन्द्रियैश्चरन् ।
आत्मवश्यैर्विधेयात्मा प्रसादमधिगच्छति ।६४।

Raagadwesha viyuktaistu vishayaanindryaischaran;
Aatmavasyair vidheyaatmaa prasaadamadhigacchati.

64. But the self-controlled Sage, though moving among the sense-objects, with his senses restrained and free from attachment and hatred, goes to Peace.

प्रसादे सर्वदुःखानां हानिरस्योपजायते ।
प्रसन्नचेतसो ह्याशु बुद्धिः पर्यवतिष्ठते ।६५।

Prasaade sarvaduhkhaanaam haanir asyopajaaaayate;
Prasanna chetaso hyaasu buddhih paryavatishthate.

65. In that peace of the mind all sorrows are brought to
their cessation, because the intellect of the Sage, whose
mind is full of bliss, becomes established in Brahman.

नास्ति बुद्धिरयुक्तस्य न चायुक्तस्य भावना ।
न चाभावयतः शान्तिरशान्तस्य कुतः सुखम् ६६

Naasti buddhir ayuktasya na chaayuktasya bhaavanaa;
Na chaabhaavayatah saantir asaantasya kutah sukham.

66. There is no intuitive intellect for one who is not
united with the Higher Self, and there is no meditative
movement in the unsteady mind; and to the unmedi-
tative there is no peace. How can there be happiness to
one who is without peace?

इन्द्रियाणां हि चरतां यन्मनोऽनु विधीयते ।
तदस्य हरति प्रज्ञां वायुर्नावमिवाम्भसि ।६७।

Indriyaanaam hi charataam yanmanonuvidheeyate;
Tadasya harati prajnaam vaayur naavam ivaambhasi.

67. Whatever wandering sense the mind follows after, it (the sense) robs the mind of its intuitive vision, just as the wind carries away a boat on the waters.

तस्माद्यस्य महाबाहो निगृहीतानि सर्वशः ।
इन्द्रियाणीन्द्रियार्थेभ्यस्तस्य प्रज्ञा प्रतिष्ठिता ॥

Tasmaad yasya mahaabaaho nigriheetaani sarvasah;
Indriyaaneendriyaarthebhyas tasya prajnaa pratishthitaa.

68. Therefore, O Mighty Armed Arjuna, one whose senses are completely restrained from the sense-objects, his intuitive wisdom is firmly established.

या निशा सर्वभूतानां तस्यां जागर्ति संयमी ।
यस्यां जाग्रति भूतानि सा निशा पश्यतो मुनेः॥

Yaa nisaa sarvabhootaanaam tasyaam jaagarti samyamee;
Yasyaam jaagrati bhoothaani saa nisaa pasyato muneh.

69. That which is night to all beings, in that a man of controlled (intuitive) mind keeps awake, but that in which all beings of the world keep awake (ignorance), is night for the Sage who sees the Self.

आपूर्यमाणमचलप्रतिष्ठं
समुद्रमापः प्रविशन्ति यद्वत् ।
तद्वत्कामा यं प्रविशन्ति सर्वे
स शान्तिमाप्नोति न कामकामी ।७०।

Aapooryamaanam achala pratistham
Samudram aapah pravisanti yadvat;
Tadwat kaamaa yam pravisanti sarve
Sa saantim aapnoti na kaama kamee.

70. Just as waters from different rivers enter into the ocean from all sides, and yet the ocean continues to be immutable, in the same way he in whom all desires enter without affecting him, he alone attains peace, not the desirer of sense-objects.

विहाय कामान्यः सर्वान्पुमांश्चरति निःस्पृहः ।
निर्ममो निरहंकारः स शान्तिमधिगच्छति ॥

Vihaaya kaamaan yah sarvaan pumaans charati nihsprihah;
Nirmamo nirahankaarah sa saantim adhigacchati.

71. Having abandoned all desires, he who moves without the feeling of mine-ness, without egoism and without craving, he attains the supreme peace (of Self-realization).

एषा ब्राह्मी स्थिति: पार्थ नैनां प्राप्य विमुह्यति ।
स्थित्वास्यामन्तकालेऽपि ब्रह्मनिर्वाणमृच्छति ॥

Eshaa brahmee sthithih paartha nainaam praapya vimuhyati;
Sthitwaa syaamanta kaalepi brahmanirvaanamricchati.

72. Such is the state of Self-realization, O Arjuna. Having attained this, a Yogi is not deluded. Being established in this even at the moment of death, he attains the Absolute State of Liberation.

ॐ तत्सदिति श्रीमद्भगवद्गीतासूपनिषत्सु ब्रह्मविद्यायां
योगशास्त्रे श्रीकृष्णार्जुनसंवादे सांख्ययोगो
नाम द्वितीयोऽध्याय: ॥२॥

*Om tat sat iti srimad bhagavad gitaasoopanishatsu
brahmavidyaayaam yogashaastre sri krishnaarjunasamvaade
samkhyayogo naama dwitiyo'dhyaayah.*

Om Tat Sat.
Thus, in the Upanishad of the Bhagavad Gita,
the knowledge of Supreme Brahman, the scripture of Yoga,
the dialogue between Sri Krishna and Arjuna,
ends the second chapter entitled,
"The Yoga of Integral Knowledge."

तस्मादसक्तः सततं कार्यं कर्म समाचर ।
असक्तो ह्याचरन्कर्म परमाप्नोति पूरुषः ।।१९।।

अथ तृतीयोऽध्यायः

Atha Tritiyo'dhyaayah

Chapter 3

Karma Yogah

The Yoga of Action

In the absence of proper insight, Karma or action gives rise to bondage. But when one performs action selflessly, detached from its fruit, in the spirit of surrender to God, and with a profound insight into the nature of the Self, the same action is converted into Karma Yoga—a purifying process leading to Liberation or Freedom from the cycles of birth and death.

अर्जुन उवाच

ज्यायसी चेत्कर्मणस्ते मता बुद्धिर्जनार्दन ।
तत्किं कर्मणि घोरे मां नियोजयसि केशव ॥१॥

Arjuna uvaacha
Jyaayasee chet karmanaste mataa buddhir janaardana;
Tat kim karmaani ghore maam niyojayasi kesava.

1. Arjuna said: O Janardana, if you say the intellect lit up with the light of wisdom is superior to the path of selfless action, then why do you lead me, O Keshava, to the performance of terrible Karmas?

व्यामिश्रेणेव वाक्येन बुद्धिं मोहयसीव मे ।
तदेकं वद निश्चित्य येन श्रेयोऽहमाप्नुयाम्॥२॥

Vyaamisreneva vaakyena buddhim mohayaseeva me;
Tad ekam vada nischitya yena sreyo'ham aapnuyaam.

2. By your apparently involved statements, you are confusing my intellect. Therefore, please tell me definitely which path will lead me to the highest blessedness.

श्रीभगवानुवाच
लोकेऽस्मिन्द्विविधा निष्ठा पुरा प्रोक्ता मयानघ ।
ज्ञानयोगेन सांख्यानां कर्मयोगेन योगिनाम्॥३॥

Sree Bhagavaan uvaacha
Loke'smin dwividhaa nishthaa puraa proktaa mayaanagha;
Jnaanayogena samkhyaanaam karmayogena yoginaam.

3. Lord Krishna replied: O sinless Arjuna, since ancient
times I have taught two paths: the Yoga of Knowledge for
those who are qualified for Samkhya (attainment of
Brahmakara Vritti or intuitive revelation of the Self), and
the Yoga of Action for those qualified for action.

न कर्मणामनारम्भान्नैष्कर्म्यं पुरुषोऽश्नुते ।
न च संन्यसनादेव सिद्धिं समधिगच्छति ॥४॥

Na karmanaam anaarambhaan naishkarmyam purusho'snute;
Na cha sannyasanaad eva siddhim samadhigacchati.

4. By merely performing action, one does not qualify
himself for the Path of Knowledge (characterized by the
renunciation of all actions), nor does he attain perfection
or Self-realization by the mere act of receiving the vows of
renunciation.

न हि कश्चित्क्षणमपि जातु तिष्ठत्यकर्मकृत् ।
कार्यते ह्यवशः कर्म सर्वः प्रकृतिजैर्गुणैः ॥५॥

Na hi kaschit kshanamapi jaatu tishthatyakarmakrit;
Kaaryate hyavasah karma sarvah prakritijair gunaih.

5. No one can stay without action even for a single moment. The Gunas born of Prakriti (through attachment and hatred) impel a person to constantly perform actions.

कर्मेन्द्रियाणि संयम्य य आस्ते मनसा स्मरन् ।
इन्द्रियार्थान्विमूढात्मा मिथ्याचार: स उच्यते।।

Karmendriyaani samyamya ya aaste manasaa smaran;
Indriyaarthaan vimoodhaatmaa mithyaachaarah sa uchyate.

6. Those who have restrained the organs of actions, but continue to think of the objects of the senses, are foolish and hypocritical.

यस्त्विन्द्रियाणि मनसा नियम्यारभतेऽर्जुन।
कर्मेन्द्रियै: कर्मयोगमसक्त:स विशिष्यते ।।७।।

Yastwindriyaani manasaa niyamyaarabhate'rjuna;
Karmendriyaih karmayogam asaktah sa visishyate.

7. O Arjuna, one who has restrained his mind and senses, and engages his organs of action in the performance of actions enjoined in the scriptures, is far superior to the former.

नियतं कुरु कर्म त्वं कर्म ज्यायो ह्यकर्मणः ।
शरीरयात्रापि च ते न प्रसिद्ध्येदकर्मणः ॥८॥

Niyatam kuru karma twam karma jyaayo hyakarmanah;
Sareera yaatraapi cha te na prasiddhyed akarmanah.

8. Therefore, perform your duties in daily life. It is far better to act than to be inactive. By being inactive, you cannot even maintain the needs of your physical body.

यज्ञार्थात्कर्मणोऽन्यत्र लोकोऽयं कर्मबन्धनः ।
तदर्थं कर्म कौन्तेय मुक्तसङ्गः समाचर ॥९॥

Yajnaarthaat karmano'nyatra loko'yam karmabandhanah;
Tadartham karma kaunteya muktasangah samaachara.

9. Only those actions bind a person which are not performed for the sake of sacrifice (for pleasing God). Therefore, O Son of Kunti, perform Karmas without

attachment and with dexterity, for the sake of the Divine Self.

सहयज्ञाः प्रजाः सृष्ट्वा पुरोवाच प्रजापतिः ।
अनेन प्रसविष्यध्वमेष वोऽस्त्विष्टकामधुक् ।१०।

Sahayajnaah prajaah srishtwaa purovaacha prajaapatih;
Anena prasavishyadhwam esha vo'stvishtakaamadhuk.

10. In ancient times, Prajapati (the creator), having created Yajna (sacrifice) along with all beings, said, "May you prosper with the help of Sacrifice. May Sacrifice yield all your desires."

देवान्भावयतानेन ते देवा भावयन्तु वः ।
परस्परं भावयन्तः श्रेयः परमवाप्स्यथ ।११।

Devaan bhaavayataanena te devaa bhaavayantu vah;
Parasparam bhaavayantah sreyah parama avaapsyatha.

11. May you satisfy the gods by the performance of sacrifice. In turn, may the gods (thus satisfied) enhance your fulfillment. Thus assisting each other, may you attain the highest good in the form of Self-realization.

इष्टान्भोगान्हि वो देवा दास्यन्ते यज्ञभाविताः ।
तैर्दत्तानप्रदायैभ्यो यो भुङ्क्ते स्तेन एव सः १२

Ishtaan bhogaan hi vo devaa daasyante yajnabhaavitaah;
Tair dattaan apradaayaibhyo yo bhungte stena eva sah.

12. The gods, pleased by Yajna, will bestow upon you the objects of your desire. Those who enjoy the objects given by the gods without offering Yajna to them are thieves.

यज्ञशिष्टाशिनः सन्तो मुच्यन्ते सर्वकिल्बिषैः ।
भुञ्जते ते त्वघं पापा ये पचन्त्यात्मकारणात् ॥

Yajnasishtaasinah santo muchyante sarva kilbishaih;
Bhunjate te twagham paapaa ye pachantyaatma kaaranat.

13. Those good men who eat only what is left from the sacrifice are freed from all sins. But those evil men who prepare food for themselves alone are eaters of sin.

अन्नाद्भवन्ति भूतानि पर्जन्यादन्नसंभवः ।
यज्ञाद्भवति पर्जन्यो यज्ञः कर्मसमुद्भवः ॥१४॥

Annaad bhavanti bhootaani parjanyaad anna sambhavah;
Yajnaad bhavati parjanyo yajnah karma samudbhavah.

14. From food there arise the bodies of beings and from rain comes food. It is Yajna that gives rise to rain, while Yajna is born of action

कर्म ब्रह्मोद्भवं विद्धि ब्रह्माक्षरसमुद्भवम् ।
तस्मात्सर्वगतं ब्रह्म नित्यं यज्ञे प्रतिष्ठितम् ।।१५।।

Karma brahmodbhavam viddhi brahmaakshara samudbhavam;
Tasmaat sarvagatam brahma nityam yajne pratishthitam.

15. Know that Karma proceeds from the Brahma (Vedas), and the Vedas emanate from the Divine Self. Therefore, the all-pervading, Eternal Brahman is seated in Yajna.

एवं प्रवर्तितं चक्रं नानुवर्तयतीह यः ।
अघायुरिन्द्रियारामो मोघं पार्थ स जीवति ।।१६।।

Evam pravartitam chakram naanuvartayateeha yah;
Aghaayur indriyaaraamo mogham paartha sa jeevati.

16. One who does not follow this wheel that is set in motion by the Divine Self, O Arjuna, though delighting in sensual pleasures, is steeped in sinfulness and lives in vain.

यस्त्वात्मरतिरेव स्यादात्मतृप्तश्च मानवः।
आत्मन्येव च संतुष्टस्तस्य कार्यं न विद्यते ।१७।

Yastwaatmaratir eva syaad aatmatriptascha maanavah;
Aatmanyeva cha santushtas tasya kaaryam na vidyate.

17. For one who delights in the Self, is satisfied by the Self, and is contented with the Self, there exists no more action that needs to be performed.

नैव तस्य कृतेनार्थो नाकृतेनेह कश्चन ।
न चास्य सर्वभूतेषु कश्चिदर्थव्यपाश्रयः ।१८।

Naiva tasya kritenaartho naakriteneha kaschana;
Na chaasya sarvabhooteshu kaschidartha vyapaasrayah.

18. Performance or nonperformance of action does not serve any purpose for one who delights in the Self,

because such an enlightened Sage does not depend upon any being for any interest of his own.

तस्मादसक्तः सततं कार्यं कर्म समाचर ।
असक्तो ह्याचरन्कर्म परमाप्नोति पूरुषः ॥१९॥

Tasmaad asaktah satatam kaaryam karma samaachara;
Asakto hyaacharan karma param aapnoti poorushah.

19. Therefore, perform your duties without attachment to the fruits of action, for one who performs actions without attachment attains Liberation.

कर्मणैव हि संसिद्धिमास्थिता जनकादयः ।
लोकसंग्रहमेवापि संपश्यन्कर्तुमर्हसि ॥२०॥

Karmanaiva hi samsiddhim aasthitaa janakaadayah;
Lokasangraham evaapi sampasyan kartum arhasi.

20. Janaka and others attained perfection by following the Yoga of Action. Even from the point of view of maintaining the world, you must perform actions.

यद्यदाचरति श्रेष्ठस्तत्तदेवेतरो जनः ।
स यत्प्रमाणं कुरुते लोकस्तदनुवर्तते ॥२१॥

Yadyad aacharati sreshthas tattadevetaro janah;
Sa yat pramaanam kurute lokastad anuvartate.

21. Whatever a great man does, the same is followed by others. Whatever he sets as an example, the same the world emulates.

न मे पार्थास्ति कर्तव्यं त्रिषु लोकेषु किंचन ।
नानवाप्तमवाप्तव्यं वर्त एव च कर्मणि ॥२२॥

Na me paarthaasti kartavyam trishu lokeshu kimchana;
Naanavaaptam avaaptavyam varta eva cha karmani.

22. O Partha, I have no need to perform any work in the three worlds, because there is nothing to be attained by Me. Yet I keep Myself engaged in action.

यदि ह्यहं न वर्तेयं जातु कर्मण्यतन्द्रितः ।
मम वर्त्मानुवर्तन्ते मनुष्याः पार्थ सर्वशः ॥२३॥

Yadi hyaham na varteyam jaatu karmanyatandritah;
Mama vartmaanuvartante manushyaah paartha sarvasah.

23. O Arjuna, Son of Pritha, if I did not engage Myself tirelessly in action, human beings would follow my example in every way possible.

उत्सीदेयुरिमे लोका न कुर्यां कर्म चेदहम् ।
संकरस्य च कर्ता स्यामुपहन्यामिमाः प्रजाः २४

Utseedeyur ime lokaa na kuryaam karma ched aham;
Sankarasya cha kartaa syaam upahanyaam imaah prajaah.

24. Should I not perform work, these worlds would be destroyed. I would cause confusion of the castes, and thus destroy all these beings.

सक्ताः कर्मण्यविद्वांसो यथा कुर्वन्ति भारत ।
कुर्याद्विद्वांस्तथासक्तश्चिकीर्षुर्लोकसंग्रहम् ॥२५॥

Saktaah karmanyavidwaamso yathaa kurvanti bhaarata;
Kuryaad vidwaam stathaa saktas chikeershur lokasangraham.

25. O Bharata, while the ignorant peform action with attachment, the wise should also perform actions, but without attachment and for the welfare of the world.

न बुद्धिभेदं जनयेदज्ञानां कर्मसङ्गिनाम् ।
जोषयेत्सर्वकर्माणि विद्वान्युक्तः समाचरन्।२६।

Na buddhibhedam janayed ajnaanaam karmasanginaam;
Yojayet sarva karmaani vidwaan yuktah samaacharan.

26. One should not unsettle the intellect of those who are attached to action. A wise man should gently lead them to action, while he himself performs actions with a controlled mind.

प्रकृतेः क्रियमाणानि गुणैः कर्माणि सर्वशः ।
अहंकारविमूढात्मा कर्ताहमिति मन्यते ॥२७॥

Prakriteh kriyamaanaani gunaih karmaani sarvasah;
Ahamkaara vimoodhaatmaa kartaaham iti manyate.

27. All actions are performed by the Gunas of Prakriti. But if one's intellect is dull due to the development of egoism, he feels that, "I am the doer."

तत्त्वविच्तु महाबाहो गुणकर्मविभागयो: ।
गुणा गुणेषु वर्तन्त इति मत्वा न सज्जते ।२८।

Tathwavittu mahaabaaho gunakarma vibhaagayoh;
Gunaa guneshu vartante iti matwaa na sajjate.

28. But, O Great-armed Arjuna, one who knows the Truth about the Gunas, the Karmas, and the actionless Self is not attached, since he knows that the Gunas operate among the Gunas.

प्रकृतेर्गुणसंमूढा: सज्जन्ते गुणकर्मसु ।
तानकृत्स्नविदो मन्दान्कृत्स्नविन्न विचालयेत् ॥

Prakriter gunasammudhaah sajjante guna karmasu;
Taan akritsnavido mandaan kritsnavin na vichaalayet.

29. Deluded by the Gunas of Nature, ignorant men are attached to the actions arising out of the Gunas. Those who are in the possession of the whole Truth should not confuse those who are in the possession of imperfect knowledge.

मयि सर्वाणि कर्माणि संन्यस्याध्यात्मचेतसा ।
निराशीर्निर्ममो भूत्वा युध्यस्व विगतज्वर: ॥

Mayi sarvaani karmaani samnyasyaadhyaatma chetasaa;
Niraaseer nirmamo bhootwa yudhyaswa vigatajwarah.

30. Having surrendered all actions to Me, with your mind illumined by spiritual vision, you should fight without desire, free from the sense of mineness, and devoid of the fever of mental worries.

ये मे मतमिदं नित्यमनुतिष्ठन्ति मानवाः ।
श्रद्धावन्तोऽनसूयन्तो मुच्यन्ते तेऽपि कर्मभिः ॥

Ye me matam idam nityam anutisthanti maanavaah;
Sraddhaavanto'nasooyanto muchyante te'pi karmabhih.

31. Those who are endowed with faith and are free from the vice of finding fault with My teachings, they too attain freedom from all actions by following the path revealed by Me.

ये त्वेतदभ्यसूयन्तो नानुतिष्ठन्ति मे मतम् ।
सर्वज्ञानविमूढांस्तान्विद्धि नष्टानचेतसः ॥३२॥

Ye twetad abhyasooyanto naanutishthanti me matam;
Sarvajnaanavimoodhaam staan viddhi nashtaan achetasah.

32. But those who do not follow My teaching and are afflicted with the vice of finding fault in it, know them to be dull-witted and deluded in every form of knowledge. They are heading towards their own destruction (through loss of self-effort).

सदृशं चेष्टते स्वस्याः प्रकृतेर्ज्ञानवानपि ।
प्रकृतिं यान्ति भूतानि निग्रहः किं करिष्यति ।।

Sadrisam cheshtate swasyaah prakriter jnaanavaan api;
Prakritim yaanti bhootaani nigrahah kim karishyati.

33. Even the wise follow the dictates of Nature, what to speak of all living beings who obey their instincts implicitly. Therefore, what can restraint do?

इन्द्रियस्येन्द्रियस्यार्थे रागद्वेषौ व्यवस्थितौ ।
तयोर्न वशमागच्छेत्तौ ह्यस्य परिपन्थिनौ ।।३४।।

Indriyasyendriyasyaarthe raagadweshau vyavasthitau;
Tayor na vasam aagacchet tau hyasya paripanthinau.

34. Raga and Dwesha pertaining to the sense-objects abide in the senses. One should not come under their sway, because they are like highway robbers.

श्रेयान् स्वधर्मो विगुणः परधर्मात्स्वनुष्ठितात् ।
स्वधर्मे निधनं श्रेयः परधर्मो भयावहः ।।३५।।

Sreyaan swadharmo vigunah paradharmaat swanushthitaat;
Swadharme nidhanam sreyah paradharmo bhayaavahah.

35. Better to perform one's own duty even though imperfectly than to perform the duties of others in a perfect manner. It is better to give up one's life while performing one's own duty, rather than to perform the duty of others which leads to fearful consequences.

अर्जुन उवाच
अथ केन प्रयुक्तोऽयं पापं चरति पूरुषः ।
अनिच्छन्नपि वार्ष्णेय बलादिव नियोजितः ।।

Arjuna uvaacha
Atha kena prayukto'yam paapam charati poorushah;
Anicchann api vaarshneya balaad iva niyojitah.

36. Arjuna asked: O Krishna, what makes a person commit a sinful deed even against his will, as if he were compelled by force?

श्रीभगवानुवाच

काम एष क्रोध एष रजोगुणसमुद्धवः ।

महाशनो महापाप्मा विद्धयेनमिह वैरिणम् ॥

Sree Bhagavaan uvaacha
Kaama esha krodha esha rajoguna samudbhavah;
Mahaasano mahaapaapmaa viddhyenam iha vairinam.

37. Sri Bhagavan Krishna replied: It is Kama (desire) as well as Krodha (anger) arising out of Rajas (passion and externalization). This Kama is a great eater and a great sinner. Know this to be your enemy in this world.

धूमेनाव्रियते वह्निर्यथादर्शो मलेन च ।

यथोल्बेनावृतो गर्भस्तथा तेनेदमावृतम् ॥३८॥

Dhoomenaavriyate vahnir yathadarso malena cha;
Yatholbenaavrito garbhas tathaa tenedam aavritam.

38. Just as smoke veils fire, dust particles cover a mirror, or the amnion envelops an embryo, so desire veils knowledge.

आवृतं ज्ञानमेतेन ज्ञानिनो नित्यवैरिणा ।
कामरूपेण कौन्तेय दुष्पूरेणानलेन च ।३९।

Aavritam jnaanam etena jnaanino nityavairinaa;
Kaamaroopena kaunteya dushpoorenaanalena cha.

39. O Son of Kunti, wisdom is enveloped by desire, this constant enemy of the wise, which is as insatiable as fire.

इन्द्रियाणि मनो बुद्धिरस्याधिष्ठानमुच्यते ।
एतैर्विमोहयत्येष ज्ञानमावृत्य देहिनम् ।४०।

Indriyaani mano buddhir asyaadhishthaanam uchyate;
Etair vimohayatyesha jnaanam aavritya dehinam.

40. The senses, mind and intellect are said to be its dwelling places. Through these, it deludes the ignorant who are identified with their bodies.

तस्मात्त्वमिन्द्रियाण्यादौ नियम्य भरतर्षभ ।
पाप्मानं प्रजहि ह्येनं ज्ञानविज्ञाननाशनम् ॥४१॥

Tasmaat twam indriyaanyaadau niyamya bharatarshabha;
Paapmaanam prajahi hyenam jnaana vijnaana naasanam.

41. Therefore, O Best of the Bharatas (descendants of
King Bharata), having first subdued the Indriyas, slay this
sinful enemy, the destroyer of knowledge and realization.

इन्द्रियाणि पराण्याहुरिन्द्रियेभ्यः परं मनः ।
मनसस्तु परा बुद्धिर्यो बुद्धेः परतस्तु सः ॥४२॥

Indriyaani paraanyaahuh indriyebhyah param manah;
Manasas tu paraa buddhiryo buddheh paratastu sah.

42. The Sages say that the senses (Indriyas) are higher
than the objects, while higher still than the senses is the
mind. The intellect is higher than the mind, and even
higher than the intellect is the Supreme Self.

एवं बुद्धेः परं बुद्ध्वा संस्तभ्यात्मानमात्मना ।
जहि शत्रुं महाबाहो कामरूपं दुरासदम् ॥४३॥

Evam buddheh param buddhwa samstabhyatmaanam aatmanaa;
Jahi satrum mahaabaaho kaamaroopam duraasadam.

43. Thus, O Great-armed Arjuna, kowing that which is higher than the intellect, with your mind under your control, you should slay this enemy, desire, which is so difficult to conquer.

ॐ तत्सदिति श्रीमद्भगवद्गीतासूपनिषत्सु ब्रह्म-
विद्यायां योगशास्त्रे श्रीकृष्णार्जुनसंवादे
कर्मयोगो नाम तृतीयोऽध्याय: ॥३॥

Om tat sat iti srimad bhagavad gitaasoopanishatsu brahmavidyaayaam yogashaastre sri krishnaarjunasamvaade karmayogo naama tritiyo'dhyaayah.

Om Tat Sat.
Thus, in the Upanishad of the Bhagavad Gita,
the knowledge of Supreme Brahman, the scripture of Yoga,
the dialogue between Sri Krishna and Arjuna,
ends the third chapter entitled,
"The Yoga of Action."

ब्रह्मार्पणं ब्रह्म हविर्ब्रह्माग्नौ ब्रह्मणा हुतम् ।
ब्रह्मैव तेन गन्तव्यं ब्रह्मकर्मसमाधिना ॥२४॥

अथ चतुर्थोऽध्यायः

Atha Chaturtho'dhyaayah

Chapter 4

Jnana Vibhaga Yogah

The Yoga of Wisdom

Lord Krishna gives the key to the mystic art of Karma Yoga. When Karma is blended with Vikarma (special discipline), one is led to Akarma (a state where Karma is trasncended). Endowed with this art, a Karma Yogi continues performing actions which purify his heart and are conducive to the good of society. Various disciplines have been outlined in this chapter.

श्रीभगवानुवाच

इमं विवस्वते योगं प्रोक्तवानहमव्ययम् ।
विवस्वान्मनवे प्राह मनुरिक्ष्वाकवेऽब्रवीत्॥१॥

Sree Bhagavaan uvaacha
Imam vivaswate yogam proktavaan aham avyayam;
Vivaswaan manave praaha manur ikhswakave'braveet.

1. Sri Bhagavan Krishna said: This imperishable Yoga was first proclaimed by Me to the Sun God. The Sun God, in turn, taught this to Sage Manu, and from Manu it was received by King Ikshwaku.

एवं परम्पराप्राप्तमिमं राजर्षयो विदुः ।
स कालेनेह महता योगो ॑ नष्टः परंतप ॥२॥

Evam paramparaa praaptam imam raajarshayo viduh;
Sa kaaleneha mahataa yogo nashtah parantapa.

2. O Scorcher of Foes (Arjuna), the Royal Sages knew this Yoga as it was handed down from one to another (in regular succession from King Ikshwaku). But due to the lapse of time, this tradition has been lost.

स एवायं मया तेऽद्य योगः प्रोक्तः पुरातनः ।
भक्तोऽसि मे सखा चेति रहस्यं ह्येतदुत्तमम् ।३।

Sa evaayam mayaa te'dya yogah proktah puraatanah;
Bhakto'si me sakhaa cheti rahasyam hyetad uttamam.

3. You are my friend and devotee. Therefore, I have declared the same ancient Yoga to you, which is a supreme secret.

अर्जुन उवाच

अपरं भवतो जन्म परं जन्म विवस्वतः ।
कथमेतद्विजानीयां त्वमादौ प्रोक्तवानिति ॥४॥

Arjuna uvaacha
Aparam bhavato janma param janma vivaswatah;
Katham etadvijaaneeyaam twam aadau proktavaan iti.

4. Arjuna asked: You were born much later, while Vivaswan (the Sun God) was born in the more distant past. How am I to understand that you taught this knowledge to the Sun God in the beginning stages of creation?

श्रीभगवानुवाच

बहूनि मे व्यतीतानि जन्मानि तव चार्जुन ।
तान्यहं वेद सर्वाणि न त्वं वेत्थ परंतप ॥५॥

Sree Bhagavaan uvaacha
Bahooni me vyatitani janmaani tava chaarjuna;
Taanyaham veda sarvaani natwam vettha parantapa.

5. Sri Bhagavan said: O Arjuna, I and you have passed through numerous embodiments. I know them all, but, O Destroyer of Foes, you do not know them.

अजोऽपि सन्नव्ययात्मा भूतानामीश्वरोऽपि सन्।
प्रकृतिं स्वामधिष्ठाय संभवाम्यात्ममायया ॥६॥

Ajo'pi sannavyayaatmaa bhootaanaam eeswaro'pi san;
Prakritim swaam'adhishthaaya sambhavaamyaatmamaayayaa

6. I am unborn, imperishable, and the Lord of all beings. Yet, by controlling My own Prakriti, I embody myself by My own Maya.

यदा यदा हि धर्मस्य ग्लानिर्भवति भारत।
अभ्युत्थानमधर्मस्य तदात्मानं सृजाम्यहम्॥७॥

Yadaa yadaa hi dharmasya glaanir bhavati bhaarata;
Abhyutthaanam adharmasya tadatmaanam srijaamyaham.

7. Whenever virtue declines and unrighteousness rises, I manifest Myself as an embodied being.

परित्राणाय साधूनां विनाशाय च दुष्कृताम् ।
धर्मसंस्थापनार्थाय संभवामि युगे युगे ।।८।।

Paritraanaaya saaddhunaam vinaasaaya cha dushkritaam;
Dharma samsthaapanaarthaaya sambhavaami yuge yuge.

8. To protect the Saints and Sages, to destroy the evil-doers and to establish Dharma (righteousness), I am born from age to age.

जन्म कर्म च मे दिव्यमेवं यो वेत्ति तत्त्वतः ।
त्यक्त्वा देहं पुनर्जन्म नैति मामेति सोऽर्जुन ।।

Janmakarma cha me divyamevam yo vetti tatwatah;
Tyaktwa deham punarjanma naiti maameti so'arjuna.

9. O Arjuna, My birth and My actions are divine. Whoever knows this truly will not be born again after shedding this physical body. He will come to Me.

वीतरागभयक्रोधा मन्मया मामुपाश्रिताः ।
बहवो ज्ञानतपसा पूता मद्भावमागताः ।।१०।।

Veetaraagabhayakrodha manmayaa maam upaasritaah;
Bahavo jnaana tapasaa pootaa madbhaavam aagataah.

10. Free from attachment, fear and anger, with their minds absorbed in Me, purified by the austerity of wisdom, many have attained My Being.

ये यथा मां प्रपद्यन्ते तांस्तथैव भजाम्यहम् ।
मम वर्त्मानुवर्तन्ते मनुष्याः पार्थ सर्वशः॥११॥

Ye yathaa maam prapadyante taans tathaiva bhajaamyaham;
Mama vartmaanuvartante manushyaah paartha sarvasah.

11. O Partha, however a person adores Me, in the same manner I bestow My grace on him. All human beings follow My path in various ways.

काङ्क्षन्तः कर्मणां सिद्धि यजन्त इह देवताः ।
क्षिप्रं हि मानुषे लोके सिद्धिर्भवति कर्मजा ॥

Kaangshantah karmanaam siddhim yajanta iha devataah;
Kshipram hi maanushe loke siddhir bhavati karmajaa.

12. Desirous of success in various actions, people worship other gods, because in this human world success in action is gained easily.

चातुर्वर्ण्यं मया सृष्टं गुणकर्मविभागशः ।
तस्य कर्तारमपि मां विद्धयकर्तारमव्ययम् ॥

Chaaturvarnyam mayaa srishtam gunakarma vibhagasah;
Tasya kartaaram api maam vidhyakartaaram avyayam.

13. The four classes of human beings have been created by Me, along with the Gunas and Karmas. Though I am their creator, know Me to be actionless and imperishable.

न मां कर्माणि लिम्पन्ति न मे कर्मफले स्पृहा ।
इति मां योऽभिजानाति कर्मभिर्न स बध्यते ॥

Na maam karmaani limpanti na me karmaphale sprihaa;
Iti maam yo'bhijaanaati karmabhir na sa badhyate.

14. Actions do not touch Me, nor am I desirous of the fruits of action. Whoever knows Me thus is not bound by actions.

एवं ज्ञात्वा कृतं कर्म पूर्वैरपि मुमुक्षुभिः ।
कुरु कर्मैव तस्मात्त्वं पूर्वैः पूर्वतरं कृतम् ॥१५॥

Evam jnaatwaa kritam karma poorvair api mumukshubhih;
Kuru karmaiva tasmat twam poorvaih poorvataram kritam.

15. Thus knowing, seekers of Liberation performed Karma in ancient times. And even before them, others also performed Karma. Therefore, perform your duty.

किं कर्म किमकर्मेति कवयोऽप्यत्र मोहिताः ।
तत्ते कर्म प्रवक्ष्यामि यज्ज्ञात्वा मोक्ष्यसेऽशुभात्

Kim karma kim akarmeti kavayo'pyatra mohitaah;
Tat te karma pravakshyaami yajjnaatwaa mokshyase'subhat.

16. Even wise men are confused about Karma (action) and Akarma (inaction). Therefore, I will declare to you decisively the nature of Karma and Akarma, knowing which, you will be free from the evil of the world-process.

कर्मणो ह्यपि बोद्धव्यं बोद्धव्यं च विकर्मणः ।
अकर्मणश्च बोद्धव्यं गहना कर्मणो गतिः ॥१७॥

Karmano hyapi boddhavyam boddhavyam cha vikarmanah;
Akarmanas cha boddhavyam gahanaa karmano gatih.

17. One must know the nature of Karma (action), Vikarma (special action), and Akarma (inaction), because the way of work is difficult to understand.

कर्मण्यकर्म यः पश्येदकर्मणि च कर्म यः ।
स बुद्धिमान्मनुष्येषु स युक्तः कृत्स्नकर्मकृत् ॥

Karmanyakarma yah pasyed akarmani cha karma yah;
Sa buddhimaan manushyeshu sa yuktah kritsnakarmakrit.

18. One who sees inaction in action and action in inaction is wise among men. He is endowed with Yoga and has performed all that is to be performed.

यस्य सर्वे समारम्भाः कामसंकल्पवर्जिताः ।
ज्ञानाग्निदग्धकर्माणं तमाहुः पण्डितं बुधाः ॥

Yasya sarve samaarambhaah kaamasankalpa varjitaah;
Jnaanaagni dagdhakarmaanam tam aahuh panditam budhaah.

19. He whose undertakings are free from Kama (desire) and Samkalpa (ego-sense), and whose actions are burnt up by the fire of wisdom, him the wise call an enlightened person.

त्यक्त्वा कर्मफलासङ्गं नित्यतृप्तो निराश्रयः ।
कर्मण्यभिप्रवृत्तोऽपि नैव किञ्चित्करोति सः ॥

Tyaktwaa karmaphalaasangam nityatripto niraasrayah;
Karmanyabhipravritto'pi naiva kinchit karoti sah.

20. Having renounced attachment to action and its fruits, he who is eternally contented and free from dependence, even though he may be engaged in action, does nothing at all.

निराशीर्यतचित्तात्मा   त्यक्तसर्वपरिग्रहः ।
शारीरं केवलं कर्म कुर्वन्नाप्नोति किल्बिषम् ॥

Niraaseer yatachittatma tyaktasarvaparigrahah;
Saareeram kevalam karma kurvannapnoti kilbisham.

21. Devoid of cravings, with the body and mind under his control, having renounced all objects of pleasure, a Yogi

performs actions only to maintain the body. He does not enter into the evil of the world-process.

यदृच्छालाभसंतुष्टो द्वन्द्वातीतो विमत्सरः ।
समः सिद्धावसिद्धौ च कृत्वापि न निबध्यते ॥

Yadricchaalaabhasantushto dwandwaateeto vimatsarah;
Samah siddhaavasiddhau cha kritwaapi na nibadhyate.

22. If one is satisfied with whatever comes without his egoistic effort, and is beyond the pairs of opposites, and if he is also free from jealousy, and balanced in success and failure, then even while acting, he is not bound.

गतसङ्गस्य मुक्तस्य ज्ञानावस्थितचेतसः ।
यज्ञायाचरतः कर्म समग्रं प्रविलीयते ॥२३॥

Gatasangasya muktasya jnanaavasthitachetasah;
Yajnaayaacharatah karma samagram pravileeyate.

23. For one who is liberated, whose mind is firmly established in wisdom, who is absolutely detached from the fruits of action, and who acts in the spirit of sacrifice, all actions dissolve along with their fruits.

ब्रह्मार्पणं ब्रह्म हविर्ब्रह्माग्नौ ब्रह्मणा हुतम् ।
ब्रह्मैव तेन गन्तव्यं ब्रह्मकर्मसमाधिना ॥२४॥

Brahmaarpanam brahma havir brahmagnau brahmanaa hutam;
Brahmaiva tena gantavyam brahma karma samaadhinaa.

24. One who sees Brahman as the oblation, Brahman as the clarified butter to be offered into the fire of Brahman by Brahman Himself, he verily holds the perpetual vision of Brahman in action! Thus seeing, he attains Brahman.

दैवमेवापरे यज्ञं योगिनः पर्युपासते ।
ब्रह्माग्नावपरे यज्ञं यज्ञेनैवोपजुह्वति ॥२५॥

Daivam evaapare yajnam yoginah paryupaasate;
Brahmaagnavapare yajnam yajnenaivopajuhwati.

25. Some Yogis perform sacrifice to please the Gods, while others offer the self to be sacrificed by the Self into the fire of Brahman.

श्रोत्रादीनीन्द्रियाण्यन्ये संयमाग्निषु जुह्वति ।
शब्दादीन्विषयानन्य इन्द्रियाग्निषु जुह्वति ॥

Srotraadeenindriyaanyanye samyamaagnishu juhwati;
Sabdaadeen vishayaananya indriyaagnishu juhwati.

26. Some Yogis offer the ear and other senses into the fire
of Samyama, while others offer the objects into the fire of
the senses.

सर्वाणीन्द्रियकर्माणि प्राणकर्माणि चापरे ।
आत्मसंयमयोगाग्नौ जुह्वति ज्ञानदीपिते ॥२७॥

Sarvaanindriya karmaani praanakarmaani chaapare;
Aatmasamyamayogaagnau juhwati jnaanadeepite.

27. Some Yogis offer the functions of all the senses and
Pranas into the fire of the Yoga of self-restraint (Samyama
on the Self) which shines with the luminosity of wisdom.

द्रव्ययज्ञास्तपोयज्ञा योगयज्ञास्तथापरे ।
स्वाध्यायज्ञानयज्ञाश्च यतयः संशितव्रताः ॥२८॥

Dravyayajnaas tapoyajnaa yogayajnaastathaapare;
Swaadhyaayajnaan yajnaascha yatayah samsitavrataah.

28. Some perform sacrifice pertaining to material objects. Some perform the Yajna of austerity; some offer the Yajna of Swadhyaya and the Yajna of knowledge. Some are devoted to the Yajna of the eight limbs of Raja Yoga. And some rare souls keep firm vows, practising the great virtues in an unrestricted manner.

अपाने जुह्वति प्राणं प्राणेऽपानं तथापरे ।
प्राणापानगती रुद्ध्वा प्राणायामपरायणाः ॥

Apaane juhwati praanam praane'paanam tathaapare;
Praanaapaana gatee ruddhwaa praanaayaamaparaayanaah.

29. Some offer Prana (ingoing breath) unto Apana (outgoing breath). Others offer Apana unto Prana, while others are engaged in the cessation of Prana and Apana by the Pranayama (restraint of breath).

अपरे नियताहाराः प्राणान्प्राणेषु जुह्वति ।
सर्वेऽप्येते यज्ञविदो यज्ञक्षपितकल्मषाः ॥३०॥

Apare niyataahaaraah praanaan praaneshu juhwati;
Sarve'pyete yajnavido yajnakshapita kalmashaah.

30. Some, having regulated their food, offer their Pranas (as organs of action) unto the Pranas (the vital forces). All those Yogis know sacrifice and have burnt up their sins in the fire of sacrifice.

यज्ञशिष्टामृतभुजो यान्ति ब्रह्म सनातनम् ।
नायं लोकोऽस्त्ययज्ञस्य कुतोऽन्यः कुरुसत्तम ॥

Yajnasishtaamritabhujo yaanti brahma sanaatanam;
Naayam loko'styayajnasya kuto'nyah kurusattama.

31. (Only) those who eat the nectarine remnant of sacrifice go to the eternal Brahman. Even this world cannot be secured by one who does not sacrifice. So how could one (who does not sacrifice) hope for the world of Brahman, Oh Best of the Kurus (Arjuna).

एवं बहुविधा यज्ञा वितता ब्रह्मणो मुखे ।
कर्मजान्विद्धि तान्सर्वानेवं ज्ञात्वा विमोक्ष्यसे ॥

Evam bahuvidhaa yajnaa vitataa brahmano mukhe;
Karmajaan viddhi taan sarvaan evam jnaatwaa vimokshyase.

32. Thus, from the very mouth of Brahman (the Vedas) many such sacrifices have proceeded. Know them all to be born of Karma. Thus knowing, you will attain Liberation.

श्रेयान्द्रव्यमयाद्यज्ञाज्ज्ञानयज्ञः   परंतप ।
सर्वं कर्माखिलं पार्थ ज्ञाने परिसमाप्यते ॥

Sreyaan dravyamayaadyajnaaj jnaanayajnah parantapa;
Sarvam karmaakhilam paartha jnaane parisamaapyate.

33. The sacrifice of knowledge, O Scorcher of Foes, is better than the sacrifice of material objects, because all actions (sacrifices), without exception, terminate in knowledge.

तद्विद्धि प्रणिपातेन परिप्रश्नेन सेवया ।
उपदेक्ष्यन्ति ते ज्ञानं ज्ञानिनस्तत्त्वदर्शिनः ॥

Tadviddhi pranipaatena pariprasnena sevayaa;
Upadekshyanti te jnaanam jnaaninas tatwadarsinah.

34. Learn this by humble prostration, spiritual enquiry and service, and the Self-realized Sages, who possess scriptural knowledge, will instruct you in wisdom.

यज्ज्ञात्वा न पुनर्मोहमेवं यास्यसि पाण्डव ।
येन भूतान्यशेषेण द्रक्ष्यस्यात्मन्यथो मयि ॥

Yajjnaatwa na punarmoham evam yaasyasi paandava;
Yena bhootaanyaseshena drakshyasyaatmanyatho mayi.

35. Having known this (wisdom), O Arjuna, you will
never enter into delusion again. You will behold all
beings within your very Self, as well as in Me.

अपि चेदसि पापेभ्यः सर्वेभ्यः पापकृत्तमः ।
सर्वं ज्ञानप्लवेनैव वृजिनं संतरिष्यसि ॥३६॥

Api chedasi paapebhyah sarvebhyah paapakrittamah;
Sarvam jnaanaplavenaiva vrijinam santarishyasi.

36. Even if you were the greatest of all sinners, you could
cross over all sins by adopting the boat of wisdom.

यथैधांसि समिद्धोऽग्निर्भस्मसात्कुरुतेऽर्जुन ।
ज्ञानाग्निः सर्वकर्माणि भस्मसात्कुरुते तथा ॥

Yathaidhaamsi samiddho'gnir bhasmasaat kurute'rjuna;
Jnaanaagnih sarvakarmaani bhasmasaat kurute tathaa.

37. Oh Arjuna, just as blazing fire turns fuel into ashes, so the fire of wisdom turns all actions into ashes.

न हि ज्ञानेन सदृशं पवित्रमिह विद्यते ।
तत्स्वयं योगसंसिद्धः कालेनात्मनि विन्दति ॥

Na hi jnaanena sadrisam pavitram iha vidyate;
Tat swayam yogasamsiddhah kaalenatmani vindati.

38. There is nothing in this world as pure as wisdom. One who has perfected himself by the practice of Karma Yoga attains this (wisdom) within his very Self in the fullness of time.

श्रद्धावाँल्लभते ज्ञानं तत्परः संयतेन्द्रियः ।
ज्ञानं लब्ध्वा परां शान्तिमचिरेणाधिगच्छति ॥

Sraddhaavaan labhate jnaanam tatparah samyatendriyah;
Jnaanam labdhvaa param santimachirenaadhigacchati.

39. One who is filled with faith, devoted to the pursuits of knowledge, and endowed with self-control attains wisdom. Having attained it, he hastens to everlasting peace.

अज्ञश्चाश्रद्दधानश्च संशयात्मा विनश्यति ।
नायं लोकोऽस्ति न परो न सुखं संशयात्मनः ॥

Ajnaschaasraddadhaanas cha samsayaatmaa vinasyati;
Naayam loko'sti na paro na sukham samsayaatmanah.

40. But one who is ignorant, devoid of faith, and overcome by doubts, perishes. There is neither this world, nor the other world—no happiness anywhere for the soul that has a doubting nature.

योगसंन्यस्तकर्माणं ज्ञानसंछिन्नसंशयम् ।
आत्मवन्तं न कर्माणि निबध्नन्ति धनंजय ॥

Yogasamnyasta karmaanam jnaanasamcchinnasamsayam;
Aatmavantam na karmaani nibadhnanti dhananjaya.

41. O Conqueror of Wealth (Arjuna), if one attains renunciation by the practise of Yoga (Karma Yoga), dispels all doubt by wisdom, and becomes established in the Self, he is never bound by Karmas (actions).

तस्मादज्ञानसंभूतं हृत्स्थं ज्ञानासिनात्मनः ।
छित्त्वैनं संशयं योगमातिष्ठोत्तिष्ठ भारत ॥४२॥

Tasmaad ajnaanasambhootam hritstham jnaanaasinaatmanah;
Chhitwainam samsayam yogam aatishthottishtha bhaarata.

42. Therefore, O Bharata, use the sword of wisdom to destroy this doubt which is born of ignorance even within your heart, and arise for the pursuit of Yoga.

ॐ तत्सदिति श्रीमद्भगवद्गीतासूपनिषत्सु ब्रह्मविद्यायां
योगशास्त्रे श्रीकृष्णार्जुनसंवादे **ज्ञानविभाग**
योगो नाम चतुर्थोऽध्यायः ॥ ४ ॥

Om tat sat iti srimad bhagavad gitaasoopanishatsu
brahmavidyaayaam yogashaastre sri krishnaarjunasamvaade
jnanavibhaagayogo naama chaturtho'dhyaayah.

Om Tat Sat.
Thus, in the Upanishad of the Bhagavad Gita,
the knowledge of Supreme Brahman, the scripture of Yoga,
the dialogue between Sri Krishna and Arjuna,
ends the fourth chapter entitled,
"The Yoga of Wisdom."

अथ पञ्चमोऽध्यायः

Atha Panchamo'dhyaayah

Chapter 5

Karma Sanyasa Yogah

The Yoga of Renunciation of Action

A profound insight into the two aspects of spiritual movement—Yoga and Samkhya—is given. Yoga implies a blend of action and devotion (Karma and Bhakti) while Samkhya suggests the path of Jnana or knowledge. For majority of people, a blend of Karma and Bhakti is important for the attainment of the heights of Jnana where the very ego is renounced.

अर्जुन उवाच

संन्यासं कर्मणां कृष्ण पुनर्योगं च शंससि ।
यच्छ्रेय एतयोरेकं तन्मे ब्रूहि सुनिश्चितम् ॥१॥

Arjuna uvaacha
Samnyaasam karmanaam krishna punar yogam cha samsasi;
Yachchreya etayorekam tanme broohi sunischitam.

1. Arjuna asked: O Krishna, you teach renunciation of action, and at the same time, the Yoga of action. Please tell me decisively, which is the better of the two?

श्रीभगवानुवाच
संन्यासः कर्मयोगश्च निःश्रेयसकरावुभौ ।
तयोस्तु कर्मसंन्यासात्कर्मयोगो विशिष्यते ॥

Sree Bhagavaan uvaacha
Samnyaasah karmayogascha nisreyasakaraa vubhau;
Tayostu karmasamnyaasaat karmyogo visishyate.

2. Sri Bhagavan Krishna replied: Both renunciation of action and Karma Yoga lead one to the highest goal, Liberation. However, of these two, Karma Yoga is better than the path of renunciation.

ज्ञेयः स नित्यसंन्यासी यो न द्वेष्टि न काङ्क्षति ।
निर्द्वन्द्वो हि महाबाहो सुखं बन्धात्प्रमुच्यते ।३।

Jneyah sa nityasamnyaasi yo na dweshti na kaangshati;
Nirdwandwo hi mahaabaaho sukham bandhaat pramuchyate.

3. O Great-armed Arjuna, one who neither hates nor desires must be considered an eternal Sanyasi. Since he does not experience the pairs of oppossites, he becomes free from bondage easily.

सांख्ययोगौ पृथग्बालाः प्रवदन्ति न पण्डिताः ।
एकमप्यास्थितः सम्यगुभयोर्विन्दते फलम् ॥

Saankhya yogau prithagbaalaah pravadanti na panditaah;
Ekam apyaasthitah samyag ubhayor vindate phalam.

4. Children (the ignorant) alone speak of Samkhya (the path of renunciation) as different from Yoga (the path of action); the enlightened do not hold this view. Whoever proceeds along either one of the two must attain Liberation, the goal of both.

यत्सांख्यैः प्राप्यते स्थानं तद्योगैरपि गम्यते ।
एकं सांख्यं च योगं च यः पश्यति स पश्यति ॥

Yatsaankhyaih praapyate sthaanam tad yogair api gamyate;
Ekam saankhyam cha yogam cha yah pasyati sa pasyati.

5. The goal that is acquired by renunciates is the same that is attained by Karma Yogis. Whoever sees Samkhya and Yoga as one, indeed sees rightly.

संन्यासस्तु महाबाहो दुःखमाप्तुमयोगतः ।
योगयुक्तो मुनिर्ब्रह्म नचिरेणाधिगच्छति ॥६॥

Samnyaasastu mahaabaaho dukham aaptum ayogatah;
Yogayukto munir brahma na chirenaadhigacchati.

6. But, O Mighty-armed Arjuna, without Karma Yoga the path of Sanyasa is beset with troubles. The Sage who pursues Yoga (having attained renunciation) hastens to the attainment of Brahman.

योगयुक्तो विशुद्धात्मा विजितात्मा जितेन्द्रियः।
सर्वभूतात्मभूतात्मा कुर्वन्नपि न लिप्यते ॥७॥

Yogayukto visuddhaatmaa vijitaatmaa jitendriyah;
Sarvabhootaatmaabhootaatmaa kurvannapi na lipyate.

7. Perfected in Yoga (of action), with a pure heart, having control over the body and mastery over the senses, he beholds the Self in all beings. Such a Sage is untouched by actions, even though he continues performing them.

नैव किंचित्करोमीति युक्तो मन्येत तच्चवित् ।
पश्यञ्शृण्वन्स्पृशञ्जिघ्रन्नश्नन्गच्छन्स्वपञ्श्वसन्॥

Naiva kinchit karomeeti yukto manyeta tatwavit;
Pasyan srinvan sprisan jighran nasnan gacchan swapan swasan.

8. A knower of Truth who is united with God, feels that "I do nothing at all." While seeing, hearing, touching, smelling, tasting (eating), walking, sleeping,

प्रलपन्विसृजन्गृह्णन्नुन्मिषन्निमिषन्नपि   ।
इन्द्रियाणीन्द्रियार्थेषु वर्तन्त इति धारयन् ।९।

Pralapan visrijan grihnan unmishan nimishannapi;
Indriyaanindriyaartheshu vartanta iti dhaarayan.

9. Breathing, speaking, grasping, letting go, opening and

ब्रह्मण्याधाय कर्माणि सङ्गं त्यक्त्वा करोति यः ।
लिप्यते न स पापेन पद्मपत्रमिवाम्भसा ॥१०॥

Brahmanyaadhaaya karmaani sangam tyaktwaa karoti yah;
Lipyate na sa paapena padmapatram ivaambhasaa.

10. He who performs actions by invoking Brahman and
by renouncing attachment to the fruit of action, is not
touched by sin, even as a lotus leaf remains untouched by
water.

कायेन मनसा बुद्ध्या केवलैरिन्द्रियैरपि ।
योगिनः कर्म कुर्वन्ति सङ्गं त्यक्त्वात्मशुद्धये ॥

Kaayena manasaa budhyaa kevalair indriyair api;
Yoginah karma kurvanti sangam tyaktwatmasuddhaye.

11. A Yogi (following the Yoga of action) continues to
perform actions merely with his body, mind, intellect
and senses. With detachment he performs actions for the
purity of his heart.

युक्तःकर्मफलं त्यक्त्वा शान्तिमाप्नोति नैष्ठिकीम् ।
युक्तः कामकारेण फले सक्तो निबध्यते ॥१२॥

Yuktah karmaphalam tyaktwaa saantim aapnoti naishthikeem;
Ayuktah kaamakaarena phale sakto nibadhyate.

12. One who is devoted to Yoga (Karma Yoga) attains peace by renouncing the fruits of action. But one who is not united with Karma Yoga is impelled by desires, attached to the fruits of action, and therefore, goes to bondage.

सर्वकर्माणि मनसा संन्यस्यास्ते सुखं वशी ।
नवद्वारे पुरे देही नैव कुर्वन्न कारयन् ॥१३॥

Sarvakarmaani manasaa samnyasyaaste sukham vasee;
Navadwaare pure dehi naiva kurvan na kaarayan.

13. The embodied soul who has controlled his body and senses, and who has mentally renounced all actions, though abiding in the nine-gated city, does not work, nor does he cause any work to be done.

न कर्तृत्वं न कर्माणि लोकस्य सृजति प्रभुः।
न कर्मफलसंयोगं स्वभावस्तु प्रवर्तते ॥१४॥

Na kartritwam na karmaani lokasya srijati prabhuh;
Na karmaphala samyogam swabhaavas tu pravartate.

14. The Divine Self does not create "doership" in people, nor does He work; He does not create the relationship between the works and their fruits. It is Prakriti that sustains these.

नादत्ते कस्यचित्पापं न चैव सुकृतं विभुः ।
अज्ञानेनावृतं ज्ञानं तेन मुह्यन्ति जन्तवः ॥१५॥

Naadatte kasyachit paapam na chaiva sukritam vibhuh;
Ajnaanenaavritam jnaanam tena muhyanti jantavh.

15. The All-pervading Divinity does not take the sin or the virtue of anyone. It is because knowledge is veiled by ignorance that individual souls are deluded.

ज्ञानेन तु तदज्ञानं येषां नाशितमात्मनः ।
तेषामादित्यवज्ज्ञानं प्रकाशयति तत्परम् ॥१६॥

Jnaanena tu tad ajnaanam yesham naasitam aatmanah;
Teshaam aadityavat jnaanam prakaasayati tatparam.

16. For those whose ignorance has been destroyed by the knowledge of the Self, wisdom shines forth like the sun, revealing the Reality of the Transcendental Self.

तद्बुद्धयस्तदात्मानस्तन्निष्ठास्तत्परायणाः।
गच्छन्त्यपुनरावृत्तिं ज्ञाननिर्धूतकल्मषाः ।।१७।।

Tadbuddhyas tadaatmaanas tannishthaas tatparaayanaah;
Gacchantyapunaraavrittim jnaana nirdhoota kalmashaah.

17. Those who have their intellect centered in the Self, and who are supremely devoted to the Self, destroy all sins by knowledge and attain that state of Liberation whence there is no return (to the world-process of repeated birth and death).

विद्याविनयसंपन्ने ब्राह्मणे गवि हस्तिनि ।
शुनि चैव श्वपाके च पण्डिताः समदर्शिनः।।१८।।

Vidyaavinaya sampanne braahmane gavi hastini;
Suni chaiva svapaake cha panditaah samadarsinah.

18. The enlightened Sages behold the same Self in Brahmins who are endowed with knowledge and humility, as in cows and elephants, or even in dogs and outcastes.

इहैव तैर्जितः सर्गो येषां साम्ये स्थितं मनः ।
निर्दोषं हि समं ब्रह्म तस्माद्ब्रह्मणि ते स्थिताः ॥

Ihaiva tairjitah sargo yesham saamye sthitam manah;
Nirdosham hi samam brahma tasmaat brahmani te sthitah.

19. Even in this life, the world is conquered by those whose mind is established in equality. Brahman is free from defects and is the embodiment of equality; therefore, become established in Brahman.

न प्रहृष्येत्प्रियं प्राप्य नोद्विजेत्प्राप्य चाप्रियम् ।
स्थिरबुद्धिरसंमूढो ब्रह्मविद् ब्रह्मणि स्थितः ।२०।

Na prahrishyet priyam praapya noddwijet praapya cha apriyam;
Sthirabuddhir asammoodho brahmavit brahmani sthitah.

20. The knower of Brahman has a firm intellect, is free from illusions, and is established in Brahman. He

neither rejoices when he acquires what is desirable, nor is he agitated when he encounters what is undesirable.

बाह्यस्पर्शेष्वसक्तात्मा विन्दत्यात्मनि यत्सुखम्।
स ब्रह्मयोगयुक्तात्मा सुखमक्षयमश्नुते ॥२१॥

Baahyasparseshwasaktaatmaa vindatyaatmani yat sukham;
Sa brahma yoga yuktaatmaa sukham akshayam asnute.

21. If the mind is not attached to the external objects of the world, one attains the Bliss of the Self. Having united with the Yoga of Brahman, one attains Infinite Bliss.

ये हि संस्पर्शजा भोगा दुःखयोनय एव ते।
आद्यन्तवन्तः कौन्तेय न तेषु रमते बुधः ॥२२॥

Ye hi samsparsajaa bhogaa duhkhayonaya eva te;
Aadyantavantah kaunteya na teshu ramate budhah.

22. The enjoyments obtained by the contact of the senses with their objects are the progenitors of pain. They have a beginning and an end; therefore, O Son of Kunti, the wise do not delight in them.

शक्नोतीहैव यः सोढुं प्राक्शरीरविमोक्षणात् ।
कामक्रोधोद्भवं वेगं स युक्तः स सुखी नरः ।२३।

Saknotihaiva yah sodhum praak sareera vimokshanaat;
Kaamakrodhodbhavam vegam sa yuktah sa sukhi narah.

23. One who is able to withstand the impulse of desire
and anger even before departing from the body, is verily
a Yogi and a blissful person.

योऽन्तःसुखोऽन्तरारामस्तथान्तज्योतिरेव यः ।
स योगी ब्रह्मनिर्वाणं ब्रह्मभूतोऽधिगच्छति ।२४।

Yo'antah sukho'ntaraaraamas tathaantarjyoti eva yah;
Sa yogee brahma nirvaanam brahmabhooto'dhigacchati.

24. One who finds bliss within, rejoices within, and finds
the light of wisdom within himself— such a Yogi becomes
Brahman, and attains absolute freedom (Nirvana).

लभन्ते   ब्रह्मनिर्वाणमृषयः   क्षीणकल्मषाः ।
छिन्नद्वैधा यतात्मानः सर्वभूतहिते रताः ।२५।

Labhante brahmanirvaanam rishayah khseenakalmashaah;
Chchinnadwaidhaa yataatmaanah sarvabhootahite rataah.

25. The Sages who have destroyed all their sins, who have
no doubts, who are self-controlled and devoted to the welfare of all beings, attain Nirvana in the form of Brahman.

कामक्रोधवियुक्तानां यतीनां यतचेतसाम् ।
अभितो ब्रह्मनिर्वाणं वर्तते विदितात्मनाम् ॥

Kaamakrodha viyuktaanaam yateenaam yatachetasaam;
Abhito brahma nirvaanam vartate viditatmanaam.

26. He who has no desire or anger, whose mind is under
his control, and who has realized the Self, has Liberation
even here, not to mention hereafter.

स्पर्शान्कृत्वा बहिर्बाह्यांश्चक्षुश्चैवान्तरे भ्रुवोः ।
प्राणापानौ समौ कृत्वा नासाभ्यन्तरचारिणौ॥

Sparsaan kritwaa bahir baahyaams chakshus chaivaantare bhruvoh;
Praanaapaanau samau kritwaa naasaabhyantara chaarinau.

यतेन्द्रियमनोबुद्धिर्मुनिर्मोक्षपरायणः ।
विगतेच्छाभयक्रोधो यः सदा मुक्त एव सः ॥२८॥

Yatendriya manobuddhir munir moksha paraayanah;
Vigatecchaabhaya krodho yah sadaa mukta eva sah.

27. & 28. Having shut out all external contacts, focused his eyes between the eyebrows, harmonized the Prana and Apana that flow through the nostrils, the Muni (a Sage devoted to meditation) controls his mind, intellect and senses, and is devoted to Liberation alone. One who has renounced desire and anger, is truly Liberated at all times.

मोक्तारं यज्ञतपसां सर्वलोकमहेश्वरम् ।
सुहृदं सर्वभूतानां ज्ञात्वा मां शान्तिमृच्छति ॥

Bhoktaaram yajnatapasaam sarvaloka maheswaram;
Suhridam sarvabhootaanaam jnaatwaa maam saantim ricchati.

29. I am the Enjoyer of all sacrifices and austerities, the great Lord ruling over all the worlds, and the Friend of all beings. One who realizes Me attains supreme peace.

ॐ तत्सदिति श्रीमद्भगवद्गीतासूपनिषत्सु ब्रह्मविद्यायां
योगशास्त्रे श्रीकृष्णार्जुनसंवादे कर्मसंन्यासयोगो
नाम पञ्चमोऽध्याय: ॥ ५ ॥

*Om tat sat iti srimad bhagavad gitaasoopanishatsu
brahmavidyaayaam yogashaastre sri krishnaarjunasamvaade
karmasanyasayogo naama panchamo'dhyaayah.*

Om Tat Sat.
Thus, in the Upanishad of the Bhagavad Gita,
the knowledge of Supreme Brahman, the scripture of Yoga,
the dialogue between Sri Krishna and Arjuna,
ends the fifth chapter entitled,
"The Yoga of Renunciation of Action."

उद्धरेदात्मनात्मानं नात्मानमवसादयेत् ।
आत्मैव ह्यात्मनो बन्धुरात्मैव रिपुरात्मनः ॥५॥

अथ षष्ठोऽध्यायः

Atha Shashtho'dhyaayah

Chapter 6

Atma Samyam Yogah

The Yoga of Meditation

Meditation is the most profound and effective technique in the practice of Karma and Bhakti Yogas on the one hand, and Jnana Yoga on the other. The present chapter, therefore, elaborates upon the art of practising meditaiton which is the basis of all the mystic movements of the world.

श्रीभगवानुवाच

अनाश्रितः कर्मफलं कार्यं कर्म करोति यः ।
स संन्यासी च योगी च न निरग्निर्न चाक्रियः ।१।

Sree Bhagavaan uvaacha
Anaashritah karmaphalam kaaryam karma karoti yah;
Sa sannyaasi cha yogi cha na niragnirna chaakriyah.

1. Lord Krishna said: One who performs actions without depending upon their fruits is indeed a Sanyasi and Yogi—not one who has merely renounced the sacrificial fire and the performance of rituals.

यं संन्यासमिति प्राहुर्योगं तं विद्धि पाण्डव ।
न ह्यसंन्यस्तसंकल्पो योगी भवति कश्चन ॥२॥

Yam sannyasamiti praahuryogam tam viddhi paandava;
Na hyasannyastasankalpo yogee bhavati kaschana.

2. O Arjuna, whatever the scriptures say about Sanyasa, the same also applies to Yoga. Because without renouncing the fruits of actions, no one can become a Yogi.

आरुरुक्षोर्मुनेर्योगं कर्म कारणमुच्यते ।
योगारूढस्य तस्यैव शमः कारणमुच्यते ॥३॥

Aarurukshormuneryogam karma kaaranamuchyate;
Yogaarudhasya tasyaiva shamah kaaranamuchyate.

3. For the Muni (a Yogi devoted to meditation) who is ascending the Yogic ladder, action is called the means, while for one who has ascended the ladder, serenity is described as the means (for attaining the fullness of wisdom).

यदा हि नेन्द्रियार्थेषु न कर्मस्वनुषज्जते ।
सर्वसंकल्पसंन्यासी योगारूढस्तदोच्यते ॥४॥

Yadaa hi nendriyaartheshu na karmaswanushajjate;
Sarvasankalpasannyaasi yogaarudhas tadochyate.

4. When the Sage is not attached to the objects of the senses, nor to actions, and has renounced all desires (for fruits of action), he is called Yogarudha—a Yogi who has ascended the ladder of Yoga.

उद्धरेदात्मनात्मानं नात्मानमवसादयेत् ।
आत्मैव ह्यात्मनो बन्धुरात्मैव रिपुरात्मनः ॥५॥

Uddharedaatmanaatmaanam naatmaanamavasaadayet;
Atmaiva hyaatmano bandhuratmaiva ripuraatmanah.

5. Let a Yogi lift himself by himself; he should not drown himself into a degraded condition. Because he himself is his own friend as well as his own enemy.

बन्धुरात्मात्मनस्तस्य येनात्मैवात्मना जितः ।
अनात्मनस्तु शत्रुत्वे वर्तेतात्मैव शत्रुवत् ॥६॥

Bandhuraatmaatmanastasya yenaatmaivaatmanaa jitah;
Anaatmanastu shatrutwe vartetaatmaiva shatruvat.

6. For one who has conquered his self (lower self) by his self (higher self), his very self becomes his friend. But for one who has not conquered his self, his very self turns out to be his enemy.

जितात्मनः प्रशान्तस्य परमात्मा समाहितः ।
शीतोष्णसुखदुः खेषु तथा मानापमानयोः ॥७॥

Jitaatmanah prasaantasya paramaatmaa samaahitah;
Sheetoshnasukhaduhkkheshu tathaa maanaapamaanayoh.

7. One who has conquered his self (the lower self) and has become peaceful, who remains balanced in cold and

heat, pleasure and pain, and honor and dishonor, his mind becomes centered on the Supreme Self.

ज्ञानविज्ञानतृप्तात्मा कूटस्थो विजितेन्द्रियः ।
युक्त इत्युच्यते योगी समलोष्टाश्मकाञ्चनः ॥८॥

Jnaanavijnaanatriptaatmaa kootastho vijitendriyah;
Yukta ityuchyate yogee samaloshtaashmakaanchanah.

8. That Yogi is united with the Divine Self whose mind is contented due to knowledge and realization, who is immutable due to his mastery over the senses, and for whom a clod of earth, a stone and gold are the same.

सुहृन्मित्रार्युदासीनमध्यस्थद्वेष्यबन्धुषु   ।
साधुष्वपि च पापेषु समबुद्धिर्विशिष्यते ॥९॥

Suhrinmitraaryudaaseenamadhyasthadweshyabandhushu;
Sadhushwapi cha paapeshu samabuddhirvishishyate.

9. Among the Yogis, he who has a balanced mind towards well-wishers, friends, enemies, the indifferent, the impartial, the hateful, relatives, saints as well as sinners, he excels.

योगी युञ्जीत सततमात्मानं रहसि स्थितः ।
एकाकी यतचित्तात्मा निराशीरपरिग्रहः ।।१०।

Yogee yunjeeta satatamaatmaanam rahasi sthitah;
Ekaaki yatachittaatmaa niraasheeraparigrahah.

10. A Yogi should constantly fix his mind on the Divine
Self. He should abide in solitude, keep his body and
mind under his control, and renounce desires and
cravings for possessions.

शुचौ देशे प्रतिष्ठाप्य स्थिरमासनमात्मनः ।
नात्युच्छ्रितं नातिनीचं चैलाजिनकुशोत्तरम् ।।११

Suchau deshe pratishthaapya sthiramaasanamaatmanah;
Naatyucchritam naatineecham chailaajinakushottaram.

11. In a clean spot which is neither too low nor too high,
one should spread Kusha grass, a deer skin, and a cloth,
one on top of the other. Thus, one establishes a firm seat
for the practice of meditation.

तत्रैकाग्रं मनः कृत्वा यतचित्तेन्द्रियक्रियः ।
उपविश्यासने युञ्ज्याद्योगमात्मविशुद्धये ।।१२।

Tatraikaagram manah kritwaa yatachittendriyakriyah;
Upavishyaasane yunjyaadyogamaatmavishuddhaye.

12. Having seated himself in a meditative pose and having brought the mind to a state of one-pointedness, he should attain mastery over the senses and mind, and practise Yoga (Samadhi) for the purification of the soul.

समं कायशिरोग्रीवं धारयन्नचलं स्थिरः ।
संप्रेक्ष्य नासिकाग्रं स्वं दिशश्चानवलोकयन्।१३।

Samam kaayashirogreevam dhaarayannachalam sthirah;
Samprekshya naasikaagram swam dishaschaanavalokayan.

13. Holding the body steady, keeping the middle part of the body, neck and head in a straight line, he should focus his gaze at the tip of the nose, without looking around, keeping the mind undistracted.

प्रशान्तात्मा विगतभीर्ब्रह्मचारिव्रते स्थितः ।
मनः संयम्य मच्चित्तो युक्त आसीत मत्परः ॥

Prashaantaatmaa vigatabheer brahmacharivrate sthitah;
Manah samyamya macchitto yukta aaseeta matparah.

14. Peaceful and fearless, established in the vow of Brahmacharya, with his mind subdued, his heart directed towards Me, and with wholehearted devotion to Me, let him sit intent on realizing Me.

युञ्जन्नेवं सदात्मानं योगी नियतमानसः ।
शान्तिं निर्वाणपरमां मत्संस्थामधिगच्छति ॥

Yunjannevam sadaatmaanam yogee niyatamaanasah;
Shaantim nirvaanaparamaam matsamsthaamadhigacchati.

15. Having subdued his mind, the Yogi constantly applies his mind to the Self, and consequently attains peace in the form of supreme Nirvana. Thus, he abides in Me.

नात्यश्नतस्तु योगोऽस्ति न चैकान्तमनश्नतः ।
न चाति स्वप्नशीलस्य जाग्रतो नैव चार्जुन ॥१६॥

Naatyashnatastu yogosti nachaikaantamanashnatah;
Na chaatiswapnasheelasya jaagrato naiva chaarjuna.

16. Oh Arjuna, Yoga cannot be attained by one who eats

too much, nor by one who does not eat at all. It is not for
one who sleeps too much, nor for one who does not sleep
at all.

युक्ताहारविहारस्य   युक्तचेष्टस्य   कर्मसु ।
युक्तस्वप्नावबोधस्य योगो भवति दुःखहा ।१७।

Yuktaahaaravihaarasya yuktacheshtasya karmasu;
Yuktaswapnaavabodhasya yogo bhavati duhkkhahaa.

17. If one is regulated in food and entertainment,
harmonized in performing actions, and balanced in
sleeping and waking, then he can perfect that Yoga which
leads to the cessation of pain.

यदा   विनियतं   चित्तमात्मन्येवावतिष्ठते ।
निःस्पृहः सर्वकामेभ्यो युक्त इत्युच्यते तदा ॥

Yadaa viniyatam chittamaatmanyevaavatishthate;
Nisprihah sarvakaamebhyo yukta ityuchyate tadaa.

18. When the Chitta is withdrawn from all sides and
focused on the Self alone, the Yogi becomes free from all

desires for the objects of the world, and he is called a Yukta (one who is established in Yoga).

यथा दीपो निवातस्थो नेङ्गते सोपमा स्मृता ।
योगिनो यतचित्तस्य युञ्जतो योगमात्मनः ॥

Yathaa deepo nivaatastho nengate sopamaa smiritaa;
Yogino yatachittasya yunjato yogamaatmanah.

19. Just as a lamp does not flicker restlessly in a place where there is no wind, so the mind of a Yogi that has been subdued by the practice of Yoga does not flicker due to the absence of the wind of desire.

यत्रोपरमते चित्तं निरुद्धं योगसेवया ।
यत्र चैवात्मनात्मानं पश्यन्नात्मनि तुष्यति ॥

Yatroparamate chittam niruddham yogasevayaa;
Yatra chaivaatmanaatmaanam pashyannaatmani tushyati.

20. When it is restrained by the practice of Yoga (Samadhi), the Chitta reaches the state of supreme withdrawal from the world-process. Then the Yogi seees the Self with his purified mind, and rejoices in the Self.

सुखमात्यन्तिकं यत्तद्बुद्धिग्राह्यमतीन्द्रियम् ।
वेत्ति यत्र न चैवायं स्थितश्चलति तत्त्वतः ।।२१।।

Sukhamaatyantikam yattad buddhigraahyamateendriyam;
Vetti yatra na chaivaayam sthitashchalati tattwatah.

21. The Yogi experiences Bliss that is unexcellable,
beyond the reach of the mind and senses. That Bliss can
be comprehended by the intuitive intellect alone. Having
attained this state, he does not falter from Truth (the Self).

यं लब्ध्वा चापरं लाभं मन्यते नाधिकं ततः ।
यस्मिन्स्थितो न दुःखेन गुरुणापि विचाल्यते ।।

Yam labdhwaa chaaparam laabham manyate naadhikam tatah;
Yasmin sthito na duhkkhena gurunaapi vichaalyate.

22. Having attained this state, he realizes that there is
nothing greater than it. And being established in this
state, he is not shaken, even when confronted with the
heaviest of sorrow.

तं विद्याद्दुःखसंयोगवियोगं योगसंज्ञितम् ।
स निश्चयेन योक्तव्यो योगोऽनिर्विण्णचेतसा ।।

Tam vidyaad duhkkhasamyogaviyogam yogasamjnitam;
Sa nishchayena yoktavyo yogonirvinnachetasaa.

23. Yoga should be known as that state wherein there is total separation from the plane where there is contact with pain. This Yoga should be practised with firmness and with an unwavering heart.

संकल्पप्रभवान्कामांस्त्यक्त्वा सर्वानशेषतः ।
मनसैवेन्द्रियग्रामं विनियम्य समन्ततः ॥२४॥

Sankalpaprabhavaan kaamaan tyaktwaa sarvaan aseshatah;
Manasaivendriyagraamam viniyamya samantatah.

24. A Yogi should renounce all desires that are born of egoistic will, and should restrain the senses completely by the mind.

शनैः शनैरुपरमेद्बुद्ध्या धृतिगृहीतया ।
आत्मसंस्थं मनः कृत्वा न किंचिदपि चिन्तयेत् ॥

Shanaih shanairuparamet budhyaa dhritigriheetayaa;
Aaatmasamstham manah kritwaa na kinchidapi chintayet.

25. With his intellect held firm, he should turn the Chitta (mind) away from the objects of the world in gradual stages. Once he has directed it to the Self, he should not think of anything else.

यतो यतो निश्चरति मनश्चञ्चलमस्थिरम् ।
ततस्ततो नियम्यैतदात्मन्येव वशं नयेत् ।२६।

Yato yato nishcharati manashchanchalamasthiram;
Tatastato niyamyaitat aatmanyeva vasham nayet.

26. If this mind becomes restless and distracted, for whatever reason, then let him restrain it and bring it back under the control of the purified intellect (the higher Self).

प्रशान्तमनसं ह्येनं योगिनं सुखमुत्तमम् ।
उपैति शान्तरजसं ब्रह्मभूतमकल्मषम् ।२७।

Prashaantamanasam hyenam yoginam sukhamuttamam;
Upaiti shaantarajasam brahmabhootamakalmasham.

27. Supreme Bliss is enjoyed by the Yogi who has attained

peace of mind, who has stilled the clamor of Rajas in his nature, who is sinless, and who has become identified with Brahman.

युञ्जन्नेवं सदात्मानं योगी विगतकल्मषः ।
सुखेन ब्रह्मसंस्पर्शमत्यन्तं सुखमश्नुते ।२८।

Yunjannevam sadaatmaanam yogee vigatakalmashah;
Sukhena brahmasamsparsham atyantam sukham ashnute.

28. Thus, a Yogi who maintains his mind always in Samadhi, rises beyond the evil of the world, and easily experiences the infinite Bliss of contact with Brahman.

सर्वभूतस्थमात्मानं सर्वभूतानि चात्मनि ।
ईक्षते योगयुक्तात्मा सर्वत्र समदर्शनः ।२९।

Sarvabhootasthamaatmaanam sarvabhootaani chaatmani;
Eekshate yogayuktaatmaa sarvatra samadarshanah.

29. One whose mind is purified by Yoga beholds the Self in all beings and all beings in the Self; he sees the same Self everywhere.

यो मां पश्यति सर्वत्र सर्वं च मयि पश्यति ।
तस्याहं न प्रणश्यामि स च मे न प्रणश्यति ।३०।

Yo maam pashyati sarvatra sarvam cha mayi pashyati;
Tasyaaham na pranashyaami sa cha me ne pranashyati.

30. For one who sees Me everywhere, and sees all beings
in Me, I am never destroyed for him, nor is he ever
destroyed for Me.

सर्वभूतस्थितं यो मां भजत्येकत्वमास्थितः ।
सर्वथा वर्तमानोऽपि स योगी मयि वर्तते ।३१।

Sarvabhootasthitam yo maam bhajatyekatwamaasthitah;
Sarvathaa vartamaanopi sa yogee mayi vartate.

31. If one worships Me seated in all beings, with the
vision of oneness, then whatever work he may do, he ever
abides in Me.

आत्मौपम्येन सर्वत्र समं पश्यति योऽर्जुन ।
सुखं वा यदि वा दुःखं स योगी परमो मतः ॥

Aaatmaupamyena sarvatra samam pashyati yo'rjuna;
Sukham vaa yadi vaa duhkkham sa yogee paramo matah.

32. O Arjuna! The Yogi who sees the likeness of himself in all and thus maintains equal vision in pleasure and pain, he is considered the highest Yogi.

अर्जुन उवाच

योऽयं योगस्त्वया प्रोक्तः साम्येन मधुसूदन ।
एतस्याहं न पश्यामि चञ्चलत्वात्तिथितिं स्थिराम्॥

Arjuna uvaacha
Yoyam yogastwayaa proktah saamyena madhusoodana;
Yetasyaaham na pashyaami chanchalatwaat sthitim sthiraam.

33. Arjuna asked: O Madhusudana (Krishna, the Destroyer of the Demon Madhu), I do not see how it is possible to maintain the steady state of Yogic equanimity which you have taught. This mind is ever so restless!

चञ्चलं हि मनः कृष्ण प्रमाथि बलवद्दृढम् ।
तस्याहं निग्रहं मन्ये वायोरिव सुदुष्करम् ।३४।

Chanchalam hi manah krishna pramaathi balavad dridham;
Tasyaaham nigraham manye vaayoriva sudushkaram.

34. Verily, O Krishna, the mind is fickle, impetuous and turburlent. To me it seems more difficult to control the mind than it is to control the wind.

श्रीभगवानुवाच

असंशयं महाबाहो मनो दुर्निग्रहं चलम् ।
अभ्यासेन तु कौन्तेय वैराग्येण च गृह्यते ।।३५।।

Sree Bhagavaan uvaacha
Asamshayam mahaabaaho mano durnigraham chalam;
Abhyaasena tu kaunteya vairaagyena cha grihyate.

35. Bhagavan Krishna said: Indeed the mind is restless and difficult to control, but can be brought under control by the exercise of Abhyasa (repeated effort) and Vairagya (dispassion).

असंयतात्मना योगो दुष्प्राप इति मे मतिः ।
वश्यात्मना तु यतता शक्योऽवाप्तुमुपायतः ।।

Asamyataatmanaa yogo dushpraapa iti me matih;
Vashyaatmanaa tu yatataa shakyovaaptumupaayatah.

36. It is my opinion that Yoga is difficult for anyone who is lacking self-control. But it can be attained by one who has mastered his lower self if he adopts the proper means.

अर्जुन उवाच

अयतिः   श्रद्धयोपेतो   योगाच्चलितमानसः ।

अप्राप्य योगसंसिद्धिं कां गतिं कृष्ण गच्छति ॥

Arjuna uvaacha
Ayatis shraddhayopeto Yogaacchalitamaanasah;
Apraapya yogasamsiddhim kaam gatim krishna gacchati.

37. Arjuna asked: O Krishna, he who is unable to control himslef despite his faith, whose mind wanders away from the state of Yoga, thus failing to attain Yogic perfection, what end does he meet?

कच्चिन्नोभयविभ्रष्टश्छिन्नाभ्रमिव   नश्यति ।

अप्रतिष्ठो महाबाहो विमूढो ब्रह्मणः पथि ॥

Kacchinnobhayavibhrashtas cchinnabhramiva nashyati;
Apratishtho mahaabaaho vimoodho brahmanah pathi.

38. O Great-armed Krishna, since he has fallen from both the path of Karma and that of Jnana, and has been deluded on the path to Brahman, does he not perish like a cloud that has been rent asunder by the wind, without finding any support?

एतन्मे संशयं कृष्ण छेत्तुमर्हस्यशेषतः ।
त्वदन्यः संशयस्यास्य छेत्ता न ह्युपपद्यते ॥

Yetanme samshayam Krishna cchettumarhasyasheshatah;
Twadanyah samshayasyaasya cchettaa na hyupapadyate.

39. This is my doubt, O Krishna. Please rend it asunder, because it is not possible for anyone except you to dispel this doubt.

श्रीभगवानुवाच
पार्थ नैवेह नामुत्र विनाशस्तस्य विद्यते ।
न हि कल्याणकृत्कश्चिद्दुर्गतिं तात गच्छति ॥

Sree Bhagavaan uvaacha
Paartha naiveha naamutra vinaashas tasya vidyate;
Nahi kalyaanakrit kaschit durgatim taata gacchati.

40. Lord Krishna answered: O Arjuna, a Yogi is never destroyed, neither in this world nor in the next. O Friend, whoever does good does not tread the path of grief.

प्राप्य पुण्यकृतां लोकानुषित्वा शाश्वतीः समाः ।
शुचीनां श्रीमतां गेहे योगभ्रष्टोऽभिजायते ॥

Praapya punyakritaam lokaanushitwaa shaashwateeh samaah;
Shucheenam shreemataam gehe yogabhrashtobhijaayate.

41. Having fallen from Yoga (after death), a Yogi enjoys heavenly worlds for everlasting years, and then, he is born in the house of those who are pure and prosperous.

अथवा योगिनामेव कुले भवति धीमताम् ।
एतद्धि दुर्लभतरं लोके जन्म यदीदृशम् ॥४२॥

Athavaa yoginaameva kule bhavati dheemataam;
Yetaddhi durlabhataram loke janma yadeedrisham.

42. Or he may even be born in the family of wise Yogis. Such a birth in this world is the most difficult to attain.

तत्र तं बुद्धिसंयोगं लभते पौर्वदेहिकम् ।
यतते च ततो भूयः संसिद्धौ कुरुनन्दन ॥४३॥

Tattra tam buddhisamyogam labhate paurvadehikam;
Yatate cha tato bhooyah samsiddhau kurunandana.

43. O Delighter of Kuru's Race, when he is reborn, he is
united with the intellect that he had cultivated in his past
lives. So he endeavors again to attain the higher rungs of
Yoga leading to Liberation.

पूर्वाभ्यासेन तेनैव ह्रियते ह्यवशोऽपि सः ।
जिज्ञासुरपि योगस्य शब्दब्रह्मातिवर्तते ॥४४॥

Poorvaabhyaasena tenaiva hriyate hyavashopi sah;
Jignaasurapi yogasya shabdabrahmaativartate.

44. Driven by his past Yogic practice, he is drawn to Yoga
even in spite of himself. For even an enquirer on the path
of Yoga goes beyond the worlds that are promised by the
ritualistic portion of the Vedas.

प्रयत्नाद्यतमानस्तु योगी संशुद्धकिल्बिषः ।
अनेकजन्मसंसिद्धस्ततो याति परां गतिम् ॥४५॥

Prayatnaadyatamaanastu yogee samshuddhakilbishah;
Anekajanmasamsiddhas tato yaati paraam gatim.

45. Having perfected Yogic states through many lives, in every birth exercising more self-effort than before, a Yogi brings about the removal of mental impurities, and consequently, attains the supreme goal.

तपस्विभ्योऽधिको योगी ज्ञानिभ्योऽपि मतोऽधिकः ।
कर्मिभ्यश्चाधिको योगी तस्माद्योगी भवार्जुन ॥४६॥

Tapaswibhyo'dhiko yogee jnaanibhyo'pi mato'dhikah;
Karmibhyaschaadhiko yogee tasmaad yogee bhavaarjuna.

46. O Arjuna, a Yogi is greater than an ascetic, better than a man of wisdom (an intellectual), and superior to those who are devoted to the path of action. Therefore, become a Yogi!

योगिनामपि सर्वेषां मद्गतेनान्तरात्मना ।
श्रद्धावान्भजते यो मां स मे युक्ततमो मतः ।४७।

Yoginaamapi sarveshaam madgatenaantaraatmanaa;
Shraddhaavaan bhajate yo maam sa me yuktatamo matah.

47. And even among Yogis, those who are endowed with faith, whose inner self is merged in Me, and who thus worship Me, are the highest of all. This is my opinion.

ॐ तत्सदिति श्रीमद्भगवद्गीतासूपनिषत्सु ब्रह्म-
विद्यायां योगशास्त्रे श्रीकृष्णार्जुनसंवादे आत्म-
संयमयोगो नाम षष्ठोऽध्यायः ॥ ६ ॥

Om tat sat iti srimad bhagavad gitaasoopanishatsu
brahmavidyaayaam yogashaastre sri krishnaarjunasamvaade
aatmasamyamyogo naama shashtho'dhyaayah.

Om Tat Sat.
Thus, in the Upanishad of the Bhagavad Gita,
the knowledge of Supreme Brahman, the scripture of Yoga,
the dialogue between Sri Krishna and Arjuna,
ends the sixth chapter entitled,
"The Yoga of Meditation."

चतुर्विधा भजन्ते मां जनाः सुकृतिनोऽर्जुन ।
आर्तो जिज्ञासुरर्थार्थी ज्ञानी च भरतर्षभ ॥१६॥

अथ सप्तमोऽध्यायः

Atha Saptamo'dhyaayah

Chapter 7

Jnana Vijnana Yogah

The Yoga of Wisdom and Realization

Lord Krishna teaches the mystic art of developing devotion to God. God possesses a twofold nature: Matter and Spirit. Matter is His lower nature while Spirit is His higher nature. A devotee must develop the art of worshipping God through every part of his personality: reason, emotion, will and action.

श्रीभगवानुवाच
मय्यासक्तमनाः पार्थ योगं युञ्जन्मदाश्रयः ।
असंशयं समग्रं मां यथा ज्ञास्यसि तच्छृणु ।।१।।

Sree Bhagavaan uvaacha:
Mayyaasaktamanaah paartha yogam yunjanmadaashrayah;
Asamshayam samagram maam yathaa jnaasyasi tatcchrinu.

1. Bhagavan Krishna said: With your mind attached to Me, with Me as your refuge, O Partha, how you will know Me fully, without any doubt, that may you hear from Me.

ज्ञानं तेऽहं सविज्ञानमिदं वक्ष्याम्यशेषतः ।
यज्ज्ञात्वा नेह भूयोऽन्यज्ज्ञातव्यमवशिष्यते ।२।

Jnaanam te'ham savijnaanam idam vakshyaamyaseshatah;
Yajgnaatwaa neha bhooyonyat jnaatavyamavashishyate.

2. I will fully instruct you regarding this knowledge together with realization; having known which nothing more shall remain here to be known.

मनुष्याणां सहस्त्रेषु कश्चिद्यतति सिद्धये ।
यततामपि सिद्धानां कश्चिन्मां वेत्ति तत्त्वतः ।३।

Manushyaanaam sahasreshu kaschidyatati siddhaye;
Yatataamapi siddhaanaam kaschinmaam vetti tatwatah.

3. Among thousands of men one rare soul strives for perfection, and among those who strive with success, one perchance knows Me in truth.

भूमिरापोऽनलो वायुः खं मनो बुद्धिरेव च ।
अहंकार इतीयं मे भिन्ना प्रकृतिरष्टधा ॥ ४ ॥

Bhhoomiraaponalo vaayuh kham mano buddhireva cha;
Ahamkaara iteeyam me bhinnaa prakritirashtadhaa.

4. Earth, Water, Fire, Air, Ether, Mind, Intellect and Ego-principle—these eight divisions go to constitute my Prakriti (the Lower Nature).

अपरेयमितस्त्वन्यां प्रकृतिं विद्धि मे पराम् ।
जीवभूतां महाबाहो ययेदं धार्यते जगत् ॥ ५ ॥

Apareyamitastwanyaam prakritim viddhi me paraam;
Jeevabhootaam mahaabaaho yayedam dhaaryate jagat.

5. This is my Lower Nature, O Mighty-armed Arjuna! Different from this is My Higher Nature which is the soul, by which this entire world is sustained.

एतद्योनीनि भूतानि सर्वाणीत्युपधारय ।
अहं कृत्स्नस्य जगतः प्रभवः प्रलयस्तथा ॥ ६ ॥

Yetadyoneeni bhootaani sarvaaneetyupadhaaraya;
Aham kritsnasya jagatah prabhavah pralayastathaa.

6. These two (Prakritis of Mine) are the source of all
beings. Thus, I am the origin of this entire world as well
as its dissolution.

मत्तः परतरं नान्यत्किञ्चिदस्ति धनंजय ।
मयि सर्वमिदं प्रोतं सूत्रे मणिगणा इव ॥७॥

Mattah parataram naanyat kinchidasti dhananjaya;
Mayi sarvamidam protam sootre maniganaa iva.

7. O Conqueror of Wealth, there is nothing here higher
than Me. All this is strung on Me like clusters of gems on a
string.

रसोऽहमप्सु कौन्तेय प्रभास्मि शशिसूर्ययोः ।
प्रणवः सर्ववेदेषु शब्दः खे पौरुषं नृषु ॥८॥

Rasohamapsu kaunteya prabhaasmi shashisooryayoh;
Pranavas sarvavedeshu shabdah khe paurusham nrishu.

8. O Son of Kunti! I am the taste in the waters, I am the light in the sun and the moon; I am Pranava (Om) in the Vedas, the sound in the Ether element, and manliness in men.

पुण्यो गन्धः पृथिव्यां च तेजश्चास्मि विभावसौ ।
जीवनं सर्वभूतेषु तपश्चास्मि तपस्विषु ॥९॥

Punyo gandhah prithivyaam cha tejashchasmi vibhaavasau;
Jeevanam sarvabhooteshu tapashchaasmi tapaswishu.

9. I am the pure fragrance in earth, I am the effulgence in fire, I am the life in all living beings, I am the austerity in the ascetics.

बीजं मां सर्वभूतानां विद्धि पार्थ सनातनम् ।
बुद्धिर्बुद्धिमतामस्मि तेजस्तेजस्विनामहम् ॥१०॥

Beejam maam sarvabhootaanaam viddhi paartha sanaatanam;
Buddhir buddhimataamasmi tejastejaswinaamaham.

10. O Partha, know Me to be the eternal seed of all beings. I am the intellect in the wise, the valor of those who are valiant.

बलं बलवतां चाहं कामरागविवर्जितम् ।
धर्माविरुद्धो भूतेषु कामोऽस्मि भरतर्षभ॥११॥

Balam balavataam chaaham kaamaraagavivarjitam;
Dharmaaviruddho bhooteshu kaamosmi bharatarshabha.

11. O Best of the Bharatas! Among the strong, I am their strength, that is devoid of lust and passion. Among all beings I am the desire that is not opposed to Dharma (the ethical law).

ये चैव सात्त्विका भावा राजसास्तामसाश्च ये ।
मत्त एवेति तान्विद्धि न त्वहं तेषु ते मयि॥१२॥

Ye chaiva saattvikaa bhaavaa raajasaastaamasaashcha ye;
Matta eveti taanviddhi natwaham teshu te mayi.

12. Whatever beings (or objects) that are Satwic, Rajasic or Tamasic, know them to have proceeded from Me. I am not in them, but they are in Me.

त्रिभिर्गुणमयैर्भावैरेभिः सर्वमिदं जगत् ।
मोहितं नाभिजानाति मामेभ्यः परमव्ययम्।१३।

Tribhirgunamayair bhaavairebhis sarvamidam jagat;
Mohitam naabhijaanaati maamebhyah paramavyayam.

13. Deluded by these three modes of nature, all this
world does not know Me who am different from them
and immutable.

दैवी ह्येषा गुणमयी मम माया दुरत्यया ।
मामेव ये प्रपद्यन्ते मायामेतां तरन्ति ते।१४।

Daivee hyeshaa gunamayee mama maayaa duratyayaa;
Maameva ye prapadyante maayaametaam taranti te.

14. This Divine Maya of Mine composed of the three
Gunas is difficult to cross over, but those who surrender
to Me, they alone are able to cross it.

न मां दुष्कृतिनो मूढाः प्रपद्यन्ते नराधमाः ।
माययापहृतज्ञाना आसुरं भावमाश्रिताः।१५।

Na maam dushkritino moodhaah prapadyante naraadhamaah;
Maayayaapahritajnaanaa aasuram bhaavamaashritaah.

15. The evil-doers sustained by dull and demoniac nature, with their intellect deluded by Maya, the lowest type of men, do not worship Me.

चतुर्विधा भजन्ते मां जनाः सुकृतिनोऽर्जुन।
आर्तो जिज्ञासुरर्थार्थी ज्ञानी च भरतर्षभ।१६।

Chaturvidhaa bhajante maam janaas sukritinorjuna;
Aarto jijnaasurartharthee jnaanee cha bharatarshabha.

16. O Best of the Bharatas! There are four types of virtuous men who worship Me—Arta (distressed), Jinjasu (enquirer), Artharthi (desirer of wealth), and Jnani (the man of wisdom).

तेषां ज्ञानी नित्ययुक्त एकभक्तिर्विशिष्यते।
प्रियो हि ज्ञानिनोऽत्यर्थमहं स च मम प्रियः।१७।

Teshaam jnaanee nityayukta ekabhaktirvishishyate;
Priyo hi jnaaninotyartham aham sacha mama priyah.

17. Of these four the Jnani who is ever united with God, and has one-pointed devotion to God is the best. Because, I am supremely dear to the man of wisdom, and he is dear to Me.

उदाराः सर्व एवैते ज्ञानी त्वात्मैव मे मतम् ।
आस्थितः स हि युक्तात्मा मामेवानुत्तमां गतिम्।।

Udaaraas sarva evaite jnaanee twaatmaiva me matam;
Asthitas sa hi yuktaatmaa maamevaanuttamaam gatim.

18. All these (four types) are indeed the best; however, I consider the man of wisdom as My very Self. For with his mind fully established in My Self, he considers Me as his highest goal.

बहूनां जन्मनामन्ते ज्ञानवान्मां प्रपद्यते ।
वासुदेवः सर्वमिति स महात्मा सुदुर्लभः ।१९।

Bahoonaam janmanaamante jnaanavaanmaam prapadyate;
Vaasudevas sarvamiti sa mahaatmaa sudurlabhah.

19. After many lives (of progressive spiritual evolution), one acquires wisdom and worships Me with the vision that "Vasudeva alone is all this." It is extremely difficult to find such a great soul.

कामैस्तैस्तैर्हृतज्ञानाः प्रपद्यन्तेऽन्यदेवताः ।
तं तं नियममास्थाय प्रकृत्या नियताः स्वया ॥

Kaamaistaistairhritajnaanah prapadyante anyadevatah;
Tam tam niyamamaasthaaya prakrityaa niyataas swayaa.

20. But those whose minds are overpowered by numerous desires, are constrained by their own nature to worship different gods by observing different rites.

यो यो यां यां तनुं भक्तः श्रद्धयार्चितुमिच्छति ।
तस्य तस्याचलां श्रद्धां तामेव विदधाम्यहम् ॥

Yo yo yaam yaam tanum bhaktas shraddhayaarchitumicchati;
Tasya tasyaachalaam shraddhaam taameva vidadhaamyaham.

21. Whatever divine form a devotee wishes to worship with faith, I intensify his faith in that very form.

स तया श्रद्धया युक्तस्तस्याराधनमीहते ।
लभते च ततः कामान्मयैव विहितान्हि तान् ॥

Sa tayaa shraddhayaa yuktastasyaaraadhanameehate;
Labhate cha tatah kaamaan mayaiva vihitaan hitaan.

22. Endowed with that faith, he worships that form, but it is I who (assuming that form of the Deity) bestow upon him the fulfillment of his desires.

अन्तवत्तु फलं तेषां तद्भवत्यल्पमेधसाम् ।
देवान्देवयजो यान्ति मद्भक्ता यान्ति मामपि ॥

Antavattu phalam teshaam tadbhavatyalpamedhasaam;
Devaan devayajo yaanti madbhaktaa yaanti maamapi.

23. But these worshippers possessing dull intellect attain perishable fruits. The worshippers of Gods go to the Gods, while those who are My devotees come to Me.

अव्यक्तं व्यक्तिमापन्नं मन्यन्ते मामबुद्धयः ।
परं भावमजानन्तो ममाव्ययमनुत्तमम् ॥२४॥

Avyaktam vyaktimaapannam manyante maamabuddhayah;
Param Bhaavamajaananto mamaavyayamanuttamam.

24. Men lacking understanding consider Me who am Unmanifest as having manifestation; they do not know My Higher Nature that is immutable and unexcellable.

नाहं प्रकाशः सर्वस्य योगमायासमावृतः ।
मूढोऽयं नाभिजानाति लोको मामजमव्ययम् २५

Naaham prakaashah sarvasya yogamaayaasamaavritah;
Moodhoyam naabhijaanaati loko maamajamavyayam.

25. Veiled as am I by My Yoga Maya, I am not revealed to all. This deluded world does not know Me who am the Unborn, the Imperishable.

वेदाहं समतीतानि वर्तमानानि चार्जुन ।
भविष्याणि च भूतानि मां तु वेद न कश्चन ॥

Vedaaham samateetaani vartamaanaani chaarjuna;
Bhavishyaani cha bhootani maam tu veda na kashchana.

26. O Arjuna, I know all beings of the past, present and future, but no one knows Me.

इच्छाद्वेषसमुत्थेन   द्वन्द्वमोहेन   भारत ।
सर्वभूतानि संमोहं सर्गे यान्ति परन्तप ।।२७।।

Icchaadweshasamutthena dwandwamohena bhaarata;
Sarvabhootaani sammoham sarge yaanti parantapa.

27. O Bharata! All beings at the time of their birth come under the sway of the delusion of pairs of opposites caused by desire and hatred. O Parantapa!

येषां त्वन्तगतं पापं जनानां पुण्यकर्मणाम् ।
ते द्वन्द्वमोहनिर्मुक्ता भजन्ते मां दृढव्रताः ।।

Yeshaam twantagatam paapam janaanaam punyakarmanaam;
Te dwandwamohanirmuktaa bhajante maam dridhavrataah.

28. But, those virtuous souls whose sins have terminated, free of the delusion of the pairs of opposites, worship Me, steadfast in their resolve.

जरामरणमोक्षाय मामाश्रित्य यतन्ति ये ।
ते ब्रह्म तद्विदुः कृत्स्नमध्यात्मं कर्म चाखिलम् ॥

Jaraamaranamokshaaya maamaashritya yatanti ye;
Te brahma tadviduh kritsnam adhyaatmam karma chaakhilam.

29. Those who having taken refuge in Me strive for the cessation of age and death, they know Brahman fully, and have the whole knowledge of the Self and all action.

साधिभूताधिदैवं मां साधियज्ञं च ये विदुः ।
प्रयाणकालेऽपि च मां ते विदुर्युक्तचेतसः ।३०।

Saadhibhootaadhidaivam maam saadhiyajnam cha ye viduh;
Prayaanakaalepi cha maam te vidur yuktachetasah.

30. Those who know Me as Adhibhuta (with relation to elements), as Adhidaiva (with relation to gods) and Adhiyajna (with relation to sacrifices), they with their minds centered in Me, happen to know Me even at the time of their death.

ॐ तत्सदिति श्रीमद्भगवद्गीतासूपनिषत्सु ब्रह्म-
विद्यायां योगशास्त्रे श्रीकृष्णार्जुनसंवादे ज्ञान-
विज्ञानयोगो नाम सप्तमोऽध्यायः ॥७॥

Om tat sat iti srimad bhagavad gitaasoopanishatsu
brahmavidyaayaam yogashaastre sri krishnaarjunasamvaade
jnaanavijnaanayogo naama saptamo'dhyaayah.

Om Tat Sat.
Thus, in the Upanishad of the Bhagavad Gita,
the knowledge of Supreme Brahman, the scripture of Yoga,
the dialogue between Sri Krishna and Arjuna,
ends the seventh chapter entitled,
"The Yoga of Wisdom and Realization."

अनन्यचेताः सततं यो मां स्मरति नित्यशः ।
तस्याहं सुलभः पार्थ नित्ययुक्तस्य योगिनः ॥

अथाष्टमोऽध्यायः

Atha Ashtamo'dhyaayah

Chapter 8

Akshara Brahma Yogah

The Yoga of Imperishable Brahman

This chapter presents the philosophical insight by which a devotee may focus all his attention towards the intensification of Samskaras (impressions) that will help him to remember God even at the time of death. If God becomes the ruling thought of his mind at the time of death, he will not be born again.

अर्जुन उवाच
किं तद्ब्रह्म किमध्यात्मं किं कर्म पुरुषोत्तम ।
अधिभूतं च किं प्रोक्तमधिदैवं किमुच्यते ॥१॥

Arjuna uvaacha
Kim tadbrahma kim adhyaatmam kimn karma purushottama,
Adhibhootam cha kim proktam adhidaivam kimuchyate.

1. Arjuna asked: O Purushottama (the best of souls)! What is Brahman? What is Adhyatma? What is Karma? What is said to be Adhibhuta and what is Adhidaiva?

अधियज्ञः कथं कोऽत्र देहेऽस्मिन्मधुसूदन ।
प्रयाणकाले च कथं ज्ञेयोऽसि नियतात्मभिः ।२।

Adhiyajnah katham kotra dehesmin madhusudana;
Prayaanakaale cha katham jneyosi niyataatmabhih.

2. What is Adhiyajna here in this body? O Madhusudana! And how are You to be known at the time of death by those who are self-controlled?

श्रीभगवानुवाच
अक्षरं ब्रह्म परमं स्वभावोऽध्यात्ममुच्यते ।
भूतभावोद्भवकरो विसर्गः कर्मसंज्ञितः ।।३।।

Sree Bhagavaan uvaacha
Aksharam Brahma Paramam swabhaavodhyaatmamuchyate;
Bhootabhaavodbhavakaro visargah karmasamjnitah.

3. Lord Krishna said: The Supreme Brahman is Akshara—
the Imperishable. Adhyatma or the Subjective Self (in the
individual) is His very own Nature. That creative force is
known as Karma which is the cause of the existence and
the manifestation of all beings.

अधिभूतं क्षरो भावः पुरुषश्चाधिदैवतम् ।
अधियज्ञोऽहमेवात्र देहे देहभृतां वर ॥४॥

Adhibhootam ksharo bhaavah purushashchaadhidaivatam;
Adhiyajno'hamevaatra dehe dehabhritaam vara.

4. Adhibhuta (the world of elements) is My perishable
nature, Adhidaiva (the world of gods) is the Purusha (the
Cosmic Self). O best among the embodied beings!
Adhiyajna (the presiding Deity of sacrifices) is Myself
abiding in all beings.

अन्तकाले च मामेव स्मरन्मुक्त्वा कलेवरम् ।
यः प्रयाति स मद्भावं याति नास्त्यत्र संशयः ॥५॥

Antakaale cha maameva smaran muktwaa kalevaram;
Yah prayaati sa madbhaavam yaati naastyatra samshayah.

5. Whoever leaves his body remembering Me at the time of death attains to My being, there is no doubt in this.

यं यं वापि स्मरन्भावं त्यजत्यन्ते कलेवरम् ।
तं तमेवैति कौन्तेय सदा तद्भावभावितः ॥६॥

Yam yam vaapi smaran bhaavam tyajatyante kalevaram;
Tam tamevaiti kaunteya sadaa tadbhaavabhaavitah.

6. At the time of death whoever thinks of any being, to that being he goes, being overpowered by the thought thereof.

तस्मात्सर्वेषु कालेषु मामनुस्मर युध्य च ।
मय्यर्पितमनोबुद्धिर्मामेवैष्यस्यसंशयम् ॥७॥

Tasmaat sarveshu kaaleshu maamanusmara yudhya cha;
Mayyarpitamanobuddhirmaamevaishyasyasamshayam.

7. Therefore, remember Me at all times and fight. With your mind and intellect surrendered to Me you will attain Me without doubt.

अभ्यासयोगयुक्तेन चेतसा नान्यगामिना।
परमं पुरुषं दिव्यं याति पार्थानुचिन्तयन्॥८॥

Abhyaasayogayuktena chetasaa naanyagaamina;
Paramam purusham divyam yaati parthaanuchintayan.

8. O Partha! taking recourse to the Yoga of Abhyasa
(repeated practice of meditation), possessing a mind that
does not go elsewhere, and constantly dwelling upon Me,
one goes to the Effulgent Self—the Supreme Purusha.

कविं   पुराणमनुशासितार-
मणोरणीयांसमनुस्मरेद्यः   ।
सर्वस्य   धातारमचिन्त्यरूप-
मादित्यवर्णं   तमसः   परस्तात् ॥ ९ ॥

Kavim puraanamanushaasitaaram
Anoraneeyaamsamanusmaredyah;
Sarvasya dhaataaramachintyaroopam
Aaadityavarnam tamasah parastaat.

9. Whoever thinks of the Divine Self who is omniscient,
the ancient, the ruler of all, the subtler than the subtlest,
the supporter of all, of form inconceivable, effulgent like
the sun, beyond darkness, (he attains the Absolute Self).

प्रयाणकाले मनसाचलेन
भक्त्या युक्तो योगबलेन चैव ।
भ्रुवोर्मध्ये प्राणमावेश्य सम्यक्
स तं परं पुरुषमुपैति दिव्यम् ॥१०॥

Prayaanakaale manasaachalena
Buddhya yukto yogabalena chaiva;
Bhruvormadhye praanamaaveshya samyak
Sa tam param purusham upaiti divyam.

10. Whoever does so at the time of death, with an
unshakable mind, endowed with devotion, by fixing his
Pranas at the center between the eyebrows by the power
of Yoga, he attains that Supreme Effulgent Purusha.

यदक्षरं वेदविदो वदन्ति
विशन्ति यद्यतयो वीतरागाः ।
यदिच्छन्तो ब्रह्मचर्यं चरन्ति
तत्ते पदं संग्रहेण प्रवक्ष्ये ॥११॥

Yadaksharam vedavido vadanti
Vishanti yadyatayo veetaraagah;
Yadicchanto Brahmacharyam charanti
Tatte padam samgrahena pravakshye.

11. That which is called Akshara (the Imperishable) by the knowers of the Vedas, into which the striving Yogis, free of passion enter, aspiring for which, they practise Brahmacharya, that supreme goal I shall explain to you in brief.

सर्वद्वाराणि संयम्य मनो हृदि निरुध्य च।
मूर्ध्न्याधायात्मनः प्राणमास्थितो योगधारणाम्

Sarvadwaaraani samyamya mano hridi nirudhya cha;
Moordhnyaadhaayaatmanah praanamaasthito yogadhaaranaam.

12. Having restrained all the senses, drawing the mind into the heart, and keeping the Pranas centered at the space between the eyebrows, steady in the practice of Yogic concentration.

ओमित्येकाक्षरं ब्रह्म व्याहरन्मामनुस्मरन् ।
यः प्रयाति त्यजन्देहं स याति परमां गतिम् ॥

Omityekaksharam Brahma vyaaharanmaamanusmaran;
Yah prayaati tyajan deham sa yaati paramaam gatim.

13. Uttering the one-syllabled Om that denotes Brahman, thinking of Me, the Yogi who departs from his body attains the Supreme Goal.

अनन्यचेताः सततं यो मां स्मरति नित्यशः ।
तस्याहं सुलभः पार्थ नित्ययुक्तस्य योगिनः ॥

*Ananyachetaah satatam yo maam smarati nityashah;
Tasyaaham sulabhah paartha nityayuktasya yoginah.*

14. He who remembers Me constantly with his mind unflinchingly devoted to Me, for that ever controlled Yogi I am easy of attainment, O Partha!

मामुपेत्य पुनर्जन्म दुःखालयमशाश्वतम् ।
नाप्नुवन्ति महात्मानः संसिद्धिं परमां गताः ॥

*Maamupetya punarjanma dukhaalayamashaashwatam;
Naapnuvanti mahaatmaanah samsiddhim paramaam gataah.*

15. Having attained Me, and thus having reached the highest goal, these great souls are not born again in this world which is the abode of pain and is non-eternal.

आब्रह्मभुवनाल्लोकाः   पुनरावर्तिनोऽर्जुन ।
मामुपेत्य तु कौन्तेय पुनर्जन्म न विद्यते ॥१६॥

Aabrahmabhuvanaallokah punaraavartinorjuna;
Maamupeteya tu kaunteya punarjanma na vidyate.

16. All the worlds up to the highest Brahma-Loka are
characterized by the return of the soul. But he who
attains Me for him there is no more of rebirth, O Son of
Kunti!

सहस्रयुगपर्यन्तमहर्यद्ब्रह्मणो   विदुः   ।
रात्रिं युगसहस्रान्तां तेऽहोरात्रविदो जनाः ॥

Sahasrayugaparyantam aharyad brahmano viduh;
Raatrim yugasahasraantaam tehoraatravido janaah.

17. Those who know that the day of Brahma extends for a
thousand Yugas, and His night lasts for another thousand Yugas, they are the knowers of day and night.

अव्यक्ताद्व्यक्तयः सर्वाः प्रभवन्त्यहरागमे ।
रात्र्यागमे प्रलीयन्ते तत्रैवाव्यक्तसंज्ञके ॥१८॥

Avyaktaadvyaktayah sarvaah prabhavantyaharaagame;
Raatryaagame praleeyante tatraivaavyaktasamjnake.

18. With the coming of the day, all these manifested beings and objects proceed from the unmanifest, and with the coming of the night all these enter into the state of dissolution known as the unmanifest.

भूतग्रामः स एवायं भूत्वा भूत्वा प्रलीयते ।
रात्र्यागमेऽवशः पार्थ प्रभवत्यहरागमे ॥१९॥

Bhootagraamah sa evaayam bhootwaa bhootwaa praleeyate;
Raatryagame'vashah paartha prabhavatyaharaagame.

19. Thus, O Partha, these beings come forth again and again with the coming of the day, and are helplessly led to dissolution (in the unmanifest) at the coming of the night.

परस्तस्मात्तु भावोऽन्योऽव्यक्तोऽव्यक्तात्सनातनः ।
यः स सर्वेषु भूतेषु नश्यत्सु न विनश्यति ॥२०॥

Parastasmaat tu bhaavonyo avyaktovyaktaatsanaatanah;
Yah sa sarveshu bhooteshu nashyatsu na vinashyati.

20. Higher than this unmanifest there exists yet another Unmanifest—the Eternal Being who is not destroyed when all beings perish.

अव्यक्तोऽक्षर इत्युक्तस्तमाहुः परमां गतिम् ।
यं प्राप्य न निवर्तन्ते तद्धाम परमं मम ॥२१॥

Avyaktokshara ityuktastamaahuh paramaam gatim;
Yam praapya na nivartante taddhaama paramam mama.

21. This Unmanifest Being is called the Imperishable, which they (the scriptures) declare as the Supreme Goal. That is My highest abode reaching which, one does not return to this world again.

पुरुषः स परः पार्थ भक्त्या लभ्यस्त्वनन्यया ।
यस्यान्तःस्थानि भूतानि येन सर्वमिदं ततम् ॥

Purushah sa parah paartha bhaktyaa labhyastwananyayaa;
Yasyaantasthaani bhootaani yena sarvamidam tatam.

22. Within Whom abide all these beings, by Whom all this is pervaded, that Supreme Being is attainable by unswerving devotion to Him alone, O Partha!

यत्र काले त्वनावृत्तिमावृत्तिं चैव योगिनः ।
प्रयाता यान्ति तं कालं वक्ष्यामि भरतर्षभ ॥

Yatra kaale twanaavrittim aavrittim chaiva yoginah;
Prayaataa yaanti tam kaalam vakshyaami bharatarshabha.

23. O Best of Bharatas, I shall explain to you the time departing in which the Yogis (devoted to Sakamya Karma) return to this world, and the time in which they (who are devoted to Niskamya Karma) do not return.

अग्निर्ज्योतिरहः शुक्लः षण्मासा उत्तरायणम् ।
तत्र प्रयाता गच्छन्ति ब्रह्म ब्रह्मविदो जनाः ॥

Agnirjyotirahah suklah shanmaasaa uttaraayanam;
Tatra prayaata gacchanti Brahma brahmavido janaah.

24. The Yogis (devoted to Niskamya Karma) depart at a time that is characterized by fire, light, day, the bright half of the month, the six months of he northern course of the Sun, and thus they who know Brahman go to Brahman.

धूमो रात्रिस्तथा कृष्णः षण्मासा दक्षिणायनम् ।
तत्र चान्द्रमसं ज्योतिर्योगी प्राप्य निवर्तते ॥

Dhoomo ratristathaa krishnah shanmaasaa dakshinaayanam;
Tatra chaandramasam jyotiryogee praapya nivartate.

25. The other Yogis (devoted to Sakamya Karma) depart at a time that is characterized by smoke, night, the dark fortnight, the six months of the southern course of the Sun, and thus they reach the worlds of the Moon, and from there they return (to the world-process).

शुक्लकृष्णे गती ह्येते जगतः शाश्वते मते ।
एकया यात्यनावृत्तिमन्ययावर्तते पुनः ॥२६॥

Shuklakrishne gatee hyete jagatah saashwate mate;
Ekayaa yaatyanaavrittim anyayaavartate punah.

26. These two paths—the path of Light and that of Darkness are considered beginningless. Following the path of Light one does not return, while following the path of darkness one returns.

नैते सृती पार्थ जानन्योगी मुह्यति कश्चन।
तस्मात्सर्वेषु कालेषु योगयुक्तो भवार्जुन॥

Naite sritee paartha jaananyogi muhyati kashchana;
Tasmaat sarveshu kaaleshu yogayukto bhavaarjuna.

27. The Yogi who knows these two paths is never deluded, O Partha. Therefore, O Arjuna, become devoted to Yoga at all times.

वेदेषु यज्ञेषु तपःसु चैव
दानेषु यत्पुण्यफलं प्रदिष्टम्।
अत्येति तत्सर्वमिदं विदित्वा
योगी परं स्थानमुपैति चाद्यम्॥२८॥

Vedeshu yajneshu tapahssu chaiva
Daaneshu yatpunyaphalam pradishtam;
Atyeti tatsarvamidam viditwaa
Yogi param sthaanamupaiti chaadyam.

28. For the Yogi having known this goes beyond the fruits of meritorious deeds such as the study of the Vedas, performance of sacrifices, practice of austerities, and acts of charity. For he attains the Supreme Abode—the Ancient Source (of the entire creation).

ॐ तत्सदिति   श्रीमद्भगवद्गीतासूपनिषत्सु   ब्रह्म-
विद्यायां योगशास्त्रे श्रीकृष्णार्जुनसंवादे अक्षर-
ब्रह्मयोगो नामाष्टमोऽध्याय: ॥ ८ ॥

*Om tat sat iti srimad bhagavad gitaasoopanishatsu
brahmavidyaayaam yogashaastre sri krishnaarjunasamvaade
aksharabrahmayogo naama ashtamo'dhyaayah.*

Om Tat Sat.
Thus, in the Upanishad of the Bhagavad Gita,
the knowledge of Supreme Brahman, the scripture of Yoga,
the dialogue between Sri Krishna and Arjuna,
ends the eighth chapter entitled,
"The Yoga of Imperishable Brahman."

अनन्याश्चिन्तयन्तो मां ये जनाः पर्युपासते ।
तेषां नित्याभियुक्तानां योगक्षेमं वहाम्यहम् ॥

अथ नवमोऽध्यायः

Atha Navamo'dhyaayah

Chapter 9

Raja Vidya Raja Guhya Yogah

The Yoga of Kingly Knowledge and Mystic Secret

There is a mystic secret by which one may attain Liberation even in this very life. This secret lies in relating to God everything one does. A devotee should surrender not only his outer actions but even his inner thoughts—not only the positive thoughts but even the impurities of his heart at the Feet of the Lord. This is the secret of spiritual transformation.

श्रीभगवानुवाच

इदं तु ते गुह्यतमं प्रवक्ष्याम्यनसूयवे ।
ज्ञानं विज्ञानसहितं यज्ज्ञात्वा मोक्ष्यसेऽशुभात् ।।

Sree Bhagavaan uvaacha
Idam tu te guhyatamam pravakshyaamyanasooyave;
Jnaanam vijnaanasahitam yajjnaatwa mokshyasesubhat.

1. Sri Bhagavan Krishna said: I will declare to you who are devoid of cavilling, the greatest secret in the form of the indirect and direct knowledge of Brahman, knowing which you will attain freedom from the evil of the world-process.

राजविद्या राजगुह्यं पवित्रमिदमुत्तमम् ।
प्रत्यक्षावगमं धर्म्यं सुसुखं कर्तुमव्ययम् ॥२॥

Raajavidyaa raajaguhyam pavitramidamuttamam;
Pratyakshaavagamam dharmyam susukham kartumavyayam.

2. This knowledge is the King of all knowledges, the King of all secrets, the best among all purifier, fit to be realized directly by (intuition), of highest merit, very easy of attainment, and yet imperishable.

अश्रद्दधानाः पुरुषा धर्मस्यास्य परंतप ।
अप्राप्य मां निवर्तन्ते मृत्युसंसारवर्त्मनि ॥३॥

Ashradhadhaanaah purushaa dharmasyaasya parantapa;
Apraapya maam nivartante mrityusamsaaravartmani.

3. O scorcher of your foes, one who is devoid of faith in this Dharma (the intuitional knowledge of the Self), without attaining Me, he continues to wander in the world of death.

मया ततमिदं सर्वं जगदव्यक्तमूर्तिना ।
मत्स्थानि सर्वभूतानि न चाहं तेष्ववस्थितः ॥

Mayaa tatamidam sarvam jagadavyaktamoortinaa;
Matsthaani sarvabhootaani na chaaham teshvavasthitah.

4. The entire world is pervaded by Me in My unmanifest form; all beings exist in me, but I do not abide in them.

न च मत्स्थानि भूतानि पश्य मे योगमैश्वरम् ।
भूतभृन्न च भूतस्थो ममात्मा भूतभावनः ॥५॥

Na cha matsthaani bhootaani pashya me yogamaishwaram;
Bootabhrinna cha bhootastho mamaatmaa bhootabhaavanah.

5. Even these beings do not exist in Me (in reality).
Behold My Divine Glory. Though I am the material
cause as well as sustainer and creator of all beings yet I do
not dwell in them.

यथाकाशस्थितो नित्यं वायुः सर्वत्रगो महान् ।
तथा सर्वाणि भूतानि मत्स्थानीत्युपधारय ॥

Yathaakaashasthito nityam vaayus sarvatrago mahaan;
Tathaa sarvaani bhootani matsthaaneetyupadhaaraya.

6. Just as the mighty wind that moves everywhere abides
in the sky, in the same way all beings abide in Me; thus
should you understand.

सर्वभूतानि कौन्तेय प्रकृतिं यान्ति मामिकाम् ।
कल्पक्षये पुनस्तानि कल्पादौ विसृजाम्यहम् ॥

Sarvabhootaani kaunteya prakritim yaanti maamikaam;
Kalpakshaye punastaani kalpaadau visrijaamyaham.

7. O Son of Kunti, all beings merge into My Prakriti at the
end of the Kalpa, and with the commencement of the
next Kalpa it is I who send them forth.

प्रकृतिं स्वामवष्टभ्य विसृजामि पुनः पुनः ।
भूतग्राममिमं कृत्स्नमवशं प्रकृतेर्वशात् ॥८॥

Prakritim swaamavashtabhya visrijaami punah punah;
Bhootagraamamimam kritsnamavasham prakritervashaat.

8. Keeping Prakriti under My control, I, again and again, send forth these beings which are helplessly under the control of Prakriti.

न च मां तानि कर्माणि निबध्नन्ति धनंजय ।
उदासीनवदासीनमसक्तं तेषु कर्मसु ॥९॥

Na cha maam taani karmaani nibadhnanti dhananjaya;
Udaasseenavadaaseenamasaktam teshu karmasu.

9. O conqueror of wealth, I am like one who is indifferent, unattached to those actions (of creation, sustenance and dissolution); those actions do not bind Me.

मयाध्यक्षेण प्रकृतिः सूयते सचराचरम् ।
हेतुनानेन कौन्तेय जगद्विपरिवर्तते ॥१०॥

Mayaa'dhyakshena prakritih sooyate sacharaacharam;
Hetunaanena kaunteya jagadwiparivartate.

10. Presided by Me, Prakriti brings forth the creation of beings consisting of movables and immovables. O Son of Kunti, it is for this reason that the world continues to undergo (endless modifications).

अवजानन्ति मां मूढा मानुषीं तनुमाश्रितम् ।
परं भावमजानन्तो मम भूतमहेश्वरम् ॥११॥

Avajaananti maam moodhaah maanusheem tanumaashritam;
Param bhaavamajaananto mama bhootamaheshwaram.

11. The dull-witted are unable to understand Me who manifest in human form. They do not know My transcendental nature as the great Lord of all beings.

मोघाशा मोघकर्माणो मोघज्ञाना विचेतसः ।
राक्षसीमासुरीं चैव प्रकृतिं मोहिनीं श्रिताः ॥

Moghaashaa moghakarmaano moghajnaanaa vichetasah;
Raakshaseemaasureem chaiva prakritim mohineem shritaah.

12. Endowed with vain desires, vain actions, vain knowledge, devoid of discrimination and intelligence, they continue to be deluded sustained by the deluding nature of the demons and the Asuras.

महात्मानस्तु मां पार्थ दैवीं प्रकृतिमाश्रिताः ।
भजन्त्यनन्यमनसो ज्ञात्वा भूतादिमव्ययम् ॥

Mahaatmaanastu maam paartha daiveem prakritimaashritaah;
Bhajantyananyamanaso jnaatwaa bhootaadimavyayam.

13. But, O Partha, the great souls taking refuge in My divine nature worship Me at all times knowing Me to be the imperishable nature of all beings.

सततं कीर्तयन्तो मां यतन्तश्च दृढव्रताः ।
नमस्यन्तश्च मां भक्त्या नित्ययुक्ता उपासते ॥

Satatam keertayanto maam yatantashcha dhridhavrataah;
Namasyantashcha maam bhaktyaa nityayuktaa upaasate.

14. Glorifying Me at all times, steadfast in great vows, those great souls strive to know Me; endowed with devotion, they bow down to Me and worship Me.

ज्ञानयज्ञेन चाप्यन्ये यजन्तो मामुपासते ।
एकत्वेन पृथक्त्वेन बहुधा विश्वतोमुखम् ॥

Jnaanayajnena chaapyanye yajanto maamupaasate;
Ekatwena prithaktwena bahudhaa vishwatomukham.

15. Others worship Me with Jnana Yajna (with the
sacrifice of knowledge) in the form of oneness, or with a
sense of separation (with the feeling of master and
servant), or with the manifold aspects of My Being.

अहं क्रतुरहं यज्ञः स्वधाहमहमौषधम् ।
मन्त्रोऽहमहमेवाज्यमहमग्निरहं हुतम् ॥१६॥

Aham kraturaham yajnah swadhaahamahamaushadham;
Mantrohamahamevaajyam ahamagniraham hutam.

16. I am Kratu, I am Yajna, I am Swadha, I am the
medicinal herb, I am the sacred Mantra, the clarified
butter that is poured in fire; as well as I am the fire, and
the very act of offering oblation.

पिताहमस्य जगतो माता धाता पितामहः ।
वेद्यं पवित्रमोंकार ऋक्साम यजुरेव च ॥१७॥

Pitaahamasya jagato maataa dhaataa pitaamahah;
Vedyam pavritramomkaara riksaama yajureva cha.

17. I am the Father of the universe; I am the Mother, the sustainer, as well as the Grandfather. I am the goal of Vedic knowledge, I am the sacred Om, I am verily the Vedas in the form of Rik, Yaju and Sama.

गतिर्भर्ता प्रभुः साक्षी निवासः शरणं सुहृत् ।
प्रभवः प्रलयः स्थानं निधानं बीजमव्ययम् ॥

Gatirbhartaa prabhuh saakshee nivaasah sharanam suhrit;
Prabhavah pralayah sthaanam nidhaanam beejamavyayam.

18. I am the Final Goal, the Nourisher of all beings, the Lord of creation, the Witnessing Self, the Supreme Abode, the Refuge of all, the Supreme Well-wisher. I am the origin and the dissolution of the universe, I am also the sustainer, the supreme treasure, and the imperishable seed.

तपाम्यहमहं वर्षं निगृह्णाम्युत्सृजामि च ।
अमृतं चैव मृत्युश्च सदसच्चाहमर्जुन ॥१९॥

Tapaamyahamaham varsham nigrihnaamyutsrijaami cha;
Amritam chaiva mrityushcha sadasacchaahamarjuna.

19. O Arjuna, it is I who give forth heat (in the form of the sun), and draw water form the earth in order to pour it down in the form of rains. I am immortality, death, existence as well as non-existence.

त्रैविद्या मां सोमपाः पूतपापा
यज्ञैरिष्ट्वा स्वर्गतिं प्रार्थयन्ते ।
ते पुण्यमासाद्य सुरेन्द्रलोक-
मश्नन्ति दिव्यान्दिवि देवभोगान् २०

Traividyaa maam somapaah pootapaapaa
Yajnairishtwaa swargatimn praarthayante;
Te punyamaasaadya surendraloka-
Mashnanti divyaan divi devabhogaan.

20. Those who follow the ritualistic portion of the three Vedas, and drink the Soma juice, they with their mind sanctified by sacrifice pray for the enjoyment of heavenly worlds, and as a result of meritorious deeds, they attain the heavens where they enjoy divine pleasures.

ते तं भुक्त्वा स्वर्गलोकं विशालं
क्षीणे पुण्ये मर्त्यलोकं विशन्ति ।
एवं   त्रयीधर्ममनुप्रपन्ना
गतागतं कामकामा लभन्ते ॥२१॥

*Te tam bhuktwaa swargalokam vishaalam
Ksheene punye martyalokam vishanti;
Evam trayeedharmamanuprapannaa
Gataagatam kaamakaamaa labhante.*

21. With the exhaustion of meritorious deeds, having enjoyed the expansive pleasures of the heavens, they fall into human world. Thus the followers of ritualistic portion of the Vedas continue to come and go driven by their desires.

अनन्याश्चिन्तयन्तो मां ये जनाः पर्युपासते ।
तेषां नित्याभियुक्तानां योगक्षेमं वहाम्यहम् ॥

*Ananyaasshchintayanto maam ye janaah paryupaasate;
Teshaam nityaabhiyuktaanaam yogakshemam vahaamyaham*

22. But those who worship Me by meditating upon Me with a vision of non-separateness, and who are ceaselessly devoted to Me, I look after their Yoga and Kshema.

येऽप्यन्यदेवता भक्ता यजन्ते श्रद्धयान्विताः ।
तेऽपि मामेव कौन्तेय यजन्त्यविधिपूर्वकम् ॥

Ye apyanyadevataa bhaktaa yajante shraddhayaanvitaah;
Te'pi maameva kaunteya yajantyavidhipoorvakam.

23. Even the devotees of other Gods who practise devotion with faith are in fact worshipping Me alone but not according to the direct path.

अहं हि सर्वयज्ञानां भोक्ता च प्रभुरेव च ।
न तु मामभिजानन्ति तत्त्वेनातश्च्यवन्ति ते ॥

Aham hi sarvayajnaanaam bhoktaa cha prabhureva cha;
Na tu maamabhijaananti tatwenaatashchyavanti te.

24. I am the enjoyer of all sacrifices, as well as the Lord. Those who worship many Gods, they do not know Me truly, therefore they continue to fall (into repeated embodiments).

यान्ति देवव्रता देवान्पितॄन्यान्ति पितृव्रताः ।
भूतानि यान्ति भूतेज्या यान्ति मद्याजिनोऽपि माम्

Yaanti devavrataa devaan pitreenyaanti pitrivrataah;
Bhootaani yaanti bhootejyaa yaanti madyaajinopi maam.

25. The worshipper of Gods go to the Gods, the worshipper of Forefathers to the Forefathers, and the worshipper of spirits go to the spirits but those who worship Me, they come to Me.

पत्रं पुष्पं फलं तोयं यो मे भक्त्या प्रयच्छति ।
तदहं भक्त्युपहृतमश्नामि प्रयतात्मनः ॥२६॥

Patram pushpam phalam toyam yo me bhaktyaa prayacchati;
Tadaham bhaktyupahritamashnaami prayataatmanah.

26. Whoever offers even a leaf, or a flower, or a fruit or just water with devotion to Me, I accept that offering of love from my pure-hearted devotee.

यत्करोषि यदश्नासि यज्जुहोषि ददासि यत् ।
यत्तपस्यसि कौन्तेय तत्कुरुष्व मदर्पणम् ॥२७॥

Yatkaroshi yadashnaasi yajjuhoshi dadaasi yat;
Yattapasyasi kaunteya tatkurushva madarpanam.

27. O son of Kunti, whatever you eat, whatever you offer as an oblation, whatever you give, and whatever austerity you may practise, do that as an offering to Me.

शुभाशुभफलैरेवं मोक्ष्यसे कर्मबन्धनैः ।
संन्यासयोगयुक्तात्मा विमुक्तो मामुपैष्यसि ॥

Shubhaashubhaphalairevam mokshyase karmabandhanaih;
Sannyasayogayuktaatmaa vimukto maamupaishyasi.

28. Thus, you will become free from the bondage of good and evil Karmas, and being united with the Yoga of renunciation, liberated even in life, you will attain Me.

समोऽहं सर्वभूतेषु न मे द्वेष्योऽस्ति न प्रियः ।
ये भजन्ति तु मां भक्त्या मयि ते तेषु चाप्यहम् ॥

Samoham sarvabhooteshu na me dweshyosti na priyah;
Ye bhajanti tu maam bhaktyaa mayi te teshu chaapyaham.

29. I am equally present in all being. I have neither like nor dislike towards anyone. But those who worship Me with devotion, I am in them, and they are in Me.

अपि चेत्सुदुराचारो भजते मामनन्यभाक् ।
साधुरेव स मन्तव्यः सम्यग्व्यवसितो हि सः ॥

Api chetsuduraachaaro bhajate maamananyabhaak;
Saadhureva sa mantavyah samyagvyavasito hi sah.

30. Even if the worst of evil-doers were to worship Me
with a single-minded devotion, he must be considered a
righteous person, because he has rightly resolved.

क्षिप्रं भवति धर्मात्मा शश्वच्छान्ति निगच्छति ।
कौन्तेय प्रति जानीहि न मे भक्तः प्रणश्यति ॥

Kshipram bhavati dharmaatmaa shashwacchaantim nigacchati;
Kaunteya pratijaaneehi na me bhaktah pranashyati.

31. He hastens to become a righteous soul and attains the
unceasing peace (of liberation). O son of Kunti, know it
for certain that my devotee is never destroyed.

मां हि पार्थ व्यपाश्रित्य येऽपि स्युः पापयोनयः ।
स्त्रियो वैश्यास्तथा शूद्रास्तेऽपि यान्ति परां गतिम्

Maam hi paartha vyapaashritya yepi syuh paapayonayah;
Striyo vaisyaastathaa soodraaste'pi yaanti paraam gatim.

32. O Arjuna, those who take refuge in Me, whether men born in a lowly class, or women, or Vaishyas, or Shudras, even they are sure to attain the highest goal.

किं पुनर्ब्राह्मणाः पुण्या भक्ता राजर्षयस्तथा ।
अनित्यमसुखं लोकमिमं प्राप्य भजस्व माम् ॥

Kim punarbrahmanaah punyaa bhaktaa raajarshayastatha;
Anityamasukhamlokam imam praapya bhajaswa maam.

33. Then, what to speak of those devotees who are holy Brahmins or the royal sages? Having attained this transient and joyless world, you should worship Me.

मन्मना भव मद्भक्तो मद्याजी मां नमस्कुरु ।
मामेवैष्यसि युक्त्वैवमात्मानं मत्परायणः ॥

Manmanaa bhava madbhakto madyaajee maam namaskuru;
Maamevaishyasi yuktwaivamaatmaanam matparaayanah.

34. Fix your mind in Me, be devoted to Me, worship Me, and bow down to Me. Having thus surrendered yourself to Me, with your spirit united with Me, you will surely attain Me.

ॐ तत्सदिति श्रीमद्भगवद्गीतासूपनिषत्सु ब्रह्मविद्यायां
योगशास्त्रे श्रीकृष्णार्जुनसंवादे राजविद्याराजगुह्य-
योगो नाम नवमोऽध्यायः ॥ ९ ॥

Om tat sat iti srimad bhagavad gitaasoopanishatsu brahmavidyaayaam yogashaastre sri krishnaarjunasamvaade raajavidyaaraajaguhyayogo naama navamo'dhyaayah.

Om Tat Sat.
Thus, in the Upanishad of the Bhagavad Gita,
the knowledge of Supreme Brahman, the scripture of Yoga,
the dialogue between Sri Krishna and Arjuna,
ends the ninth chapter entitled,
"The Yoga of Kingly Knowledge and Mystic Secret."

अहं सर्वस्य प्रभवो मत्तः सर्वं प्रवर्तते ।
इति मत्वा भजन्ते मां बुधा भावसमन्विताः ॥

अथ दशमोऽध्यायः

Atha Dashamo'dhyaayah

Chapter 10

Vibhuti Yogah

The Yoga of Divine Glories

The divine glories are described so that the mind of the devotee may turn to God at all times and in all things. To begin with a devotee sees the Glories of God in the majestic things of nature—the Sun, the Ocean, the Himalayas and others, but later he beholds His Glories even in the smallest and most insignificant objects of the world.

श्रीभगवानुवाच

भूय एव महाबाहो शृणु मे परमं वचः ।
यत्तेऽहं प्रीयमाणाय वक्ष्यामि हितकाम्यया ।।१।।

Sree Bhagavaan uvaacha
Bhooya eva mahaabaaho srinu me paramam vachah;
Yatte'ham preeyamaanaaya vakshyaami hitakaamyayaa.

1. Lord Krishna said: O mighty-armed Arjuna, listen again to My supreme instruction, which for doing good to you I shall declare to you who are delighting in My words.

न मे विदुः सुरगणाः प्रभवं न महर्षयः ।
अहमादिर्हि देवानां महर्षीणां च सर्वशः ॥२॥

Na me viduh suraganaah prabhavam na maharshayah;
Ahamaadirhi devaanaam maharsheenaam cha sarvashah.

2. Neither the host of Gods nor Rishis know My Glory, for I am in everyway the Origin of Gods and Rishis.

यो मामजमनादिं च वेत्ति लोकमहेश्वरम् ।
असंमूढः स मर्त्येषु सर्वपापैः प्रमुच्यते ॥३॥

Yo maamajamanaadim cha vetti lokamaheshwaram;
Asammoodhah sa martyeshu sarvapaapaih pramuchyate.

3. He who knows Me as unborn, beginningless, the Great Lord of all the worlds, he among human beings, undeluded, becomes free from all sins.

बुद्धिर्ज्ञानमसंमोहः क्षमा सत्यं दमः शमः ।
सुखं दुःखं भवोऽभावो भयं चाभयमेव च ॥४॥

Buddhirjnaanamasammohah kshamaa satyam damah shamah;
Sukham duhkham bhavo'bhaavo bhayam chaabhayameva cha.

4. Intellect (understanding), wisdom, lack of delusion, forgiveness (endurance), truth, control of senses, control of mind, pleasure, pain, existence and non-existence, fear and fearlessness (these proceed from Me alone).

अहिंसा समता तुष्टिस्तपो दानं यशोऽयशः ।
भवन्ति भावा भूतानां मत्त एव पृथग्विधाः ॥५॥

Ahimsaa samataa tushtistapo daanam yasho'yashah;
Bhavanti bhaavaa bhootaanaam matta eva prithagvidhaah.

5. Non-violence, equanimity, contentment, austerity, charity, fame and infamy—these different conditions of beings proceed from Me alone.

महर्षयः सप्त पूर्वे चत्वारो मनवस्तथा ।
मद्भावा मानसा जाता येषां लोक इमाः प्रजाः ॥

Maharshayah sapta poorve chatwaaro manavastathaa;
Madbhaava maanasaa jaata yeshaam loka imaah prajaah.

6. The ancient seven Sages and four Manus from whom all these beings have emerged were born of My Mind, and they existed with their minds immersed in Me.

एतां विभूतिं योगं च मम यो वेत्ति तत्त्वतः ।
सोऽविकम्पेन योगेन युज्यते नात्र संशयः ॥७॥

Yetaam vibhootim yogam cha mama yo vetti tattwatah;
So'vikampena yogena yujjyate naatra samshayah.

7. Whoever knows truly My Divine Glories and My Yoga, he becomes endowed with the Yoga of unflinching wisdom, there is no doubt in this.

अहं सर्वस्य प्रभवो मत्तः सर्वं प्रवर्तते ।
इति मत्वा भजन्ते मां बुधा भावसमन्विताः ॥

Aham sarvasya prabhavo mattah sarvam pravartate;
Iti matwaa bhajante maam budhaa bhaavasamanvitaah.

8. I am the origin of all beings; all this has proceeded from Me. Thus knowing, the wise meditate upon Me with profound devotion.

मच्चित्ता मद्गतप्राणा बोधयन्तः परस्परम् ।
कथयन्तश्च मां नित्यं तुष्यन्ति च रमन्ति च ॥

Macchittaa madgatapraanaa bodhayantah parasparam;
Kathayantashcha maam nityam tushyanti cha ramanti cha.

9. With their mind wholly devoted to Me, with their Pranas (senses) entirely dedicated to Me, enlightening each other and conversing about Me, they enjoy contentment and bliss.

तेषां सततयुक्तानां भजतां प्रीतिपूर्वकम् ।
ददामि बुद्धियोगं तं येन मामुपयान्ति ते ॥१०॥

Teshaam satatayuktaanaam bhajataam preetipoorvakam;
Dadaami Buddhiyogam tam yena maamupayaanti te.

10. To them whose minds rest in the Divine Self, who worship Me ceaselessly with devotion, I give the Yoga of Wisdom by which they attain Me.

तेषामेवानुकम्पार्थमहमज्ञानजं   तमः ।
नाशयाम्यात्मभावस्थो ज्ञानदीपेन भास्वता ॥

Teshaamevaanukampaarthamahamajnaanajam tamah;
Naashayaamyaatmabhaavastho jnaanadeepena bhaaswataa.

11. As an act of divine compassion, dwelling within their self, I destroy the darkness born of ignorance with the shining lamp of wisdom.

अर्जुन उवाच
परं ब्रह्म परं धाम पवित्रं परमं भवान् ।
पुरुषं शाश्वतं दिव्यमादिदेवमजं विभुम् ॥१२॥

Arjuna uvaacha
Param Brahma param dhaama pavitram paramam bhavaan;
Purusham saashvatam divyamaadidevamajam vibhum.

12. Arjuna said: You are Supreme Brahman, Supreme Abode, Supremely Purifier. You are the Spirit, Eternal, Effulgent, the Unborn, the First of the Gods, and the All-pervading.

आहुस्त्वामृषयः सर्वे देवर्षिर्नारदस्तथा ।
असितो देवलो व्यासः स्वयं चैव ब्रवीषि मे ॥

Aahustwaam rishayah sarve devarshirnaaradastathaa;
Asito devalo vyaasah swayam chaiva braveeshi me.

13. Thus all the Sages, including Divine Narada, Asita, Devala, Vyasa have declared about You; and You are stating the same fact by Yourself.

सर्वमेतद्रृतं मन्ये यन्मां वदसि केशव ।
न हि ते भगवन्व्यक्तिं विदुर्देवा न दानवाः ॥

Sarvametadritam manye yanmaam vadasi keshava;
Nahi te bhagavan vyaktim vidurdevaa na daanavaah.

14. O Keshava, whatever you say to me, I know to be true. O Lord, even the Gods and Demons do not know Your Glory.

स्वयमेवात्मनात्मानं वेत्थ त्वं पुरुषोत्तम ।
भूतभावन भूतेश देवदेव जगत्पते ॥१५॥

Swayamevaatmanaatmaanam vettha twam purushottama;
Bhootabhaavana bhootesha devadeva jagatpate.

15. O best among all spirits, the God of Gods, the Origin
of all beings, the Controller of all, the Ruler of the worlds,
You alone know Your essence by Your own self.

वक्तुमर्हस्यशेषेण दिव्या ह्यात्मविभूतयः ।
याभिर्विभूतिभिर्लोकानिमांस्त्वं व्याप्य तिष्ठसि ॥

Vaktumarhasyasheshena divyaa hyaatmavibhootayah;
Yaabhir vibhootibhirlokaanimaamstwam vyaapya tishthasi.

16. You stand having pervaded these worlds by Your
Divine Glories; You alone can describe them fully.

कथं विद्यामहं योगिंस्त्वां सदा परिचिन्तयन् ।
केषु केषु च भावेषु चिन्त्योऽसि भगवन्मया ॥

Katham vidyaamaham yogimstwaam sadaa parichintayan;
Keshu keshu cha bhaaveshu chintyosi bhagavanmayaa.

17. O Yogin, how am I to know You by constantly meditating upon You. O Lord, in what various aspects of Yours am I to dwell upon You?

विस्तरेणात्मनो योगं विभूतिं च जनार्दन ।
भूयः कथय तृप्तिर्हि शृण्वतो नास्ति मेऽमृतम्॥

Vistarenaatmano yogam vibootim cha janaardana;
Bhooyah kathaya triptirhi srunvato naasti me'mritam.

18. O Janardana (sought by all beings for the fulfillment of their desires), please do describe to me again Your Yoga (divine powers) and Vibhutis (divine glories), for my ears are never satisfied with hearing Your nectarine words.

श्रीभगवानुवाच
हन्त ते कथयिष्यामि दिव्या ह्यात्मविभूतयः ।
प्राधान्यतः कुरुश्रेष्ठ नास्त्यन्तो विस्तरस्य मे ॥

Sree Bhagavaan uvaacha
Hanta te kathayishyaami divyaa hyaatmavibhootayah;
Praadhaanyatah kurushreshtha naastyanto vistarasya me.

19. The Blessed Lord said: Very well, O Arjuna—the best among the Kurus, I will describe those of My Divine Glories which are prominent, because there is no end to My Glories.

अहमात्मा गुडाकेश सर्वभूताशयस्थितः ।
अहमादिश्च मध्यं च भूतानामन्त एव च ॥२०॥

Ahamaatmaa gudaakesha sarvabhootaashayasthitah;
Ahmaadishcha madhyam cha bhootaanaamanta eva cha.

20. O Gudakesha, I am the Self seated in the heart of all living beings. I am also the beginning, the middle and the end of all beings.

आदित्यानामहं विष्णुर्ज्योतिषां रविरंशुमान् ।
मरीचिर्मरुतामस्मि नक्षत्राणामहं शशी ॥२१॥

Aadityaanaamaham vishnur jyotishaam raviramshumaan;
Mareechirmarutaamasmi nakshatraanaamaham shashee.

21. I am Vishnu among the Adityas, the radiant sun among the luminaries; among the Maruts (spirits pre-

siding over wind) I am Marichi, among the stars I am the Moon.

वेदानां सामवेदोऽस्मि देवानामस्मि वासवः ।
इन्द्रियाणां मनश्चास्मि भूतानामस्मि चेतना ॥

Vedaanaam saamavedosmi devaanaam asmi vaasavah;
Indriyaanaam manashchaasmi bhootaanaamasmi chetanaa.

22. I am Sama Veda among the Vedas, Indra among the Gods, Mind among the Indriyas (senses of perception), and consciousness among the living beings.

रुद्राणां शंकरश्चास्मि वित्तेशो यक्षरक्षसाम् ।
वसूनां पावकश्चास्मि मेरुः शिखरिणामहम् ॥

Rudraanaam shankarashchaasmi vittesho yaksharakshasaam;
Vasoonam paavakashchaasmi merus shikharinaamaham.

23. Among the Rudras, I am Shankara; among the Yakshas and Rakshasas, I am Kubera—the Lord of Wealth. Among the Vasus, I am the Fire-God, and among the mountains, I am Meru.

पुरोधसां च मुख्यं मां विद्धि पार्थ बृहस्पतिम् ।
सेनानीनामहं स्कन्दः सरसामस्मि सागरः ॥

Purodhasaam cha mukhyam maam viddhi paartha brihaspatim;
Senaaneenaamaham skandah sarasaamasmi saagarah.

24. O Partha, know Me to be Brihaspati among the divine priests, Skanda among the generals (of divine army), and ocean among the lakes (and rivers).

महर्षीणां   भृगुरहं   गिरामस्म्येकमक्षरम् ।
यज्ञानां जपयज्ञोऽस्मि स्थावराणां हिमालयः ॥

Maharsheenaam bhriguraham giraamasmyekamaksharam;
Yajnaanaam japayajnosmi sthaavaraanaam himaalayah.

25. I am Bhrigu among the great Sages, I am the one-lettered Om among words, I am Japa Yajna among sacrifices, and the Himalayas among the immovables.

अश्वत्थः सर्ववृक्षाणां देवर्षीणां च नारदः ।
गन्धर्वाणां चित्ररथः सिद्धानां कपिलो मुनिः ॥

Aswatthah sarvavrikshaanaam devarsheenaam cha naaradah;
Gandharvaanaam chitrarathah siddhaanaam kapilo munih.

26. I am Ashwattha among the trees, the Sage Narada among the Divine Sages, Chitraratha among the Gandharvas, and Kapila Muni among the Siddhas.

उच्चैःश्रवसमश्वानां विद्धि माममृतोद्भवम् ।
ऐरावतं गजेन्द्राणां नराणां च नराधिपम् ॥

Ucchaishravasamashwaanaam viddhi maamamritodbhavam;
Airaavatam gajendraanaam naraanaam cha naraadhipam.

27. Among the horses know Me to be Uchhaihshrava that arose during the churning of the ocean; I am Airavata among the elephants, and the King among human beings.

आयुधानामहं वज्रं धेनूनामसि कामधुक् ।
प्रजनश्चास्मि कन्दर्पः सर्पाणामस्मि वासुकिः ॥

Aayudhaanaamaham vajram dhenoonaamasmi kaamadhuk;
Prajanashchaasmi kandarpah sarpaanaamasmi vaasukih.

28. Among weapons I am the thunderbolt, among the milk cows I am the Kama Dhenu, among the progenitors, I am the God of Love, and among the snakes I am Vasuki.

अनन्तश्चास्मि नागानां वरुणो यादसामहम् ।
पितृणामर्यमा चास्मि यमः संयमतामहम् ।२९।

Anantashchaasmi naagaanaam varuno yaadasaamaham;
Pitreenaamaryamaa chaasmi yamah samyamataamaham.

29. Among the Nagas, I am Ananta, and among aquatic beings, I am Varuna. Among the departed forefathers, I am Aryama; among the controllers (and governers) I am Yama (the God of Death).

प्रह्लादश्चास्मि दैत्यानां कालः कलयतामहम् ।
मृगाणां च मृगेन्द्रोऽहं वैनतेयश्च पक्षिणाम् ।।

Prahlaadashchaasmi daityaanaam kaalah kalayataamaham;
Mrigaanaam cha mrigendro'ham vainateyashcha pakshinaam.

30. Among the Daityas (demons) I am Prahlada, among the reckoners I am Time, among animals I am the Lion, among the birds I am Garuda, the son of Vinata.

पवनः पवतामस्मि रामः शस्त्रभृतामहम् ।
झषाणां मकरश्चास्मि स्रोतसामस्मि जाह्नवी ॥

Pavanah pavataamasmi raamah shastrabhritaamaham;
Jhashaanaam makarashchaasmi srotasaamasmi jaahnavee.

31. I am wind among the purifiers, Rama among the
bearers of weapon, the alligator among the fishes,
Ganges among the rivers.

सर्गाणामादिरन्तश्च   मध्यं   चैवाहमर्जुन ।
अध्यात्मविद्या विद्यानां वादः प्रवदतामहम् ॥

Sargaanaamaadirantashcha madhyam chaivaahamarjuna;
Adhyaatmavidyaa vidyaanaam vaadah pravadataamaham.

32. O Arjuna, I am the beginning, middle and end of all
this creation; I am the knowledge of Self among all forms
of knowledge, and Vada (logic) among the debators.

अक्षराणामकारोऽस्मि द्वन्द्वः सामासिकस्य च ।
अहमेवाक्षयः कालो धाताहं विश्वतोमुखः ॥

Aksharaanaamakaaro'smi dwandwah saamaasikasya cha;
Ahamevaakshayah kaalo dhaataaham vishwatomukhah.

33. Among the letters I am the letter "A," among the
compounds I am Dwandwa (the dual), among the
changing (days, months and years), I am the Imperishable Time; and among the givers of the fruits of action, I
am the All-faced Divinity.

मृत्युः सर्वहरश्चाहमुद्भवश्च भविष्यताम् ।
कीर्तिः श्रीर्वाक्च नारीणां स्मृतिर्मेधा धृतिः क्षमा

Mrityuh sarvaharashchaahamudbhavashcha bhavishyataam;
Keertih shreevaakcha naareenaam smritirmedhaa dhritih kshamaa.

34. Among the destroyers I am the all-destroying Death,
among the future developments I am prosperity, among
the qualities of feminine gender, I am fame, prosperity,
good speech, memory, intelligence, firmness and patience (the seven wives of Dharma—the God of Virtue).

बृहत्साम तथा साम्नां गायत्री छन्दसामहम् ।
मासानां मार्गशीर्षोऽहमृतूनां कुसुमाकरः ॥

Brihatsaama tathaa saamnaam gaayatree cchandasaamaham;
Maasaanaam maargasheershohamritoonaam kusumaakarah.

35. Vrihatsama am I among the hymns, Gayatri among the meters, Margashirsha among the months, and Spring among the seasons.

धूतं छलयतामस्मि तेजस्तेजस्विनामहम् ।
जयोऽस्मि व्यवसायोऽस्मि सत्त्वं सत्त्ववतामहम् ॥

Dyootam cchalayataamasmi tejastejaswinaamaham;
Jayosmi vyavasaayosmi sattvam sattvavataamaham.

36. Among the methods of deceit, I am the gambling, among the valiant ment I am their valor, among the conquerors I am their victory; I am the self-effort of those who endeavour, I am Sattwa Guna of those who are Sattwikas.

वृष्णीनां वासुदेवोऽस्मि पाण्डवानां धनंजयः ।
मुनीनामप्यहं व्यासः कवीनामुशना कविः ॥

Vrishneenaam vaasudevosmi paandavaanaam dhananjayah;
Muneenaamapyaham vyaasah kaveenaamushanaa kavih.

37. Among the Vrishnis I am Vasudeva, among the Pandavas I am Arjuna— the conqueror of wealth, among the Sages I am Vyasa, and among the poets I am the poet—Ushana.

दण्डो दमयतामस्मि नीतिरस्मि जिगीषताम् ।
मौनं चैवास्मि गुह्यानां ज्ञानं ज्ञानवतामहम् ॥

Dando damayataamasmi neetirasmi jigeeshataam;
Mounam chaivaasmi guhyaanaam jnaanam jnaanavataa-maham.

38. Among the chastisers I am the rod of chastisement, I am the statesmanship among those who seek victory, I am silence among the secrets, and knowledge among the wise.

यच्चापि सर्वभूतानां बीजं तदहमर्जुन ।
न तदस्ति विना यत्स्यान्मया भूतं चराचरम् ॥

Yachchaapi sarvabhootaanaam beejam tadahamarjuna;
Na tadasti vinaa yatsyaanmayaa bhootam charaacharam.

39. O Arjuna, I am also the seed of all beings. There is nothing among the moving and the unmoving that can exist without Me.

नान्तोऽस्ति मम दिव्यानां विभूतीनां परंतप ।
एष तूद्देशतः प्रोक्तो विभूतेर्विस्तरो मया ॥४०॥

Naantosti mama divyaanaam vibhooteenaam parantapa;
Esha tooddeshatah prokto vibhootervistaro mayaa.

40. O Destroyer of your foes, there is no end to My Divine Glories. All that I have described to you is but a small portion of My endless Glories.

यद्यद्विभूतिमत्सत्त्वं श्रीमदूर्जितमेव   वा ।
तत्तदेवावगच्छ त्वं मम तेजोंऽशसंभवम् ॥४१॥

Yadyadvibhootimatsattwam shreemadoorjitameva vaa;
Tattadevaavagaccha twam mama tejomshasambhavam.

41. Whatever being is endowed with glory, prosperity, brilliance and power, know that to have manifested from a fragment of My Divine Glory.

अथवा बहुनैतेन किं ज्ञातेन तवार्जुन ।
विष्टभ्याहमिदं कृत्स्नमेकांशेन स्थितो जगत् ॥

Athavaa bahunaitena kim jnaatena tavaarjuna;
Vishtabhyaahamidam kritsnamekaamshena sthito jagat.

42. Or, O Arjuna, what is the purpose of the detailed knowledge of My Glories? (It is sufficient to know that) I support this entire universe with a single ray of My boundless Glory.

ॐ तत्सदिति श्रीमद्भगवद्गीतासूपनिषत्सु ब्रह्म-
विद्यायां योगशास्त्रे श्रीकृष्णार्जुनसंवादे विभूति-
योगो नाम दशमोऽध्यायः ॥१०॥

Om tat sat iti srimad bhagavad gitaasoopanishatsu
brahmavidyaayaam yogashaastre sri krishnaarjunasamvaade
vibhootiyogo naama dashamo'dhyaayah.

Om Tat Sat.
Thus, in the Upanishad of the Bhagavad Gita,
the knowledge of Supreme Brahman, the scripture of Yoga,
the dialogue between Sri Krishna and Arjuna,
ends the tenth chapter entitled,
"The Yoga of Divine Glories."

अथैकादशोऽध्यायः

Atha Ekaadasho'dhyaayah

Chapter 11

Vishwaroop Darshan Yogah

The Yoga of the Cosmic Vision

The wondrous experience of Divine Consciousness is figuratively presented in this chapter. Arjuna is given the intuitive insight by which he beholds the Cosmic Form of Krishna. The central teaching of this chapter is that an aspirant should be empty of his ego, and his entire personality should become an instrument in the Divine Hands in order to carry out the Will of God. It is in the depths of surrender that his soul, rising above the normal limits of time and space, glimpses the staggering vision of God which is at once supremely beautiful and supremely terrifying.

अर्जुन उवाच

मदनुग्रहाय परमं गुह्यमध्यात्मसंज्ञितम् ।
यत्त्वयोक्तं वचस्तेन मोहोऽयं विगतो मम ॥१॥

Arjuna uvaacha
Madanugrahaaya paramam guhyamadhyaatmasamjnitam;
Yattwayoktam vachastena mohoyam vigato mama.

1. Arjuna said: O Krishna, the Supreme Secret concerning the Self which you have graciously presented before me, has dispelled my delusion.

भवाप्ययौ हि भूतानां श्रुतौ विस्तरशो मया।
त्वत्तः कमलपत्राक्ष माहात्म्यमपि चाव्ययम्।२।

Bhavaapyayau hi bhootaanaam srutau vistarasho mayaa;
Twattah kamalapatraaksha maahaatmyamapi chaavyayam.

2. O Lotus-eyed Lord, I have heard from You regarding the origin and dissolution of all beings in detail, and also about Your Imperishable Glory.

एवमेतद्यथात्थ त्वमात्मानं परमेश्वर ।
द्रष्टुमिच्छामि ते रूपमैश्वरं पुरुषोत्तम ॥३॥

Evametadyathaattha twamaatmaanam parameshwara;
Drashtumicchaami te roopamaishwaram purushottama.

3. O Supreme Being, whatever You say about Yourself is indeed so. But still, O best of the souls, I would like to behold Your Divine Form.

मन्यसे यदि तच्छक्यं मया द्रष्टुमिति प्रभो ।
योगेश्वर ततो मे त्वं दर्शयात्मानमव्ययम् ॥४॥

Manyase yadi tacchakyam mayaa drashtumiti prabho;
Yogeshwara tato me twam darshayaatmaanamavyayam.

4. If You consider that it is possible for me to behold your Divine Form, then, O Lord of Yoga, please reveal to me Your Imperishable Form.

श्रीभगवानुवाच
पश्य मे पार्थ रूपाणि शतशोऽथ सहस्रशः ।
नानाविधानि दिव्यानि नानावर्णाकृतीनि च ॥

Sree Bhagavaan uvaacha
Pashya me paartha roopaani shatashotha sahasrashah;
Naanaavidhaani divyaani naanaavarnaakriteeni cha.

5. Lord Krishna said: Behold, O Arjuna, My hundreds and thousands of divine forms, of different colors and shapes.

पश्यादित्यान्वसून्रुद्रानश्विनौ मरुतस्तथा ।
बहून्यदृष्टपूर्वाणि पश्याश्चर्याणि भारत ॥६॥

Pashyaadityaan vasoonrudraan ashwinau marutastathaa;
Bahoonyadrishtapoorvaani pashyaashcharyaani Bhaarata.

6. Behold, the sungods, the Vasus, the Rudras, the Ashwini-kumaras, and the wind-gods. Behold many more wonders that you have never seen before.

इहैकस्थं जगत्कृत्स्नं पश्याद्य सचराचरम् ।
मम देहे गुडाकेश यच्चान्यद्द्रष्टुमिच्छसि॥७॥

Ihaikastham jagatkritsnam pashyaadya sacharaacharam;
Mama dehe gudaakesha yacchaanyad drashtumicchasi.

7. O conqueror of sleep, today, even in my body behold the entire universe consisting of movables and immovables centered in Me, and also behold whatever else you would wish to see.

न तु मां शक्यसे द्रष्टुमनेनैव स्वचक्षुषा ।
दिव्यं ददामि ते चक्षुः पश्य मे योगमैश्वरम्॥८॥

Na tu maam shakyase drashtumanenaiva swachakshushaa;
Divyam dadaami te chakshuh pashya me yogamaishwaram.

8. But, you cannot behold My Divine Form with your
physical eyes, therefore, I am bestowing upon you the
intuitional vision by which you will be able to behold my
Divine Glory and Cosmic Powers.

संजय उवाच

एवमुक्त्वा ततो र जन्महायोगेश्वरो हरिः ।
दर्शयामास पार्थाय परमं रूपमैश्वरम् ॥९॥

Sanjaya uvaacha
Evamuktwaa tato raajan mahaayogeshwaro Harih;
Darshayaamaasa paarthaaya paramam roopamaishwaram.

9. Sanjaya said: O King, then Sri Hari, the Great Lord of Yoga,
thus saying revealed to Arjuna His Supreme and Divine Form.

अनेकवक्त्रनयनमनेकाद्भुतदर्शनम्
अनेकदिव्याभरणं दिव्यानेकोद्यतायुधम्।१०।

Anekavaktranayanam anekaadbhutadarshanam;
Anekadivyaabharanam divyaanekodyataayudham.

10. With numerous faces and eyes, with numerous wondrous scenes, dazzling with divine ornaments, with uplifted divine weapons (such is the form he revealed).

दिव्यमाल्याम्बरधरं दिव्यगन्धानुलेपनम् ।
सर्वाश्चर्यमयं देवमनन्तं विश्वतोमुखम् ।।११।।

Divyamaalyaambaradharam divyagandhaanulepanam;
Sarvaashcharyamayam devamanantam vishwatomukham.

11. Decked with divine garlands and wearing divine apparels, anointed with divine unguents, full of wonders, shining effulgent, with innumerable faces on all sides.

दिवि सूर्यसहस्रस्य भवेद्युगपदुत्थिता ।
यदि भाः सदृशी सा स्याद्भासस्तस्य महात्मनः।।

Divi sooryasahasrasya bhavedyugapadutthitaa;
Yadi bhaas sadrishee saa syaadbhaasastasya mahaatmanah.

12. If there were to shine forth a thousand suns in the sky, even that effulgence can hardly compare the splendor of that Mighty Being.

तत्रैकस्थं जगत्कृत्स्नं प्रविभक्तमनेकधा ।
अपश्यद्देवदेवस्य शरीरे पाण्डवस्तदा ॥१३॥

Tatraikastham jagatkritsnam pravibhaktamanekadha;
Apashyaddevadevasya shareere paandavastadaa.

13. Then Arjuna beheld in the body of that God of gods this entire universe resting in One with its numerous divisions.

ततः स विस्मयाविष्टो हृष्टरोमा धनंजयः ।
प्रणम्य शिरसा देवं कृताञ्जलिरभाषत ॥१४॥

Tatas sa vismayaavishto hrishtaromaa dhananjayah;
Pranamya shirasaa devam kritaanjalirabhaashata.

14. With hairs standing on their end, and the mind filled with awe, Arjuna bowing down with his head spoke with folded hands.

अर्जुन उवाच
पश्यामि देवांस्तव देव देहे
सर्वांस्तथा भूतविशेषसङ्घान् ।
ब्रह्माणमीशं कमलासनस्थ-
मृषींश्च सर्वानुरगांश्च दिव्यान्॥१५॥

Arjuna uvaacha
Pashyaami devaamstava deva dehe
Sarvamstathaa bhootavisheshasanghaan;
Brahmaanameesham kamalaasanastham
Risheemshcha sarvaanuragaamshcha divyaan.

15. Arjuna said: O Divine Being, I behold in Your Body all the gods, and all moving and unmoving beings, as well as Brahma seated on the lotus, the Sages and the Divine Serpents.

अनेकबाहूदरवक्त्रनेत्रं
पश्यामि त्वां सर्वतोऽनन्तरूपम् ।
नान्तं न मध्यं न पुनस्तवादिं
पश्यामि विश्वेश्वर विश्वरूप ॥१६॥

Anekabaahoodaravaktranetram
Pashyaami twaam sarvato'nantaroopam;
Naantam na madhyam na punastavaadim
Pashyaami vishweshwara vishawaroopa.

16. O Lord of the unvierse, the Deity of Cosmic Form, I behold you everywhere having countless forms, countless arms, stomachs, faces and eyes. I do not see the beginning, middle or end of Your Being.

किरीटिनं गदिनं चक्रिणं च
तेजोराशिं सर्वतो दीप्तिमन्तम् ।
पश्यामि त्वां दुर्निरीक्ष्यं समन्ता-
द्दीप्तानलार्कद्युतिमप्रमेयम् ।।१७।।

Kireetinam gadinam chakrinam cha
Tejoraashim sarvato deeptimantam;
Pashyaami twaam durnireekshyam samantaat
Deeptaanalaarkadyutimaprameyam.

17. I behold You with crown, mace and discus; a mass of luminosity, shining effulgent on all sides, difficult to behold, dazzling with radiance, even like the flaming fire, shining like the sun and moon, incomparable.

त्वमक्षरं परमं वेदितव्यं
त्वमस्य विश्वस्य परं निधानम् ।
त्वमव्ययः शाश्वतधर्मगोप्ता
सनातनस्त्वं पुरुषो मतो मे ॥१८॥

Twamaksharam paramam veditavyam
Twamasya vishwasya param nidhaanam;
Twamavyayah shaashwatadharmagoptaa
Sanaatanastwam purusho mato me.

18. You are the Imperishable Brahman, the Supreme Knowable (for spiritual aspirants); You are the best Support of the Universe, the Imperishable Protector of Eternal Religion. I consider You as the Ancient Being.

अनादिमध्यान्तमनन्तवीर्य-
मनन्तबाहुं शशिसूर्यनेत्रम् ।
पश्यामि त्वां दीप्तहुताशवक्त्रं
स्वतेजसा विश्वमिदं तपन्तम् ॥१९॥

Anaadimadhyaantamanantaveeryam
Anantabaahum shashisooryanetram;
Pashyaami twaam deeptahutaashavaktram
Swatejasaa vishwamidam tapantam.

19. I behold You as one devoid of beginning, middle and end; endowed with limitless valor, with innumerable arms, having sun and moon as Your eyes, with faces blazing with fire, scorching this world with your radiance.

द्यावापृथिव्योरिदमन्तरं हि
व्याप्तं त्वयैकेन दिशश्च सर्वाः।
दृष्ट्वाद्भुतं   रूपमुग्रं   तवेदं
लोकत्रयं प्रव्यथितं महात्मन् ॥२०॥

Dyaavaaprithivyoridamantaram hi
Vyaaptam twayaikena dishashcha sarvaah;
Drishtwaadbhutam roopamugram tavedam.
Lokatrayam pravyathitam mahaatman.

20. All the directions as well as that which is in the middle of the earth and sky are filled with You alone. O Great Soul, beholding this terrible and strange form of Yours, the three worlds are being agitated.

अमी हि त्वां सुरसङ्घा विशन्ति
केचिद्भीताः प्राञ्जलयो गृणन्ति ।

स्वस्तीत्युक्त्वा महर्षिसिद्धसङ्घाः
स्तुवन्ति त्वां स्तुतिभिः पुष्कलाभिः ॥

Amee hi twaam surasanghaah vishanti
kechit bheetaah praanjalayo grinanti;
Swasteetyuktwaa maharshisiddhasanghaah
Stuvanti twaam stutibhih pushkalaabhih.

21. The group of Gods are entering into You, some terrifired are praising You with folded hands, and Sages and Siddhas are uttering words of auspiciousness as they sing praises of You.

रुद्रादित्या वसवो ये च साध्या
विश्वेऽश्विनौ   मरुतश्चोष्मपाश्च ।
गन्धर्वयक्षासुरसिद्धसङ्घा
वीक्षन्ते त्वां विस्मिताश्चैव सर्वे॥२२॥

Rudraadityaa vasavo ye cha saadhyaa
Vishwe'shvinau marutashchoshmapaashcha;
Gandharvayakshaasurasiddhasanghaa
Veekshante twaam vismitaashchaiva sarve.

22. Rudras, Adityas, Vasus, Sadhyas, Vishwedevas, Ashwini-kumaras, Maruts and Forefathers, as well as Gandharvas, Yakshas, Rakshasas and Siddhas—all these are gazing at You with amazement and wonder.

रूपं महत्ते बहुवक्त्रनेत्रं
महाबाहो बहुबाहूरुपादम् ।
बहूदरं बहुदंष्ट्राकरालं
दृष्ट्वा लोकाः प्रव्यथितास्तथाहम् ।२३।

Roopam mahat te bahuvaktranetram
Mahaabaaho bahubaahoorupaadam;
Bahoodaram bahudamshtraakaraalam
Drishtwaa lokaah pravyathitaastathaaham.

23. Seeing Your great form with many faces, many eyes, many arms, many thighs and feet, and many terrible tusks and stomachs, O Mighty Armed, the worlds are terrified and so am I.

नभःस्पृशं दीप्तमनेकवर्णं
व्यात्ताननं दीप्तविशालनेत्रम् ।
दृष्ट्वा हि त्वां प्रव्यथितान्तरात्मा
धृतिं न विन्दामि शमं च विष्णो ।२४।

Nabhasprisham deeptamanekavarnam
Vyaattaananam deeptavishaalanetram;
Drishtwaa hi twaam pravyathitaantaraatmaa
Dhritim na vindaami shamam cha vishno.

24. O Vishnu, having seen Your form that touches the sky, effulgent with many colors, with wide opened mouths, and blazing large eyes, I tremble from the depths of my being, and am unable to find steadiness or peace.

दंष्ट्राकरालानि च ते मुखानि
दृष्ट्वैव कालानलसन्निभानि ।
दिशो न जाने न लभे च शर्म
प्रसीद देवेश जगन्निवास ॥२५॥

Damshtraakaraalaani cha te mukhaani
Drishtwaiva kaalaanalasannibhaani;
Disho na jaane na labhe cha sharma
Praseeda devesha jagannivaasa.

25. Seeing Your mouths and terrble tusks, like the fires of universal destruction, I have lost the sense of directions, and am unable to find peace. Therefore, O Refuge of the Universe, O God of gods, be gracious unto me.

अमी च त्वां धृतराष्ट्रस्य पुत्राः
सर्वे   सहैवावनिपालसङ्घैः ।
भीष्मो द्रोणः सूतपुत्रस्तथासौ
सहास्मदीयैरपि योधमुख्यैः ॥२६॥

Amee cha twaam dhritaraashtrasya putraah
Sarve sahaivaavanipaalasanghaih;
Bhishmo dronah sootaputrastathaasau
Sahaasmadeeyairapi yodhamukhyaih.

26. The sons of Dhritarashtra along with groups of kings
including Bhishma, Drona, Karna as well as heroes from
our sides (are entering into Your wide opened mouths).

वक्त्राणि ते त्वरमाणा विशन्ति
दंष्ट्राकरालानि भयानकानि ।
केचिद्विलग्ना   दशनान्तरेषु
संदृश्यन्ते चूर्णितैरुत्तमाङ्गैः ॥२७॥

Vaktraani te twaramaana vishanti
Damshtraakaraalaani bhayaanakaani;
Kechidwilagnaa dashanaantareshu
Sandrishyante choornitairuttamaangaih.

27. They are rushing into Your terrible mouths that are filled with terrible tusks, and some stick between the tusks, while others have their heads crushed by them.

यथा नदीनां बहवोऽम्बुवेगाः
समुद्रमेवाभिमुखा द्रवन्ति ।
तथा तवामी नरलोकवीरा
विशन्ति वक्त्राण्यभिविज्वलन्ति ॥

Yathaa nadeenaam bahavombuvegaah
Samudramevaabhimukhaah dravanti;
Tathah tavaamee naralokaveerah
Vishanti vaktraanyabhivijwalanti.

28. Just as torrents of many rivers hasten to enter into the ocean, in the same way these heroes of this human world are entering into Your blazing mouth from all sides.

यथा प्रदीप्तं ज्वलनं पतङ्गा
विशन्ति नाशाय समृद्धवेगाः ।
तथैव नाशाय विशन्ति लोका-
स्तवापि वक्त्राणि समृद्धवेगाः ॥२९॥

Yathaa pradeeptam jwalanam patangaa
Vishanti naashaaya samriddhavegaah;
Tathaiva naashaaya vishanti lokaas
Tavaapi vaktraani samriddhavegaah.

29. Just as moths rush into blazing fires to be consumed to ashes, in the same way all these men are rushing swiftly into Your mouth for their destruction.

लेलिह्यसे ग्रसमानः समन्ता-
ल्लोकान्समग्रान्वदनैर्ज्वलद्भिः।
तेजोभिरापूर्य   जगत्समग्रं
भासस्तवोग्राःप्रतपन्ति विष्णो॥३०॥

Lelihyase grasamaanah samantaal
Lokaan samagraan vadanair jwaladbhih
Tejobhiraapoorya jagatsamagram
Bhaasastavograah pratapanti vishno.

30. You are devouring all the worlds by Your blazing mouths, and You are licking them up, O Vishnu! Terrible effulgence is scorching the entire world with its fierce flames.

आख्याहि मे को भवानुग्ररूपो
नमोऽस्तु ते देववर प्रसीद ।
विज्ञातुमिच्छामि भवन्तमाद्यं
न हि प्रजानामि तव प्रवृत्तिम् ॥३१॥

Aaakhyaahi me ko bhavaanugraroopo
Namostu te devavara praseeda;
Vijnaatumicchaami bhavantamaadyam
Nahi prajaanaami tava pravrittim.

31. O Best among the Gods! Please tell me who are You of this terrible form? Adorations to You, may You be pleased with me. I want to know Your nature who are the cause of all beings. I do not know Your workings.

श्रीभगवानुवाच
कालोऽस्मि लोकक्षयकृत्प्रवृद्धो
लोकान्समाहर्तुमिह प्रवृत्तः ।
ऋतेऽपि त्वां न भविष्यन्ति सर्वे
येऽवस्थिताः प्रत्यनीकेषु योधाः ॥३२॥

Sree Bhagavaan uvaacha
Kaalosmi lokakshayakrit pravriddho
Lokaansamaahartumiha pravrittah;

Rite'pi twaam na bhavishynati sarve
Ye'awasthitaah pratyaneekeshu yodhah.

32. Bhagavan Krishna said: I am verily Time-spirit, fully developed, engaged in the destruction of the worlds. Even without you, these heroes assembled in hostile armies will not live.

तस्मात्त्वमुत्तिष्ठ यशो लभस्व
जित्वा शत्रून् भुङ्क्ष्व राज्यं समृद्धम् ।
मयैवैते   निहताः   पूर्वमेव
निमित्तमात्रं भव सव्यसाचिन् ॥३३॥

Tasmaat twam uttishtha yasho labhaswa
Jitwaa shatroon bhunkshwa raajyam samriddham;
Mayaivaite nihataah poorvameva
Nimittamaatram bhava savyasaachin.

33. Therefore, O Arjuna, stand up, conquer the enemies, attain victory and enjoy prosperous kingdom. I have already killed them, therefore become just an instrument (in causing their destruction).

द्रोणं च भीष्मं च जयद्रथं च
कर्णं तथान्यानपि योधवीरान् ।
मया हतांस्त्वं जहि मा व्यथिष्ठा
युध्यस्व जेतासि रणे सपत्नान् ॥३४॥

Dronam cha bheeshmam cha jayadratham cha
Karnam tathaanyaanapi yodhaveeraan;
Mayaa hataamstwam jahi maa vyathishthaa
Yudhyaswa jetaasi rane sapatnaan.

34. Destroy Drona, Bhishma, Jayadratha, Karna and other heroes who have been already killed by Me. Do not be terrified by fear. Fight. You are bound to attain victory in this battle.

संजय उवाच

एतच्छ्रुत्वा वचनं केशवस्य
कृताञ्जलिर्वेपमानः किरीटी ।
नमस्कृत्वा भूय एवाह कृष्णं
सगद्गदं भीतभीतः प्रणम्य ॥३५॥

Sanjaya uvaacha
Etacchrutwaa vachanam keshavasya
Kritaanjalirvepamaanah kireetee;

Namaskritwaa bhooya evaaha krishnam
Sagadgadam bheetahbheetah pranamya.

35. Sanjaya said: Hearing these words of Sri Krishna, with hands folded, trembling with extreme fear, Arjuna bowing his head spoke in choking voice.

अर्जुन उवाच

स्थाने हृषीकेश तव प्रकीर्त्या
जगत्प्रहृष्यत्यनुरज्यते   च ।
रक्षांसि भीतानि दिशो द्रवन्ति
सर्वे नमस्यन्ति च सिद्धसङ्घाः॥३६॥

Arjuna uvaacha
Sthaane hrisheekesha tava prakeertyaa
Jagatprahrishyatyanurajyate cha;
Rakshaamsi bheetaani disho dravanti
Sarve namasyanti cha siddhasanghaah.

36. Arjuna said: O Lord (Hrishikesh), it is befitting that the whole world is thrilled, and is filled with love for You. And terrified by You the demons are fleeing in all directions, while the host of Siddhas (enlightened beings) are bowing to You.

कस्माच्च ते न नमेरन्महात्मन्
गरीयसे ब्रह्मणोऽप्याादिकर्त्रे ।
अनन्त देवेश जगन्निवास
त्वमक्षरं सदसत्तत्परं यत् ॥३७॥

Kasmaat cha te na nameran mahaatman
Gareeyase Brahmanopyaadikartre;
Ananta devesha jagannivaasa
Twamaksharam sadasattatparam yat.

37. O Mighty Soul, Why shouldn't they adore You who
are the origin of Brahma himself, and thus, who are
greater than the great? O Infinite Lord, the God of gods,
the Abode of the universe, You are the Imperishable Self
beyond existence and non-existence.

त्वमादिदेवः पुरुषः पुराण-
स्त्वमस्य विश्वस्य परं निधानम्।
वेत्तासि वेद्यं च परं च धाम
त्वया ततं विश्वमनन्तरूप ॥३८॥

Twamaadidevah purushah puraanas
Twamasya vishwasya param niddhaanam;
Vettaasi vedyam cha param cha dhaama
Twayaa tatam vishwamanantaroopa.

38. O Countless formed Divinity, You are the First of Gods, the Supreme Being, the Ancient Self, and You are the resting place of the world. You are the knower, the knowable, and the Supreme Abode of Lord Vishnu. This entire world is pervaded by You.

वायुर्यमोऽग्निर्वरुणः शशाङ्कः
प्रजापतिस्त्वं प्रपितामहश्च ।
नमो नमस्तेऽस्तु सहस्रकृत्वः
पुनश्च भूयोऽपि नमो नमस्ते ॥३९॥

Vaayuryamognirvarunah shasaankah
Prajaapatistwam prapitaamahashcha;
Namo namastestu sahasrakritwah
Punashcha bhooyopi namo namaste.

39. You are the Father of Vayu, Yama, Agni, Varuna, Moon-God, and Hiranyagarbha (the Deity presiding over the Cosmic Mind). Thousands of adorations to You! Adorations to You again and again!

नमः पुरस्तादथ पृष्ठतस्ते
नमोऽस्तु ते सर्वत एव सर्व ।

अनन्तवीर्यामितविक्रमस्त्वं
सर्वं समाप्नोषि ततोऽसि सर्वः ॥४०॥

Namah purastaadatha prishtataste
Namostu te sarvata eva sarva;
Anantaveeryaamitavikramastwam
Sarvam samaapnoshi tatosi sarvah.

40. Adorations to You from the front, adorations to You from behind. O All-formed Deity, adorations to You from all sides! You are endowed with endless valor and limitless power. You have pervaded this universe. You are indeed all this!

सखेति मत्वा प्रसभं यदुक्तं
हे कृष्ण हे यादव हे सखेति ।
अजानता महिमानं तवेदं
मया प्रमादात्प्रणयेन वापि ॥४१॥

Sakheti matwaa prasabham yaduktam
He krishna he yaadava he sakheti;
Ajaanataa mahimaanam tavedam
Mayaa pramaadaatpranayena vaapi.

41. Not knowing Your greatness, due to my carelessness or my love for You, I have often addressed You saying, O Krishna, O Yadava, O Friend, considering You to be of equal to me.

यच्चावहासार्थमसत्कृतोऽसि
विहारशय्यासनभोजनेषु
एकोऽथवाप्यच्युत तत्समक्षं
तत्क्षामये त्वामहमप्रमेयम् ॥४२॥

Yacchaavahaasaarthamasatkritosi
Vihaarashayyasanabhojaneshu;
Ekothavaapyachyuta tatsamaksham
Tatkshaamaye twaamaham aprameyam.

42. Out of mere fun and play, whatever disrespect I have shown to You, while sleeping, sitting, and taking food, in privacy or before others, I pray, O Invincible and Boundless One, for Your forgiveness.

पितासि लोकस्य चराचरस्य
त्वमस्य पूज्यश्च गुरुर्गरीयान् ।
न त्वत्समोऽस्त्यभ्यधिकः कुतोऽन्यो
लोकत्रयेऽप्यप्रतिमप्रभाव ॥४३॥

Pitaasi lokasya charaacharasya
Twamasya poojyashcha gururgareeyaan;
Na twatsamostyabhyadhikah krito'nyo
Lokatraye'pyapratimaprabhaava.

43. O God of Incomparable Power, You are the Father of this creation consisting of movables and immovables. You are the Adorable One, the Preceptor, and the Glorious One. There is none equal to You in the three worlds, much less can any one excel You.

तस्मात्प्रणम्य प्रणिधाय कायं
प्रसादये त्वामहमीशमीड्यम् ।
पितेव पुत्रस्य सखेव सख्युः
प्रियः प्रियायार्हसि देव सोढुम् ।४४।

Tasmatpranamya pranidhaaya kaayam
Prasaadaye twaamahameeshameedyam;
Piteva putrasya sakheva sakhyuh
Priyah priyaayaarhasi deva sodhum.

44. Therefore, bowing down and prostrating myself before You, I seek Your Divine Grace, O Divine Being, forgive me just as father forgives his son, a friend forgives his friend and a lover his beloved.

अदृष्टपूर्वं हृषितोऽस्मि दृष्ट्वा
भयेन च प्रव्यथितं मनो मे ।
तदेव मे दर्शय देव रूपं
प्रसीद देवेश जगन्निवास ॥४५॥

Adrishtapoorvam hrishito'smi drishtwaa
Bhayena cha pravyathitam mano me;
Tadeva me darshaya deva roopam
Praseeda devesha jagannivaasa.

45. I am pleased to see this universal form which was
never seen by me before, and at the same time my mind is
terrified with fear. Therefore, please reveal to me Your
previous form. O God of Gods, O Refuge of the Universe, be gracious to me.

किरीटिनं गदिनं चक्रहस्त-
मिच्छामि त्वां द्रष्टुमहं तथैव ।
तेनैव रूपेण चतुर्भुजेन
सहस्रबाहो भव विश्वमूर्ते ॥४६॥

Kireetinam gadinam chakrahastam
Icchaami twaam drashtumaham tathaiva;

Tenaiva roopena chaturbhujena
Sahasrabaaho bhava vishwamoorte.

46. I wish to see You as before with crown, holding mace and discus in Your hands. O Thousand-armed! O Universal Formed! Be pleased to assume Your Four-armed Form.

श्रीभगवानुवाच

मया प्रसन्नेन तवार्जुनेदं
रूपं परं दर्शितमात्मयोगात् ।
तेजोमयं विश्वमनन्तमाद्यं
यन्मे त्वदन्येन न दृष्टपूर्वम् ॥४७॥

Sree Bhagavaan uvaacha
Mayaa prasannena tavaarjunedam
    Roopam param darshitamaatmayogaat;
Tejomayam vishwamanantamaadyam
    Yanme twadanyena na drishtapoorvam.

47. The Blessed Lord said: O Arjuna, being pleased with you, by the power of My Yoga, I have revealed to you this My Ancient Form which is luminous, universal, endless, and which has not been seen ever before by anyone other than you.

न वेदयज्ञाध्ययनैर्न दानै-
        र्न च क्रियाभिर्न तपोभिरुग्रैः ।
एवंरूपः शक्य अहं नृलोके
        द्रष्टुं त्वदन्येन कुरुप्रवीर ॥४८॥

Na vedayajnaadhyayanairna daanair
        Na cha kriyaabhirna tapobhirugraih;
Evam roopah shakya aham nriloke
        Drashtum twadanyena kurupraveera.

48. O best of the Kurus, I cannot be seen by anyone other than yourself in this human world. Neither by the study of Vedas, nor by acts of charity nor by purificatory rites, and not even by terrible austerities (can I be seen thus).

मा ते व्यथा मा च विमूढभावो
        दृष्ट्वा रूपं घोरमीदृङ्ममेदम् ।
व्यपेतभीः प्रीतमनाः पुनस्त्वं
        तदेव मे रूपमिदं प्रपश्य ॥४९॥

Maa te vyathaa maa cha vimoodhabhaavo
        Drishtwaa roopam ghorameedringmamedam;
Vyapetabheeh preetamanaah punastwam
        Tadeva me roopamidam prapashya.

49. Having seen this terrible form of Mine do not be afraid or bewildered. Rid of fear, with a cheerful heart, now behold again My previous form.

संजय उवाच

इत्यर्जुनं वासुदेवस्तथोक्त्वा
स्वकं रूपं दर्शयामास भूयः ।

आश्वासयामास च भीतमेनं
भूत्वा पुनः सौम्यवपुर्महात्मा ॥५०॥

Sanjaya uvaacha
Ityarjunam vaasudevastathoktwaa
　　Swakam roopam darshayaamaasa bhooyah;
Aaashwaasayaamaasa cha bheetamenam
　　Bhootwaa punah saumyavapurmahaatmaa.

50. Sanjaya said: Having said to Arjuna thus, Lord Krishna showed to him his former form. And having resumed His gentle form, that Great Soul comforted Arjuna who was terrified.

अर्जुन उवाच

दृष्ट्वेदं मानुषं रूपं तव सौम्यं जनार्दन ।
इदानीमस्मि संवृत्तः सचेताः प्रकृतिं गतः ॥५१॥

Arjuna uvaacha
Drishtwedam maamnusham roopam tava saumyam janaardana;
Idaaneemasmi samvrittah sachetaah prakritim gatah.

51. Arjuna said: O Janardana, having beheld Your human form, I am now free of fear, my mind is composed, I have resumed by normal awareness.

श्रीभगवानुवाच
सुदुर्दर्शमिदं रूपं दृष्टवानसि यन्मम ।
देवा अप्यस्य रूपस्य नित्यं दर्शनकाङ्क्षिणः ॥

Sree Bhagavaan uvaacha
Sudurdarshamidam roopam drishtavaanasi yanmama;
Devaa apyasya roopasya nityam darshanakaankshinah.

52. The Blessed Lord said: This form of Mine that you have seen is very difficult to behold; even gods are ever desirous of beholding this form.

नाहं वेदैर्न तपसा न दानेन न चेज्यया ।
शक्य एवंविधो द्रष्टुं दृष्टवानसि मां यथा॥५३॥

Naaham vedairna tapasaa na daanena na chejyayaa;
Shakya evamvidho drashtum drishtavaanasi maam yathaa.

53. This form of Mine which you have seen cannot be realized even by the study of Vedas, or by austerities, or by acts of charity, or by the performance of sacrifices.

भक्त्या त्वनन्यया शक्य अहमेवंविधोऽर्जुन ।
ज्ञातुं द्रष्टुं च तत्त्वेन प्रवेष्टुं च परंतप ॥५४॥

Bhaktyaa twananyayaa shakyam ahamevamvidhoarjuna;
Jnaatum drashtum cha tattwena praveshtum cha parantapa.

54. O Arjuna, the scorcher of your foes, it is by single-minded devotion alone that I can be known, seen in reality, and also entered into.

मत्कर्मकृन्मत्परमो मद्भक्तः सङ्गवर्जितः ।
निर्वैरः सर्वभूतेषु यः स मामेति पाण्डव ॥५५॥

Matkarmakrinmatparamo madbhaktah sangavarjitah;
Nirvairah sarvabhooteshu yah sa maameti paandava.

55. O Son of Pandu, he who performs actions for Me, who considers Me as the Supreme Goal, who is My devotee, and is devoid of attachments; who is without animosity towards all living beings, he alone attains Me.

ॐ तत्सदिति श्रीमद्भगवद्गीतासूपनिषत्सु ब्रह्मविद्यायां योगशास्त्रे श्रीकृष्णार्जुनसंवादे विश्वरूपदर्शनयोगो. नामैकादशोऽध्यायः ॥ ११ ॥

Om tat sat iti srimad bhagavad gitaasoopanishatsu brahmavidyaayaam yogashaastre sri krishnaarjunasamvaade vishwaroopdarshanyogo naama ekadasho'dhyaayah.

Om Tat Sat.
Thus, in the Upanishad of the Bhagavad Gita,
the knowledge of Supreme Brahman, the scripture of Yoga,
the dialogue between Sri Krishna and Arjuna,
ends the eleventh chapter entitled,
"The Yoga of the Cosmic Vision."

यो न हृष्यति न द्वेष्टि न शोचति न काङ्क्षति ।
शुभाशुभपरित्यागी भक्तिमान्यः स मे प्रियः ॥

अथ द्वादशोऽध्यायः

Atha Dwaadasho'dhyaayah

Chapter 12

Bhakti Yogah

The Yoga of Devotion

Lord Krishna teaches that for most people, the worship of the Saguna aspect of God (God with form and attributes) is easier than that of the Nirguna aspect (God without form and attributes). The Saguna worship will automatically lead one to the Nirguna worship. A series of disciplines are outlined for developing unflinching devotion to God. The characteristics of a perfected devotee are given, so that a Yogi may develop them and thus become very dear to God!

अर्जुन उवाच

एवं सततयुक्ता ये भक्तास्त्वां पर्युपासते ।
ये चाप्यक्षरमव्यक्तं तेषां के योगवित्तमाः ॥१॥

Arjuna uvaacha
Evam satatayuktaa ye bhaktaastwaam paryupaasate;
Ye chaapyaksharamavyaktam tesham ke yogavittamaah.

1. Arjuna asked: Of these two types of Yogis, those who thus worship You with form endowed with devotion, and those who are devoted to the Imperishable, the Non-manifest Brahman, which of the two worshippers is the better knower of Yoga?

श्रीभगवानुवाच

मय्यावेश्य मनो ये मां नित्ययुक्ता उपासते ।

श्रद्धया परयोपेतास्ते मे युक्ततमा मताः ॥२॥

Sree Bhagavaan uvaacha
Mayyaveshya mano ye maam nityayuktaa upaasate;
Shraddhayaa parayopetaaste me yuktatamaa mataah.

2. The Blessed Lord said: Those who having immersed their mind in Me endowed with faith, worship Me with ceaseless devotion, they are in my opinion the best skilled in Yoga.

ये त्वक्षरमनिर्देश्यमव्यक्तं पर्युपासते ।

सर्वत्रगमचिन्त्यं च कूटस्थमचलं ध्रुवम् ॥३॥

Ye twaksharamanirdeshyamavyaktam paryupaasate;
Sarvatragamachintyam cha kootasthamachalam dhruvam.

3. Those who worship the imperishable, the indefinable, the unmanifest, the all-pervading, the immutable, the immovable, the indescribable, the Eternal

संनियम्येन्द्रियग्रामं सर्वत्र समबुद्धयः ।
ते प्राप्नुवन्ति मामेव सर्वभूतहिते रताः ॥४॥

Samniyamyendriyagraamam sarvatra samabuddhayah;
Te praapnuvanti maameva sarvabhootahite rataah.

4. With their senses restrained, and endowed with balance of mind, engaged in the welfare of all beings, even they attain Me.

क्लेशोऽधिकतरस्तेषामव्यक्तासक्तचेतसाम् ।
अव्यक्ता हि गतिर्दुःखं देहवद्भिरवाप्यते ॥५॥

Kleshodhikatarasteshaamavyaktaasaktachetasaam;
Avyaktaa hi gatirduhkham dehavadbhiravaapyate.

5. But, the worshippers who are attached to the non-manifest Absolute have to encounter greater difficulties, because it is very difficult for an embodied soul to reach the Non-manifest Absolute.

ये तु सर्वाणि कर्माणि मयि संन्यस्य मत्पराः ।
अनन्येनैव योगेन मां ध्यायन्त उपासते ॥६॥

Ye tu sarvaani karmaani mayi sannyasya matparaah;
Anannyenaiva yogena maam dhyaayanta upaasate.

6. But those who having offered all actions to Me, devoted to Me, meditate upon Me with one-pointed Yoga

तेषामहं समुद्धर्ता मृत्युसंसारसागरात् ।
भवामि नचिरात्पार्थ मय्यावेशितचेतसाम् ॥

Teshaamaham samuddhartaa mrityusamsaarasaagaraat;
Bhavaami nachirat paartha mayyaaveshitachetasaam.

7. O Partha, for those whose minds are immersed in Me, I become their saviour from the ocean of death, in a very short time.

मय्येव मन आधत्स्व मयि बुद्धिं निवेशय ।
निवसिष्यसि मय्येव अत ऊर्ध्वं न संशयः ॥८॥

Mayyeva mana aadhatswa mayi buddhim niveshaya;
Nivasishyasi mayyeva ata oordhwam na samshayah.

8. Focus your mind on Me only, let your intellect be fixed on Me, you will verily abide in Me hereafter without a shadow of doubt.

अथ चित्तं समाधातुं न शक्नोषि मयि स्थिरम् ।
अभ्यासयोगेन ततो मामिच्छाप्तुं धनंजय ॥९॥

Atha chittam samaadhaatum na shaknoshi mayi sthiram;
Abhyaasayogena tato maamicchaaptum dhananjaya.

9. O conqueror of wealth, if you are unable to steady your mind on Me, then endeavor to attain Me by taking recourse to the Yoga of Abhyasa (repeated effort).

अभ्यासेऽप्यसमर्थोऽसि मत्कर्मपरमो भव ।
मदर्थमपि कर्माणि कुर्वन्सिद्धिमवाप्स्यसि ॥

Abhyaasepyasamarthosi matkarmaparamo bhava;
Madarthamapi karmaani kurvansiddhimavaapsyasi.

10. If you are unable to practise Abhyasa, then be intent upon doing actions for My sake, you will attain perfection.

अथैतदप्यशक्तोऽसि कर्तुं मद्योगमाश्रितः ।
सर्वकर्मफलत्यागं ततः कुरु यतात्मवान् ॥११॥

Athaitadapyashaktosi kartum madyogamaashritah;
Sarvakarmaphalatyaagam tatah kuru yataatmavaan.

11. And if you are unable to do even this, then taking recourse to the Yoga of Surrender, striving to control the mind and senses, renounce the fruits of all actions.

श्रेयो हि ज्ञानमभ्यासाज्ज्ञानाद्ध्यानं विशिष्यते ।
ध्यानात्कर्मफलत्यागस्त्यागाच्छान्तिरनन्तरम्

Shreyo hi jnaanamabhyaasaat jnaanaddhyaanam vishishyate;
Dhyaanaat karmaphalatyaagastyaagaatcchaantiranantaram.

12. Knowledge (indirect) is better than repeated effort (Abhyasa), and better than knowledge is Dhyana or meditation. From meditation follows renunciation of fruits of action, and from renunciation there arises ceaseless peace.

अद्वेष्टा सर्वभूतानां मैत्रः करुण एव च ।
निर्ममो निरहंकारःसमदुःखसुखः क्षमी ॥१३॥

Adweshtaa sarvabhootaanaam maitrah karuna eva cha;
Nirmamo nirahankaarah samaduhkhasukah kshamee.

13. He who is without hatred towards all beings, who is friendly and compassionate as well, who is free from the sense of mine-ness (attachment and egoism) and is equally balanced in pleasure and pain (such a devotee is dear to Me.)

संतुष्टः सततं योगी यतात्मा दृढनिश्चयः ।
मय्यर्पितमनोबुद्धिर्यो मद्भक्तः स मे प्रियः ॥

Santushtas satatam yogee yataatmaa dridhanishchayah;
Mayyarpitamanobuddhiryo madbhaktah sa me priyah.

14. He who is ever contented, united with Me, self-controlled, possessed of firm resolve, with his mind and intellect dedicated to Me, such a devotee is dear to me.

यस्मान्नोद्विजते लोको लोकान्नोद्विजते च यः ।
हर्षामर्षभयोद्वेगैर्मुक्तो यः स च मे प्रियः ॥१५॥

Yasmaanodwijate loko lokaannodwijate cha yah;
Harshamarshabhayodwegairmukto yah sa cha me priyah.

15. He by whom the world is not agitated, and he is not agitated by the world, who is free from joy, envy, fear and anxiety, he is indeed dear to Me.

अनपेक्षः शुचिर्दक्ष उदासीनो गतव्यथः ।
सर्वारम्भपरित्यागी यो मद्भक्तः स मे प्रियः ॥

Anapekshah shuchirdaksha udaaseeno gatavyathah;
Sarvaarambhaparityaagee yo madbhaktah sa me priyah.

16. He who is without expectation, pure, skilled (in spiritual movement), indifferent (to joy and sorrow), without grief, who has renounced all his Karmic involvements, such a devotee is dear to Me.

यो न हृष्यति न द्वेष्टि न शोचति न काङ्क्षति ।
शुभाशुभपरित्यागी भक्तिमान्यः स मे प्रियः ॥

Yo na hrishyati na dweshti na shochati na kaankshati;
Shubhaashubhaparityaagi bhaktimaan yah sa me priyah.

17. He who neither rejoice, nor hates, nor expects, renouncing good and evil, such a devotee is dear to Me.

समः शत्रौ च मित्रे च तथा मानापमानयोः ।
शीतोष्णसुखदुःखेषु समः सङ्गविवर्जितः ।१८।

Samah shatrau cha mitre cha tathaa maanaapamaanayoh;
Sheetoshnasukhaduhkheshu samah sangavivarjitah.

18. He who is equally balanced in the midst of friends and foes, who is the same in praise and censure, as well as cold and heat, to whom pleasure and pain are alike, and who is devoid of attachments (such a devotee is dear to me).

तुल्यनिन्दास्तुतिर्मौनी संतुष्टो येन केनचित् ।
अनिकेतः स्थिरमतिर्भक्तिमान्मे प्रियो नरः ॥

Tulyanindaastutirmaunee santushto yena kenachit;
Aniketah sthiramatir bhaktimaanme priyo narah.

19. He to whom praise and censure are alike, who is reflective, contented with everything, without a physical dwelling place, who is endowed with the steady intellect, and full of devotion, such a devotee is dear to Me.

ये तु धर्म्यामृतमिदं यथोक्तं पर्युपासते ।
श्रद्दधाना मत्परमा भक्तास्तेऽतीव मे प्रियाः ॥

Ye tu dharmyaamritamidam yathoktam paryupaasate;
Shraddadhaanaah matparamaa bhaktaasteteeva me priyaah.

20. Those who are devoted to the Immortal Dharma set forth above, endowed with faith, regarding Me as the Supreme, they— My Devotees are extremely dear to me.

ॐ तत्सदिति श्रीमद्भगवद्गीतासूपनिषत्सु ब्रह्म-
विद्यायां योगशास्त्रे श्रीकृष्णार्जुनसंवादे भक्ति-
योगो नाम द्वादशोऽध्यायः ॥ १२ ॥

Om tat sat iti srimad bhagavad gitaasoopanishatsu brahmavidyaayaam yogashaastre sri krishnaarjunasamvaade bhaktiyogo naama dwaadasho'dhyaayah.

Om Tat Sat.
Thus, in the Upanishad of the Bhagavad Gita,
the knowledge of Supreme Brahman, the scripture of Yoga,
the dialogue between Sri Krishna and Arjuna,
ends the twelfth chapter entitled,
"The Yoga of Devotion."

अथ त्रयोदशोऽध्यायः

Atha Trayodasho'dhyaayah

Chapter 13

Kshetra Kshetrajna Vibhaga Yogah

The Yoga of Distinction
Between the Field and Its Knower

When a Yogi develops a keen insight into the fact that his soul is different from the body, he becomes a better Karma Yogi, a better Bhakti Yogi and a better Jnana Yogi. In fact, he becomes more integrated in his personality. This is the main theme of this chapter.

The soul in the state of ignorance seems to be involved in sowing the seeds of Karmas in the field of matter and reaps the harvest of Karmic entanglements. But in the state of Enlightenment it discovers its identity with the Absolute Self and becomes Liberated from bondage.

अर्जुन उवाच

प्रकृति पुरुषं चैव क्षेत्रं क्षेत्रज्ञमेव च ।
एतद्वेदितुमिच्छामि ज्ञानं ज्ञेयं च केशव ॥

Arjuna uvaacha
Prakritim purusham chaiva kshetram khsetrajnameva cha;
Etadveditumicchaami jnaanam jneyam cha kesava.

Arjuna said: I wish to learn (the distinction between) Prakriti (Matter) and Purusha (Spirit); Kshetra (the Field) and Kshetrajna (the Knower of the Field); and also Knowledge and that which is to be Known, O Keshava!

श्रीभगवानुवाच

इदं शरीरं कौन्तेय क्षेत्रमित्यभिधीयते ।
एतद्यो वेत्ति तं प्राहुः क्षेत्रज्ञ इति तद्विदः ॥१॥

Sree Bhagavaan uvaacha
Idam shareeram kaunteya kshetramityabhidheeyate;
Etadyo vetti tam praahuh kshetrajna iti tadvidah.

1. The Blessed Lord said: O Arjuna, this body is known as the Field, and the One who knows this body is the Knower of the Field. Thus do the Sages say who have discerned into the nature of both.

क्षेत्रज्ञं चापि मां विद्धि सर्वक्षेत्रेषु भारत ।
क्षेत्रक्षेत्रज्ञयोर्ज्ञानं यत्तज्ज्ञानं मतं मम ॥२॥

Kshetrajnam chaapi maam viddhi sarvaksetreshu bhaarata;
Kshetrakshetrajnayorjnaanam yattatjnaanam matam mama.

2. Know Me as the Knower of the Field in all beings. It is
My view that true knowledge consists in knowing the
distinction between the Field and the Knower of the
Field.

तत्क्षेत्रं यच्च यादृक्च यद्विकारि यतश्च यत् ।
स च यो यत्प्रभावश्च तत्समासेन मे शृणु ॥३॥

Tat kshetram yatcha yaadrik cha yadvikaari yatashcha yat;
Sa cha yo yatprabhaavashcha tatsamaasena me shrinu.

3. What is the Field, what is its nature, what are its
modifications, and whence it is? And also what is the
nature of the Knower of the Field and what is His Glory?
Listen to all this from Me summarily.

ऋषिभिर्बहुधा गीतं छन्दोभिर्विविधैः पृथक् ।
ब्रह्मसूत्रपदैश्चैव हेतुमद्भिर्विनिश्चितैः ॥४॥

Rishibhirbahudhaa geetam cchandobhirvividhaih prithak;
Brahmasootrapadaishchaiva hetumadbhirvinishchitaih.

4. This (knowledge pertaining to Kshetra and Kshetrajna) has been sung by Sages in various ways, distinctly stated in different Vedic hymns, and also expressed in the well-reasoned texts of the Brahma-Sutras.

महाभूतान्यहंकारो बुद्धिरव्यक्तमेव च ।
इन्द्रियाणि दशैकं च पञ्च चेन्द्रियगोचराः ॥५॥

Mahaabhootaanyahankaaro buddhiravyaktameva cha;
Indriyaani dasaikam cha pancha chendriyagocharaah.

5. The great elements, ego-sense, intellect, and the non-manifest; the ten Indriyas (five senses and five organs of action) and mind, and the five objects of the senses;

इच्छा द्वेषः सुखं दुःखं संघातश्चेतना धृतिः ।
एतत्क्षेत्रं समासेन सविकारमुदाहृतम् ॥६॥

Ichcha dweshas sukham duhkham sanghaatashchetanaa dhritih;
Etat kshetram samaasena savikaaramudaahritam.

6. Desire, aversion, pleasure, pain, the aggregate (of body and senses), consciousness, firmness—this in brief is the Field along with its effects.

अमानित्वमदम्भित्वमहिंसा क्षान्तिरार्जवम् ।
आचार्योपासनं शौचं स्थैर्यमात्मविनिग्रहः ॥७॥

Amaanitwam adambhitwam ahimasaa kshaantiraarjavam;
Aacharyopaasanam shaucham sthairyamaatmavinigrahah.

7. Absence of pride, absence of hypocrisy, non-violence, forbearance, uprightness, service of preceptor, purity, steadiness, control over the body and senses.

इन्द्रियार्थेषु वैराग्यमनहंकार एव च ।
जन्ममृत्युजराव्याधिदुःखदोषानुदर्शनम् ॥८॥

Indriyaartheshu vairaagyamanahamkaara eva cha;
Janmamrityujaraavyaadhiduhkhadoshaanudarshanam.

8. Dispassion towards the objects of the senses, absence of egoism, and reflection upon the evils associated with birth, death, old age, disease and pain.

असक्तिरनभिष्वङ्गः　पुत्रदारगृहादिषु ।
नित्यं च समचित्तत्वमिष्टानिष्टोपपत्तिषु ॥९॥

Asaktiranabhishwangah putradaaragrihaadishu;
Nityam cha samachittatwam ishtaanishtopapttishu.

9. Detachment, absense of the feeling of mineness towards son, wife, house and the like and constant equanimity of mind in all happenings whether desirable or undesirable.

मयि चानन्ययोगेन भक्तिरव्यभिचारिणी ।
विविक्तदेशसेवित्वमरतिर्जनसंसदि　॥१०॥

Mayi chaananyayogena bhaktiravyabhichaarinee;
Viviktadeshasevitwamaratirjanasamsadi.

10. Unflinching devotion to Me through the Yoga of inseperability, abiding in solitary places, not delighting in the company of the worldly minded.

अध्यात्मज्ञाननित्यत्वं तत्त्वज्ञानार्थदर्शनम् ।
एतज्ज्ञानमिति प्रोक्तमज्ञानं यदतोऽन्यथा ॥११॥

Adhyaatmajnaananityatwam tatwajnaanaarthadarshanam;
Etatjnaanamiti proktam ajnaanam yadatonyathaa.

11. Ever devoted to spiritual knowledge, experiencing the fruit of the knowledge of truth—this is said to be knowledge, and ignorance is that which is contrary to it.

ज्ञेयं यत्तत्प्रवक्ष्यामि यज्ज्ञात्वामृतमश्नुते ।
अनादिमत्परं ब्रह्म न सत्तन्नासदुच्यते ।।१२।।

Jneyam yattatpravakshyaami yajjnaatwaamritamashnute;
Anaadimatparam brahma na sattannasaduchyate.

12. I will relate to you that which is to be known, knowing which one attains immortality. It is the Supreme Brahman, who is without beginning, who is said to be neither existent nor non-existent.

सर्वतःपाणिपादं तत्सर्वतोऽक्षिशिरोमुखम् ।
सर्वतःश्रुतिमल्लोके सर्वमावृत्य तिष्ठति ।।१३।।

Sarvatah paanipaadam tat sarvatokshishiromukham;
Sarvatah shrutimalloke sarvamaavritya tishthati.

13. With His hands and feet everwhere, head and eyes and faces everywhere, ears everywhere thus permeating all that Brahman dwells in this world.

सर्वेन्द्रियगुणाभासं   सर्वेन्द्रियविवर्जितम् ।
असक्तं सर्वभृच्चैव निर्गुणं गुणभोक्तृ च ॥१४॥

Sarvendriyagunaabhaasam sarvendriyavivarjitam;
Asaktam sarvabhricchaiva nirgunam gunabhoktri cha.

14. It is Brahman who illumines all the senses, and at the same time He is devoid of the senses. He is detached and yet is the sustainer of all. He is devoid of the Gunas and yet is their enjoyer.

बहिरन्तश्च   भूतानामचरं   चरमेव   च ।
सूक्ष्मत्वात्तद्विज्ञेयं दूरस्थं चान्तिके च तत् ॥

Bahirantashcha bhootaanaamacharam charameva cha;
Sookshmatwaat tadavijneyam doorastham chaantike cha tat.

15. That Brahman is within and outside of all beings; He is the movable as well as the immovable. Because of

subtlety, He is not known (through the senses); He is distant (for the ignorant) and very near too (for the wise).

अविभक्तं च भूतेषु विभक्तमिव च स्थितम् ।
भूतभर्तृ च तज्ज्ञेयं ग्रसिष्णु प्रभविष्णु च॥१६॥

Avibhaktam cha bhooteshu vibhaktamiva cha sthitam;
Bhootabhartri cha tadjneyam grasishnu prabhavishnu cha.

16. That Brahman is indivisible in all beings, as well as appears to be divisible. He is the sustainer of all beings, He is their destroyer as well as their origin.

ज्योतिषामपि तज्ज्योतिस्तमसः परमुच्यते ।
ज्ञानं ज्ञेयं ज्ञानगम्यं हृदि सर्वस्य विष्ठितम् ॥

Jyotishaamapi tajjyotistamasah paramuchyate;
Jnaanam jneyam jnaanagamyam hridi sarvasya vishthitam.

17. He is the Light of all lights, beyond the darkness (of ignorance). He is the knowledge, the object of knowledge and the goal of knowledge. He abides in the heart of everyone.

इति क्षेत्रं तथा ज्ञानं ज्ञेयं चोक्तं समासतः ।
मद्भक्त एतद्विज्ञाय मद्भावायोपपद्यते ॥१८॥

Iti kshetram tathaa jnaanam jneyam choktam samaasatah;
Madbhakta etadvijnaaya madbhaavaayopapadyate.

18. Thus have I explained the Field, Knowledge and the
Knowable (the Knower of the Field) in brief. My devotee
having known this attains My Being.

प्रकृतिं पुरुषं चैव विद्धयनादी उभावपि ।
विकारांश्च गुणांश्चैव विद्धि प्रकृतिसंभवान् ।१९।

Prakritim purusham chaiva vidhyanaadee ubhaavapi;
Vikaaramshcha gunaamshchaiva viddhi prakritisambhavaan.

19. Know both these— Prakriti and Purusha to be beginningless. All the Gunas and their effects have proceeded
from Prakriti.

कार्यकरणकर्तृत्वे हेतुः प्रकृतिरुच्यते ।
पुरुषः सुखदुःखानां भोक्तृत्वे हेतुरुच्यते ।२०।

Kaaryakaaranakartriwe hetuh prakritiruchyate;
Purushah sukhaduhkhaanaam bhoktritwe heturuchyate.

20. Prakriti is the cause of effect (body), instrument (senses) and their functions. Purusha (the soul) is said to be the cause of experiencing pleasure and pain.

पुरुषः प्रकृतिस्थो हि भुङ्क्ते प्रकृतिजान्गुणान् ।
कारणं गुणसङ्गोऽस्य सदसद्योनिजन्मसु ॥२१॥

Purushah prakritistho hi bhunkte prakritijaan gunaan;
Kaaranam gunasangosya sadasadyonijanmasu.

21. Purusha abiding in Prakriti enjoys the Gunas born of Prakriti. Because of its attachment to the Gunas it attains higher or lower births.

उपद्रष्टानुमन्ता च भर्ता भोक्ता महेश्वरः ।
परमात्मेति चाप्युक्तो देहेऽस्मिन्पुरुषः परः ॥

Upadrashtaanumantaa cha bhartaa bhoktaa maheshwarah;
Paramaatmeti chaapyukto dehesmin purushah parah.

22. The Supreme Being in the body is said to be the seer, approver, supporter, enjoyer, the Lord of Gods and the Supreme Self.

य एवं वेत्ति पुरुषं प्रकृतिं च गुणैः सह ।
सर्वथा वर्तमानोऽपि न स भूयोऽभिजायते ॥

Ya evam vetti purusham prakritim cha gunaih saha;
Sarvathaa vartamaanopi na sa bhooyo'bhi jaayate.

23. He who thus knows the Purusha (the Self) and Prakriti along with the Gunas, though acting in whatever way, he is not born again.

ध्यानेनात्मनि पश्यन्ति केचिदात्मानमात्मना ।
अन्ये सांख्येन योगेन कर्मयोगेन चापरे ॥२४॥

Dhyaanenaatmani pashyanti kechidaatmaanamaatmanaa;
Anye saankhyena yogena karmayogena chaapare.

24. Some behold the Self in the self by the self by meditation, others by the Yoga of Knowledge and some others by the Yoga of Action.

अन्ये त्वेवमजानन्तः श्रुत्वान्येभ्य उपासते ।
तेऽपि चातितरन्त्येव मृत्युं श्रुतिपरायणाः ॥

Anye twevamajaanantah shrutwaanyebhya upaasate;
Te'pi chaatitarntyeva mrityum shrutiparaayanaah.

25. Others who do not know this, worship the Self having
heard from others (advanced aspirants). They too devoted to listening (the teachings of the scriptures) cross
beyond the ocean of the world-process.

यावत्संजायते किंचित्सत्चवं स्थावरजङ्गमम् ।
क्षेत्रक्षेत्रज्ञसंयोगात्तद्विद्धि   भरतर्षभ ॥२६॥

Yaavat sanjaayate kinchit sattwam sthavarajangamam;
Kshetrakshetrajnasamyogaat tadviddhi bharatarshabha.

26. O best of the Bharatas (Arjuna)! Know that whatever
beings there are whether moving or unmoving, their
bodies have been produced by the conjuction of the
Field and the Knower of the Field.

समं सर्वेषु भूतेषु तिष्ठन्तं परमेश्वरम् ।
विनश्यत्स्वविनश्यन्तं यः पश्यति स पश्यति ॥

Samam sarveshu bhooteshu tishthantam parameshwaram;
Vinashyatswavinashyantam yah pashyati sa pashyati.

27. The Supreme Self abides equally in all beings; and though these beings perish that Self is imperishable. He who sees thus truly sees.

समं पश्यन्हि सर्वत्र समवस्थितमीश्वरम् ।
न हिनस्त्यात्मनात्मानं ततो याति परां गतिम् ॥

Samam pashyanhi sarvatra samavasthitameeshwaram;
Na hinastyaatmanaatmaanam tato yaati paraam gatim.

28. Because, he who sees the Self equally abiding in all beings does not hurt himself by himself, and thus, attains the Supreme Goal.

प्रकृत्यैव च कर्माणि क्रियमाणानि सर्वशः ।
यः पश्यति तथात्मानमकर्तारं स पश्यति ॥२९॥

Prakrityaiva cha karmaani kriyamaanaani sarvashah;
Yah pashyati tathaatmaanamakartaaram sa pashyati.

29. All actions, in every form, are performed by Prakriti
alone, while the Self is the non-performer of action. He
who sees thus, truly sees.

यदा   भूतपृथग्भावमेकस्थमनुपश्यति ।
तत एव च विस्तारं ब्रह्म संपद्यते तदा ॥३०॥

Yadaa bhootaprithagbhaavamekasthamanupashyati;
Tata eva cha vistaaram brahma sampadyate tadaa.

30. When he sees the multiplicity of beings rooted in the
Self, and spreading out from the Self, then he attains
Brahman.

अनादित्वान्निर्गुणत्वात्परमात्मायमव्ययः   ।
शरीरस्थोऽपि कौन्तेय न करोति न लिप्यते ॥

Anaaditwaat nirgunatwaat paramaatmaayamavyayah;
Shareerasthopi kaunteya na karoti na lipyate.

31. Being without beginning and devoid of Gunas, that
Supreme Self is immutable. O Arjuna, though abiding in
the body, that Self does not act, nor is He tainted.

यथा सर्वगतं सौक्ष्म्यादाकाशं नोपलिप्यते ।
सर्वत्रावस्थितो देहे तथात्मा नोपलिप्यते ॥३२॥

Yathaa sarvagatam saukshmyaadaakaasham nopalipyate;
Sarvatraavasthito dehe tathaatmaa nopalipyate.

32. Just as the sky, due to its expansion and subtlety, is not tainted by anything, in the same way, the Self abiding in all bodies is never tainted.

यथा प्रकाशयत्येकः कृत्स्नं लोकमिमं रविः ।
क्षेत्रं क्षेत्री तथा कृत्स्नं प्रकाशयति भारत ॥३३॥

Yathaa prakashayatyekah kritsnam lokamimam ravih;
Kshetram kshetree tathaa kritsnam prakaashayati bhaarata.

33. Just as one sun illumines this whole earth, in the same way the One Atman (the Lord of the Field) illumines entire Field, O Arjuna.

क्षेत्रक्षेत्रज्ञयोरेवमन्तरं ज्ञानचक्षुषा ।
भूतप्रकृतिमोक्षं च ये विदुर्यान्ति ते परम् ॥

Kshetrakshetrajnayorevamantaram jnaanachakshushaa;
Bhootaprakritimoksham cha ye vidur yaanti te param.

34. Whoever thus sees by the eye of wisdom the distinction between the Field and the Knower of the Field, and also the liberation of beings from Prakriti, they reach the Supreme.

ॐ तत्सदिति श्रीमद्भगवद्गीतासूपनिषत्सु ब्रह्मविद्यायां
योगशास्त्रे श्रीकृष्णार्जुनसंवादे क्षेत्रक्षेत्रज्ञविभाग-
योगो नाम त्रयोदशोऽध्यायः ॥१३॥

Om tat sat iti srimad bhagavad gitaasoopanishatsu
brahmavidyaayaam yogashaastre sri krishnaarjunasamvaade
kshetrakshetrajnavibhaagayogo naama trayodasho'dhyaayah.

Om Tat Sat.
Thus, in the Upanishad of the Bhagavad Gita,
the knowledge of Supreme Brahman, the scripture of Yoga,
the dialogue between Sri Krishna and Arjuna,
ends the thirteenth chapter entitled,
"The Yoga of Distinction between the Field and Its Knower."

समदुःखसुखः स्वस्थः समलोष्टाश्मकाञ्चनः ।
तुल्यप्रियाप्रियो धीरस्तुल्यनिन्दात्मसंस्तुतिः ॥

अथ चतुर्दशोऽध्यायः

Atha Chaturdasho'dhyaayah

Chapter 14

Gunatraya Vibhaaga Yogah

The Yoga of the Division of the Three Gunas

The teachings of the previous chapter are further elaborated in this chapter. There are three modes of Prakriti—Sattwa, Rajas and Tamas. The task before a Yogi is to overcome Rajas and Tamas by developing Sattwa in his personality. Finally he must transcend Sattwa as well, and thus become free from the Prakriti and its Gunas (the modes). He is then known as Trigunateeta—one who has transcended the Gunas.

श्रीभगवानुवाच
परं भूयः प्रवक्ष्यामि ज्ञानानां ज्ञानमुत्तमम् ।
यज्ज्ञात्वा मुनयः सर्वे परां सिद्धिमितो गताः ॥

Sree Bhagavaan uvaacha
Param bhooyah pravakshyaami jnaanaanaam jnaana-muttamam;
Yajjnaatwaa munayah sarve paraam siddhimito gataah.

1. I shall again describe to you that supreme knowledge, which is the best of all knowledges, knowing which all Sages attained perfection, being liberated from the body.

इदं ज्ञानमुपाश्रित्य मम साधर्म्यमागताः ।
सर्गेऽपि नोपजायन्ते प्रलये न व्यथन्ति च ॥२॥

Idam jnaanamupaashritya mama saadharmyamaagataah;
Sargepi nopajaayante pralaye na vyathanti cha.

2. Having taken refuge in this knowledge, and having attained oneness with Me, these Sages are neither born at the time of creation nor are they affected at the time of the universal dissolution.

मम योनिर्महद्ब्रह्म तस्मिन्गर्भं दधाम्यहम् ।
संभवः सर्वभूतानां ततो भवति भारत ॥३॥

Mama yonirmahadbrahma tasmin garbham dadhaamyaham;
Sambhavah sarvabhootaanaam tato bhavati bhaarata.

3. My womb is the Mahat (Hiranyagarbha—the Cosmic Mind) in which I place the seed of life. Thence, O Arjuna, all these beings are born.

सर्वयोनिषु कौन्तेय मूर्तय: संभवन्ति या: ।
तासां ब्रह्म महद्योनिरहं बीजप्रद: पिता ॥४॥

Sarvayonishu kaunteya moortayah sambhavanti yaah;
Taasaam Brahma mahadyoniraham beejapradah pitaa.

4. O Arjuna, whatever embodied being is born in any species, it is I who am the seed-giving Father, while Mahat is the conceiving Mother.

सत्त्वं रजस्तम इति गुणा: प्रकृतिसंभवा: ।
निबध्नन्ति महाबाहो देहे देहिनमव्ययम् ॥५॥

Sattwam rajastama iti gunaah prakitisambhavaah;
Nibadhnanti mahaabaaho dehe dehinamavyayam.

5. Sattwa, Rajas and Tamas—these Gunas arising from Prakriti create bondage for the Imperishable Atman abiding in the body, O Arjuna.

तत्र सत्त्वं निर्मलत्वात्प्रकाशकमनामयम् ।
सुखसङ्गेन बध्नाति ज्ञानसङ्गेन चानघ ॥६॥

Tattra Sattwam nirmalatwaat prakaashakamanaamayam;
Sukhasangena badhnaati jnaanasangena chaanagha.

6. Among them Sattwa due to its purity is enlightener and is the giver of health and happiness. It causes bondage by creating attachment to happiness and (relative) knowledge, O Sinless Arjuna.

रजो रागात्मकं विद्धि तृष्णासङ्गसमुद्भवम् ।
तन्निबध्नाति कौन्तेय कर्मसङ्गेन देहिनम् ॥७॥

Rajo raagaatmakam viddhi trishnaasangasamudbhavam;
Tannibadhnaati kaunteya karmasangena dehinam.

7. Rajas is of the nature of passion, and is the producer of craving and attachment. It causes bondage for the embodied by creating attachment to action.

तमस्त्वज्ञानजं विद्धि मोहनं सर्वदेहिनाम् ।
प्रमादालस्यनिद्राभिस्तन्निबध्नाति भारत ॥८॥

Tamastwajnaanajam viddhi mohanam sarvadehinaam;
Pramaadaalasyanidrabhistannibadhnaati bhaarata.

8. Know that Tamas is born of ignorance and is the deluder of all embodied beings; it causes bondage through procrastination, laziness and sleep.

सत्त्वं सुखे संजयति रजः कर्मणि भारत ।
ज्ञानमावृत्य तु तमः प्रमादे संजयत्युत ॥९॥

Sattvam sukhe sanjayati rajah karmani bhaarata;
Jnaanamaavritya tu tamah pramaade sanjayatyuta.

9. From Sattwa there arises joy, from Rajas actions; and Tamas having veiled knowledge gives rise to heedlessness.

रजस्तमश्चाभिभूय सत्त्वं भवति भारत ।
रजः सत्त्वं तमश्चैव तमः सत्त्वं रजस्तथा ।१०।

Rajastamashchaabhibhooya sattwam bhavati bhaarata;
Rajas sattwam tamashchaiva tamas sattwam rajastathaa.

10. O Bharata, Sattwa advances overpowering Rajas and Tamas. Rajas advances overpowering Sattwa and Tamas,

and similarly Tamas advances overpowering Rajas and Sattwa.

सर्वद्वारेषु देहेऽस्मिन्प्रकाश उपजायते ।
ज्ञानं यदा तदा विद्याद्विवृद्धं सत्त्वमित्युत ॥११॥

Sarvadwaareshu dehe'smin prakaasha upajaayate;
Jnaanam yadaa tadaa vidyaadvivriddham sattvamityuta.

11. When the light of knowledge shines in every gate (sense) of the body, it should be known that Sattwa is advancing.

लोभः प्रवृत्तिरारम्भः कर्मणामशमः स्पृहा ।
रजस्येतानि जायन्ते विवृद्धे भरतर्षभ ॥१२॥

Lobhah pravrittiraarambhah karmanaamashamah sprihaa;
Rajasyetaani jaayante vivriddhe bharatarshabha.

12. O Lord of the Bharatas, when Rajas advances, there arise greed, activity, undertaking of actions, restlessness, and longing.

अप्रकाशोऽप्रवृत्तिश्च प्रमादो मोह एव च ।
तमस्येतानि जायन्ते विवृद्धे कुरुनन्दन ।१३।

Aprakaashopravrittishcha pramaado moha eva cha;
Tamasyetaani jaayante vivriddhe kurunandana.

13. O Best of the Bharatas, when Tamas advances, there arise non-discrimination, inactivity, heedlessness, and mere delusion,

यदा सत्त्वे प्रवृद्धे तु प्रलयं याति देहभृत् ।
तदोत्तमविदां लोकानमलान्प्रतिपद्यते ।१४।

Yadaa sattwe pravriddhe tu pralayam yaati dehabhrit;
Tadottamavidaam lokaanamalaan pratipadyate.

14. When the embodied one dies during the predominance of Sattwa he is reborn in the pure family of the Yogis.

रजसि प्रलयं गत्वा कर्मसङ्गिषु जायते ।
तथा प्रलीनस्तमसि मूढयोनिषु जायते ।१५।

Rajasi pralayam gatwaa karmasangishu jaayate;
Tathaa praleenastamasi moodhayonishu jaayate.

15. When he dies during the predominance of Rajas he is reborn in the family of those who are attached to action. Similarly when he dies during the rise of Tamas, he is born in the wombs of the dull-witted.

कर्मणः सुकृतस्याहुः सात्त्विकं निर्मलं फलम् ।
रजसस्तु फलं दुःखमज्ञानं तमसः फलम् ।।१६।।

Karmanah sukritasyaahuh saattvikam nirmalam phalam;
Rajasastu phalam duhkhamajnaanam tamasah phalam.

16. The wise say that the fruit of virtuous actions is Sattwika and pure, the fruit of Rajas is pain, while the fruit of Tamas is ignorance.

सत्त्वात्संजायते ज्ञानं रजसो लोभ एव च ।
प्रमादमोहौ तमसो भवतोऽज्ञानमेव च ।।१७।।

Sattwaatsanjaayate jnaanam rajaso lobha eva cha;
Pramaadamohau tamaso bhavato'jnaanameva cha.

17. From Sattwa proceeds knowledge, from Rajas greed, and from Tamas heedlessness, delusion and ignorance.

ऊर्ध्वं गच्छन्ति सत्त्वस्था मध्ये तिष्ठन्ति राजसाः।
जघन्यगुणवृत्तिस्था अधो गच्छन्ति तामसाः ॥

Oordhwam gacchanti sattwasthaa madhye tishthanti raajasaah;
Jaghanyagunavrittisthaa adho gachchanti taamasaah.

18. Those who are established in Sattwa go upwards, those in Rajas stay in the middle, and the Tamasikas steeped in the worst functions of the Guna, go downwards.

नान्यं गुणेभ्यः कर्तारं यदा द्रष्टानुपश्यति ।
गुणेभ्यश्च परं वेत्ति मद्भावं सोऽधिगच्छति ॥

Naanyam gunebhyah kartaaram yadaa drashtaanupashyati;
Gunebhyashcha param vetti madbhaavam so'dhigacchati.

19. When the seer does not see any agent other than the Gunas, and knows what is beyond the Gunas, he attains My State.

गुणानेतानतीत्य त्रीन्देही देहसमुद्भवान् ।
जन्ममृत्युजरादुःखैर्विमुक्तोऽमृतमश्नुते ॥२०॥

Gunaanetaanateetya treendehi dehasamudbhavaan;
Janmamrityujaraaduhkhairvimuktoamritamashnute.

20. The individual soul having transcended the three
Gunas which give rise to the body becomes free from
birth, death, old age and the miseries of life, and attains
Immortality.

अर्जुन उवाच
कैर्लिङ्गैस्त्रीन्गुणानेतानतीतो भवति प्रभो ।
किमाचारः कथं चैतांस्त्रीन्गुणानतिवर्तते ॥

Arjuna uvaacha
Kairlingais treengunaanetaanateeto bhavati prabho;
Kimaachaarah katham chaitaanstreengunaanativarate.

21. Arjuna asked: O Lord, what are the characteristics of
him who has transcended the three Gunas, how does he
conduct himself, and how does he rise above these three
Gunas?

श्रीभगवानुवाच

प्रकाशं च प्रवृत्तिं च मोहमेव च पाण्डव ।
न द्वेष्टि संप्रवृत्तानि न निवृत्तानि काङ्क्षति ॥

Sree Bhagavaan uvaacha
Prakasham cha pravrittim cha mohameva cha paandava;
Na dweshti sampravrittaani na nivrittaani kaankshati.

22. Lord Krishna said: When Light, Activity and Delusion are prevalent, he does not hate them, when they are absent he does not long for them.

उदासीनवदासीनो गुणैर्यो न विचाल्यते ।
गुणा वर्तन्त इत्येव योऽवतिष्ठति नेङ्गते ॥२३॥

Udaaseenavadaaseeno gunairyo na vichaalyate;
Gunaa vartanta ityeva yovatishthati nengate.

23. Seated like one indifferent, he is not disturbed by the Gunas; he knows that the Gunas alone operate and not the Self, and thus, being established in the Self, he moves not.

समदुःखसुखः स्वस्थः समलोष्टाश्मकाञ्चनः ।
तुल्यप्रियाप्रियो धीरस्तुल्यनिन्दात्मसंस्तुतिः ॥

Samaduhkhasukhah swasthah samaloshtaashmakaanchanah;
Tulyapriyaapriyo dheerastulyanindaatmasamstutih.

24. Ever established in the Self, he is alike to pleasure and pain, he regards a clod of earth, a stone and a piece of gold as equal in value; he is firm in wisdom and keeps his mind balanced in conditions that are agreeable and disagreeable, treating praise and censure alike.

मानापमानयोस्तुल्यस्तुल्यो मित्रारिपक्षयो: ।
सर्वारम्भपरित्यागी गुणातीत: स उच्यते ॥

Maanaapamaanayostulyastulyo mitraaripakshayoh;
Sarvaarambhaparityaagi gunaateetah sa uchyate.

25. He is the same in honor and dishonor, alike to friend and foe; he has abandoned all Karmic involvements, he is verily called Gunateeta— the one who has gone beyond the Gunas.

मां च योऽव्यभिचारेण भक्तियोगेन सेवते ।
स   गुणान्समतीत्यैतान्ब्रह्मभूयाय कल्पते ॥

Maam cha yovyabhichaarena bhaktiyogena sevate;
Sa gunaan samateetyaitaan brahmabhooyaaya kalpate.

26. He who worships Me with unswerving devotion, he crosses over these three Gunas, and becomes qualified for becoming one with Brahman or the Absolute.

ब्रह्मणो हि प्रतिष्ठाहममृतस्याव्ययस्य च ।
शाश्वतस्य च धर्मस्य सुखस्यैकान्तिकस्य च ॥

Brahmano hi pratishthaahamamritasyaavyayasya cha;
Shaashwatasya cha dharmasya sukhasyaikaantikasya cha.

27. For I am the Abode of Brahman the Immortal, the Immutable, of Eternal Virtue and of Unending Bliss.

ॐ तत्सदिति श्रीमद्भगवद्गीतासूपनिषत्सु ब्रह्मविद्यायां
योगशास्त्रे श्रीकृष्णार्जुनसंवादे गुणत्रयविभाग-
योगो नाम चतुर्दशोऽध्यायः ॥ १४ ॥

Om tat sat iti srimad bhagavad gitaasoopanishatsu
brahmavidyaayaam yogashaastre sri krishnaarjunasamvaade
gunatrayavibhaagayogo naama chaturdasho'dhyaayah.

Om Tat Sat.

Thus, in the Upanishad of the Bhagavad Gita,
the knowledge of Supreme Brahman, the scripture of Yoga,
the dialogue between Sri Krishna and Arjuna,
ends the fourteenth chapter entitled,
"The Yoga of the Division of the Three Gunas."

अथ पञ्चदशोऽध्यायः

Atha Panchadasho'dhyaayah

Chapter 15

Purushottam Yogah

The Yoga of the Supreme Spirit

The interaction of spirit and matter has evolved the world-process. A Yogi gains insight into the nature of the Purushottama or the Supreme Being who is distinct from spirit and matter, and who permeates and sustains the three worlds. This insight enables the Yogi to possess the weapon of non-attachment by which he cuts down the mystic tree of the world-process and is established in Brahman.

श्रीभगवानुवाच

ऊर्ध्वमूलमधःशाखमश्वत्थं प्राहुरव्ययम् ।
छन्दांसि यस्य पर्णानि यस्तं वेद स वेदवित् ॥

Sree Bhagavaan uvaacha
Oordhwamoolamadhasshaakhamashwattham praahuravyayam;
Cchandaamsi yasya parnaani yastam veda sa vedavit.

1. The Blessed Lord said: The scriptures speak of the imperishable Ashwattha tree (of the world-process) with its roots above and branches below; the Vedic verses constitute its leaves. He who knows this Tree is the knower of the essence of the Vedas.

अधश्चोर्ध्वं प्रसृतास्तस्य शाखा
गुणप्रवृद्धा   विषयप्रवालाः।
अधश्च   मूलान्यनुसंततानि
कर्मानुबन्धीनि   मनुष्यलोके ॥२॥

Adhashchordhwam prasritaastasya shaakhaa
Gunapravriddhaa vishayapravaalaah;
Adhascha moolaanyanusantataani
Karmaanubandheeni manushyaloke.

2. Nourished by the Gunas (the modes of Nature) the branches of this tree, which has sense-objects for its buds, spread high and low; and its roots spread below in the world of men creating the bondage of Karma.

न रूपमस्येह तथोपलभ्यते
नान्तो न चादिर्न च संप्रतिष्ठा ।
अश्वत्थमेनं सुविरूढमूल-
मसङ्गशस्त्रेण दृढेन छित्वा ॥३॥

Na roopamasyeha tathopalabhyate
  Naanto na chaadirnacha sampratishthaa;
Ashwatthamenam suviroodhamoolam
  Asangashastrena dridhena cchitwaa.

3. The real form of this tree is not perceived here, nor does anyone see its beginning, middle or end. Having cut off this Ashwattha tree with its firmly planted roots with the weapon of detachment—

ततः पदं तत्परिमार्गितव्यं
यस्मिन्गता न निवर्तन्ति भूयः ।
तमेव चाद्यं पुरुषं प्रपद्ये
यतः प्रवृत्तिः प्रसृता पुराणी ॥४॥

Tatah padam tat parimaargitavyam
  Yasmin gataa na nivartanti bhooyah;
Tameva chaadyam purusham prapadye
  Yatah pravrittih prasritaa puraanee.

4. One should seek that Abode having attained which one does not return (to the world-process). I adore that Primeval Supreme Being from Whom proceeded this ancient activity (this tree of the world-process).

निर्मानमोहा   जितसङ्गदोषा
अध्यात्मनित्या   विनिवृत्तकामाः ।
द्वन्द्वैर्विमुक्ताः   सुखदुःखसंज्ञै-
गच्छन्त्यमूढाः पदमव्ययं तत् ॥५॥

Nirmaanamohaa jitasangadoshaa
Adhyaatmanityaa vinivrittakaamaah;
Dwandwairvimuktaah sukhaduhkhasamjnair
Gacchantyamoodhaah padamavyayam tat.

5. He who is devoid of pride and delusion, who has conquered the defect of attachment, who is ever steady in meditating upon the Self, who has turned away from worldly desires, and is free from the pairs of opposites in the form of pleasure and pain, he, the undeluded, reaches this Immutable Abode.

न तद्भासयते सूर्यो न शशाङ्को न पावकः ।
यद्गत्वा न निवर्तन्ते तद्धाम परमं मम ॥६॥

Na tadbhaasayate sooryo na shashaanko na paavakah;
Yadgatwaa na nivartante taddhaama paramam mama.

6. That is My Supreme Abode having reached which
Yogis do not return to the world-process. There the sun
does not shine, nor does the moon or fire.

ममैवांशो जीवलोके जीवभूतः सनातनः ।
मनःषष्ठानीन्द्रियाणि प्रकृतिस्थानि कर्षति ॥

Mamaivaamsho jeevaloke jeevabhootah sanaatanah;
Manah shashthaaneendriyaani prakritisthaani karshati.

7. In this world of embodied beings, a ray of My Eternal
Self exists as the individual soul which abiding in Prakriti
draws to itself the (five) senses with the mind as the sixth.

शरीरं यदवाप्नोति यच्चाप्युत्क्रामतीश्वरः ।
गृहीत्वैतानि संयाति वायुर्गन्धानिवाशयात् ॥

Shareeram yadavaapnoti yacchaapyutkraamateeshwarah;
Griheetwaitaani samyaati vaayurgandhaanivaashayaat.

8. When the Lord (of the body and senses—the Jiva) leaves this body, he draws the senses and carries them to the body that he obtains even in the same manner as the wind carries fragrance (from the flowers).

श्रोत्रं चक्षुः स्पर्शनं च रसनं घ्राणमेव च ।
अधिष्ठाय मनश्चायं विषयानुपसेवते ॥९॥

Shrotram chakshuh sparshanam cha rasanam ghraanameva cha;
Adhishthaaya manashchaayam vishayaanupasevate.

9. Depending upon sound, sight, touch, taste and smell, and the mind (as well as organs of action and Pranas) the soul enjoys the objects of the world.

उत्क्रामन्तं स्थितं वापि भुञ्जानं वा गुणान्वितम्।
विमूढा नानुपश्यन्ति पश्यन्ति ज्ञानचक्षुषः ॥

Utkraamantam sthitham vaapi bhunjaanam vaa gunaanvitam;
Vimoodhaa naanupashyanti pashyanti jnaanachakshushah.

10. Though abiding in the body, moving from one body to another, and enjoying the objects of the senses, this

soul enveloped by the Gunas is not seen by the ignorant, those who are endowed with intuitive knowledge they alone know the true nature of this soul.

यतन्तो योगिनश्चैनं पश्यन्त्यात्मन्यवस्थितम् ।
यतन्तोऽप्यकृतात्मानो नैनं पश्यन्त्यचेतसः ॥

Yatanto yoginashchainam pashyantyaatmanyavasthitam;
Yatantopyakritaatmaano nainam pashyantyachetasah.

11. The Yogis devoted to the practice of Yoga behold the Self within their own self (through the purified mind), but those who are unintelligent and undisciplined they do not behold the Self though striving.

यदादित्यगतं तेजो जगद्भासयतेऽखिलम् ।
यच्चन्द्रमसि यच्चाग्नौ तत्तेजो विद्धि मामकम् ॥

Yadaadityagatam tejo jagadbhaasayatekhilam;
Yacchandramasi yacchaagnau tattejo viddhi maamakam.

12. The effulgence that abides in the sun and illumines this universe, and that which is in the moon as well as in fire, that you should know to be Mine.

गामाविश्य च भूतानि धारयाम्यहमोजसा ।
पुष्णामि चौषधीःसर्वाःसोमो भूत्वा रसात्मकः ॥

Gaamaavishya cha bhootaani dhaarayaamyahamojasaa;
Pushnaami chaushadheeh sarvaah somo bhootwaa rasaatmakah.

13. Having entered the earth it is I who sustain all beings by My Energy, and it is I who having become the nectarine moon nourish all the herbs.

अहं वैश्वानरो भूत्वा प्राणिनां देहमाश्रितः ।
प्राणापानसमायुक्तः पचाम्यन्नं चतुर्विधम् ॥

Aham vaishwaanaro bhootwaa praaninaam dehamaashritah;
Praanaapaanasamaayuktah pachaamyannam chaturvidham.

14. Having become the Vaishwanara Fire (digestive fire) it is I who abide in all living beings, and having been united with Prana and Apana, it is I who digest the four types of food.

सर्वस्य चाहं हृदि संनिविष्टो
मत्तः स्मृतिर्ज्ञानमपोहनं च ।
वेदैश्च सर्वैरहमेव वेद्यो
वेदान्तकृद्वेदविदेव चाहम् ॥१५॥

Sarvasya chaaham hridi sannivishto
Mattas smritirjnaanamapohanam cha;
Vedaishcha sarvairahameva vedyo
Vedaantakridvedavideva chaaham.

15. I abide in the heart of all living beings. The function of memory, knowledge as well as their loss are caused by Me. It is I who am to be known by all the Vedas. I am also the knower of the Vedas as well as their Author.

द्वाविमौ पुरुषौ लोके क्षरश्चाक्षर एव च ।
क्षरः सर्वाणि भूतानि कूटस्थोऽक्षर उच्यते ॥

Dwaavimau purushau loke ksharashchaakshara eva cha;
Ksharas sarvaani bhootaani kootasthokshara uchyate.

16. There are two Purushas (beings) in this world: Kshara (the perishable) and Akshara (the imperishable). All the objects of the world are called Kshara while Prakriti sustained by the Immutable Self is called Akshara.

उत्तमः पुरुषस्त्वन्यः परमात्मेत्युदाहृतः ।
यो लोकत्रयमाविश्य बिभर्त्यव्यय ईश्वरः ॥

Uttamah purushastwanyah paramaatmetyudaahritah;
Yo lokatrayamaavishya bibhartyavyaya eeshwarah.

17. The Best of Beings, is different from these two, therefore, He is called the Supreme Self, Who though Immutable, controls all and sustains the three worlds (by His Maya Shakti).

यस्मात्क्षरमतीतोऽहमक्षरादपि   चोत्तमः ।
अतोऽस्मि लोके वेदे च प्रथितः पुरुषोत्तमः ॥

Yasmaatksharamateetohamaksharaadapi choottamah;
Ato'smi loke vede cha prathitah purushottamah.

18. Because I am beyond the perishable objects, as well as beyond the Imperishable Prakriti, therefore I am known as the Supreme Self in this world as well as in the Vedas.

यो मामेवमसंमूढो जानाति पुरुषोत्तमम् ।
स सर्वविद्भजति मां सर्वभावेन भारत ॥१९॥

Yo maamevamasammoodho jaanati purushottamam;
Sa sarvavidbhajati maam sarvabhaavena bhaarata.

19. O Bharata, the undeluded one who knows Me as Purushottama—the Supreme self, he, the wise one, worships Me with all his heart.

इति गुह्यतमं शास्त्रमिदमुक्तं मयानघ ।
एतदुबुद्ध्वा बुद्धिमान्स्यात्कृतकृत्यश्च भारत ॥

Iti guhyatamam shaastramidamuktam mayaanagha;
Etadbuddhwaa buddhimaansyaat kritakritayshcha bhaarata.

20. O Sinless Arjuna, thus have I explained to you this scripture containing the supreme secret. Having known this one becomes enlightened; thereby he has accomplished all that is to be accomplished by him.

ॐ तत्सदिति श्रीमद्भगवद्गीतासूपनिषत्सु ब्रह्मविद्यायां
योगशास्त्रे श्रीकृष्णार्जुनसंवादे पुरुषोत्तमयोगो
नाम पञ्चदशोऽध्यायः ॥ १५ ॥

Om tat sat iti srimad bhagavad gitaasoopanishatsu
brahmavidyaayaam yogashaastre sri krishnaarjunasamvaade
purushottamyogo naama panchadasho'dhyaayah.

Om Tat Sat.

Thus, in the Upanishad of the Bhagavad Gita,
the knowledge of Supreme Brahman, the scripture of Yoga,
the dialogue between Sri Krishna and Arjuna,
ends the fifteenth chapter entitled,
"The Yoga of the Supreme Spirit."

अथ षोडशोऽध्यायः

Atha Shodasho'dhyaayah

Chapter 16

Daivaasura Sampad Vibhaaga Yogah

The Yoga of Divine and Demoniacal Qualities

The unconscious of a Yogi abounds with Shubha Samskaras or pure impressions based on the rise of Sattwa. Consequently, a Yogi begins to develop the divine qualities which are known as Daivi Sampat (the divine wealth). On the other hand, those who do not follow the Yogic path continue to develop Ashubha Samskaras or impure impressions based on Rajas and Tamas. They possess demoniac wealth. By knowing the distinction between these two types of qualities, an aspirant should shun what is demoniac and develop what is divine.

श्रीभगवानुवाच

अभयं सत्त्वसंशुद्धिर्ज्ञानयोगव्यवस्थितिः ।
दानं दमश्च यज्ञश्च स्वाध्यायस्तप आर्जवम् ॥१॥

Sree Bhagavaan uvaacha
Abhayam sattwasamshuddhirjnaanayogavyavasthitih;
Daanam damashcha yajnashcha swaadhyaayastapa aarjavam.

1. The Blessed Lord said: Fearlessness, purity of the heart, steadfastness in wisdom and Yoga, charity, control of the senses, sacrifice, study of the scriptures, austerity and straightforwardness—

अहिंसा सत्यमक्रोधस्त्यागः शान्तिरपैशुनम् ।
दया भूतेष्वलोलुप्त्वं मार्दवं ह्रीरचापलम् ॥२॥

Ahimsaa satyamakrodhastyaagah shaantirapaishunam;
Dayaa bhooteshvaloluptwam maardavam hreerachaapalam.

2. Non-violence, truthfulness, absence of anger, renunciation, serenity of mind, absence of fault-finding nature, compassion towards living beings, non-covetousness, gentleness, modesty, and absense of fickleness—

तेजः क्षमा धृतिः शौचमद्रोहो नातिमानिता ।
भवन्ति संपदं दैवीमभिजातस्य भारत ॥३॥

Tejah kshamaa dhritih shauchamadroho naatimaanitaa;
Bhavanti sampadam daiveemabhijaatasya bhaarata.

3. Valor, forgiveness, fortitude, purity, absence of animosity, and freedom from pride, these are the qualities of him who is born with divine nature, O Bharata!

दम्भो दर्पोऽभिमानश्च क्रोधः पारुष्यमेव च ।
अज्ञानं चाभिजातस्य पार्थ संपदमासुरीम् ॥

Dambho darpobhimaanashcha krodhah paarushyameva cha;
Ajnaanam chaabhijaatasya paartha sampadamaasureem.

4. O Partha, he who is born with a demoniac nature in him these qualities manifest: hypocrisy, conceit, pride, anger, harsh speech and ignorance.

दैवी संपद्विमोक्षाय निबन्धायासुरी मता ।
मा शुचः संपदं दैवीमभिजातोऽसि पाण्डव ॥

Daivee sampadvimokshaaya nibandhaayaasuree mataa;
Maa shuchah sampadam daiveemabhijaatosi paandava.

5. O Arjuna, the divine qualities are for liberation, while the demoniac qualities lead one to bondage. Do not grieve, you are born with divine qualities.

द्वौ भूतसर्गौ लोकेऽस्मिन्दैव आसुर एव च ।
दैवो विस्तरशः प्रोक्त आसुरं पार्थ मे शृणु ॥६॥

Dwau bhootasargau loke'smin daiva aasura eva cha;
Daivo vistarashah prokta aasurm paartha me shrinu.

6. In this world there are two types of created beings: divine and demoniac. The divine qualities have been described in detail, now listen to the qualities of the demoniac beings.

प्रवृत्तिं च निवृत्तिं च जना न विदुरासुराः ।
न शौचं नापि चाचारो न सत्यं तेषु विद्यते ॥

Pravrittim cha nivrittim cha janaa na viduraasuraah;
Na shaucham naapi chaachaaro na satyam teshu vidyate.

7. Men born with demoniac qualities do not know the difference between what is to be done and what is not to be done. They neither have purity or right conduct, nor there is truthfulness in them.

असत्यमप्रतिष्ठं ते जगदाहुरनीश्वरम् ।
अपरस्परसंभूतं किमन्यत्कामहैतुकम् ॥८॥

Asatyamapratishtham te jagadaahuraneeshwaram;
Aparasparasambhootam kimanyat kaamahaitukam.

8. They hold that the world is rooted in untruth; it is without support, without God. It is created by mutual union, lust being the only cause, what else?

एतां दृष्टिमवष्टभ्य नष्टात्मानोऽल्पबुद्धयः ।
प्रभवन्त्युग्रकर्माणः क्षयाय जगतोऽहिताः ॥९॥

Etaam drishtimavashtabhya nashtaatmaanolpabuddhayah;
Prabhavantyugrakarmaanah kshyaaya jagato'hitaah.

9. Having adopted this vision, these lost souls endowed with little intellect, performer of violent deeds, are born as enemies of righteousness for the destruction of the world.

काममाश्रित्य दुष्पूरं दम्भमानमदान्विताः ।
मोहाद्गृहीत्वासद्ग्राहान्प्रवर्तन्तेऽशुचिव्रताः ॥

Kaamamaashritya dushpooram dambhamaanamadaanvitaah;
Mohaadgriheetvaasadgraahaan pravartanteshuchivrataah.

10. Driven by insatiable desire, filled with pride, hypocrisy and arrogance, holding evil ideas due to delusion,
they work with impure resolves.

चिन्तामपरिमेयां च प्रलयान्तामुपाश्रिताः ।
कामोपभोगपरमा एतावदिति निश्चिताः ॥ ११ ॥

Chintaamaparimeyaam cha pralayaantaamupaashritaah;
Kaamopabhogaparamaa etaavaditi nischitaah.

11. Given to innumerable worries which last only in
death, considering the enjoyments of the sense pleasures
as the highest goal, they feel convinced that this is all.

आशापाशशतैर्बद्धाः कामक्रोधपरायणाः ।
ईहन्ते कामभोगार्थमन्यायेनार्थसञ्चयान् ॥

Aashaapaashashatairbaddhaah kaamakrodhaparaayanaah;
Eehante kaamabhogaarthamanyaayenaarthasanchayaan.

12. Bound by the fetters of numerous desires, obsessed by lust and anger, they strive for acquiring wealth by adopting unrighteous means, for the sake of gratifying the senses.

इदमद्य मया लब्धमिमं प्राप्स्ये मनोरथम् ।
इदमस्तीदमपि मे भविष्यति पुनर्धनम् ॥१३॥

Idamadya mayaa labdhamimam praapsye manoratham;
Idamasteedamapi me bhavishyati punardhanam.

13. "I have obtained this today, I will fulfill this desire as well. This is already in my possession, that wealth will also come under my possession.

असौ मया हतः शत्रुर्हनिष्ये चापरानपि ।
ईश्वरोऽहमहं भोगी सिद्धोऽहं बलवान्सुखी ॥

Asau mayaa hatah shatrurhanishye chaaparaanapi;
Ishwarohamaham bhogee siddhoham balavaansukhee.

14. "I have destroyed this enemy. Others will be also destroyed by me. I am the supreme Lord, I am the enjoyer, the perfect one, I am endowed with power; I am happy.

आढ्योऽभिजनवानस्मि कोऽन्योऽस्ति सदृशो मया
यक्ष्ये दास्यामि मोदिष्य इत्यज्ञानविमोहिताः ॥

Aadhyobhijanavaanasmi konyosti sadrisho mayaa;
Yakshye daasyaami modishye ityajnaanavimohitaah.

15. "I am wealthy and born in a noble family, who is equal to me? I will perform Yajna, give wealth in charity, will rejoice." Thus deluded by ignorance—

अनेकचित्तविभ्रान्ता   मोहजालसमावृताः ।
प्रसक्ताः कामभोगेषु पतन्ति नरकेऽशुचौ ॥

Anekachittavibhraantah mohajaalasamaavritaah;
Prasaktaah kaamabhogeshu patanti narakeashuchau.

16. Confused because of many evil desires, entangled by the snares of infatuation, intensely attached to the gratification of the senses, they fall into a foul hell.

आत्मसंभाविताः स्तब्धा धनमानमदान्विताः ।
यजन्ते नामयज्ञैस्ते दम्भेनाविधिपूर्वकम्॥१७॥

Aatmasambhaavitaah stabdhaa dhanamaanamadaanvitaah;
Yajante naamayajnaiste dambhenaavidhipoorvakam.

17. Holding themselves adorable in their own eyes,
devoid of humility, intoxicated with wealth and pride,
they perform Yajnas in name only for the sake of
ostentation, without observing the scriptural injunctions.

अहंकारं बलं दर्पं कामं क्रोधं च संश्रिताः ।
मामात्मपरदेहेषु प्रद्विषन्तोऽभ्यसूयकाः ॥१८॥

Ahamkaaram balam darpam kaamam krodham cha samshritaah;
Maamaatmaparadeheshu pradwishantobhyasooyakaah.

18. Ever addicted to egoism, force, conceit, lust and
anger, they hate Me who abide in their bodies as well as in
the bodies of others, and are full of maliciousness.

तानहं द्विषतः क्रूरान्संसारेषु नराधमान् ।
क्षिपाम्यजस्त्रमशुभानासुरीष्वेव योनिषु ॥१९॥

Taanaham dwishatah krooraan samsaareshu naraadhamaan;
Kshipaamyajasramashubhaanyaasureeshweva yonishu.

19. These cruel haters of Myself, the worst among men, who are involved in sinful deeds, I hurl them into demoniac wombs.

आसुरीं योनिमापन्ना मूढा जन्मनि जन्मनि ।
मामप्राप्यैव कौन्तेय ततो यान्त्यधमां गतिम् ॥

Aasureem yonimaapanna moodhaa janmani janmani;
Maamapraapyaiva kaunteya tato yaantyadhamaam gatim.

20. O Son of Kunti, having entered into demoniac wombs, deluded from birth after birth, unable to attain Me, they continue to fall into lower births.

त्रिविधं   नरकस्येदं   द्वारं नाशनमात्मनः ।
कामः क्रोधस्तथा लोभस्तस्मादेतत्त्रयं त्यजेत् ॥

Trividham narakasyedam dwaaram naashanamaatmanah;
Kaamah krodhastathaa lobhastasmaadetattrayam tyajet.

21. There are three gates to hell which are the destroyers of the soul. They are Lust, Anger, and Greed; therefore, these three must be renounced.

एतैर्विमुक्तः कौन्तेय तमोद्वारैस्त्रिभिर्नरः ।
आचरत्यात्मनः श्रेयस्ततो याति परां गतिम् ॥

Etairvimuktah kaunteya tamodwaaraistribhirnarah;
Aacharatyaatmanas shreyastato yaati paraam gatim.

22. Freed of these three gates to hell, he promotes blessedness for his own soul, O son of Kunti, and thus attains the Supreme Abode.

यः शास्त्रविधिमुत्सृज्य वर्तते कामकारतः ।
न स सिद्धिमवाप्नोति न सुखं न परां गतिम् ॥

Yah shaastravidhimutsrijya vartate kaamakaaratah;
Na sa siddhimavaapnoti na sukham na paraam gatim.

23. He who, discarding the scriptures, conducts according to his own will, he does not attain perfection, nor happiness, nor the Supreme Goal.

तस्माच्छास्त्रं प्रमाणं ते कार्याकार्यव्यवस्थितौ ।
ज्ञात्वा शास्त्रविधानोक्तं कर्म कर्तुमिहार्हसि ॥

Tasmaat shaastram pramaanam te kaaryaakaaryavyavasthitau;
Jnaatwaa shaastravidhaanoktam karma kartumihaarhasi.

24. Therefore, let scriptures be your guide in determining what is right and what is wrong. Knowing what is in accordance with the scriptures, you must perform duties in this world.

ॐ तत्सदिति श्रीमद्भगवद्गीतासूपनिषत्सु ब्रह्म-
विद्यायां योगशास्त्रे श्रीकृष्णार्जुनसंवादे दैवासुर-
संपद्विभागयोगो नाम षोडशोऽध्यायः ॥१६॥

Om tat sat iti srimad bhagavad gitaasoopanishatsu
brahmavidyaayaam yogashaastre sri krishnaarjunasamvaade
daivaasurasampadvibhaagayogo naama shodasho'dhyaayah.

Om Tat Sat.
Thus, in the Upanishad of the Bhagavad Gita,
the knowledge of Supreme Brahman, the scripture of Yoga,
the dialogue between Sri Krishna and Arjuna,
ends the sixteenth chapter entitled,
"The Yoga of Divine and Demoniacal Qualities."

अथ सप्तदशोऽध्यायः

Atha Saptadasho'dhyaayah

Chapter 17

Shraddhaa Traya Vibhaaga Yogah

The Yoga of Threefold Faith

According to actions performed in the past, human beings are born with a specific nature (mind). His faith is according to the impressions gathered in his mind. He is led by his faith to follow the path that agrees with him. An aspirant should gain insight into the characteristics of Satwic faith as contrasted from those of Rajasic and Tamasic faith. He should emulate the qualities of Satwic faith, and avoid those of Rajasic and Tamasic faith. When Sattwic faith unfolds in his heart, he will move towards Self-realization in an effortless manner.

अर्जुन उवाच

ये शास्त्रविधिमुत्सृज्य यजन्ते श्रद्धयान्विताः ।

तेषां निष्ठा तु का कृष्ण सत्त्वमाहो रजस्तमः ॥

Arjuna uvaacha
Ye shaastravidhimutsrijya yajante shraddhayaanvitaah;
Teshaam nishthaa tu kaa krishna sattwamaaho rajastamah.

1. Those, who, setting aside the ordinances of the scriptures, worship God led by their faith alone, what is their position, O Krishna: is it Satwic, Rajasic or Tamasic?

श्रीभगवानुवाच

त्रिविधा भवति श्रद्धा देहिनां सा स्वभावजा ।

सात्त्विकी राजसी चैव तामसी चेति तां शृणु ॥

Sree Bhagavaan uvaacha
Trividhaa bhavati shraddhaa dehinaam saa swabhaavajaa;
Sattvikee raajasee chaiva taamasee cheti taam shrinu.

2. The Blessed Lord said: Faith, born of their very nature, is of three types in the embodied beings: Satwic (pure), Rajasic (impure) and Tamasic (dull). May you hear about it.

सत्त्वानुरूपा सर्वस्य श्रद्धा भवति भारत ।
श्रद्धामयोऽयं पुरुषो यो यच्छ्रद्धः स एव सः ॥

Sattvaanuroopaa sarvasya shraddhaa bhavati bhaarata;
Sraddhaamayoyam purusho yo yacchraddhah sa eva sah.

3. Faith is according to the nature of one's Chitta (the impressions that are formed in the mind-stuff from countless births.) A person is of the nature of his faith. Whatever his faith so he is, O Arjuna!

यजन्ते सात्त्विका देवान्यक्षरक्षांसि राजसाः ।
प्रेतान्भूतगणांश्चान्ये यजन्ते तामसा जनाः ॥

Yajante saattvikaa devvaanyakshrakshaamsi raajasaah;
Pretaanbhootaganaamschaanye yajante taamasaa janaah.

4. The Satwicas worship gods, the Rajasicas adore Yakshas and Rakshasas (the demigods and demons), while the Tamasicas are devoted to the lower spirits and ghosts.

अशास्त्रविहितं घोरं तप्यन्ते ये तपो जनाः ।
दम्भाहंकारसंयुक्ताः कामरागबलान्विताः ॥

Ashaastravihitam ghoram tapyante ye tapo janaah;
Dambhaahamkaarasamyuktaah kaamaraagabalaanvitaah.

5. Those who are given to hypocrisy and conceit, they, impelled by lust and attachment, perform terrible austerities which are not enjoined in the scriptures.

कर्षयन्तः शरीरस्थं भूतग्राममचेतसः ।
मां चैवान्तःशरीरस्थं तान्विद्ध्यासुरनिश्चयान् ॥

Karshayantah shareerastham bhootagraamamachetasah;
Maam chaivaantahshareerastham taanvidhyaasuranishchayaan.

6. They torture the elements (that go to form their body) and also Me (the Divine Self)—the Indweller within the body. Know them to be of demoniac resolve.

आहारस्त्वपि सर्वस्य त्रिविधो भवति प्रियः ।
यज्ञस्तपस्तथा दानं तेषां भेदमिमं शृणु ॥७॥

Aahaarastwapi sarvasya trividho bhavati priyah;
Yajnastapastathaa daanam yeshaam bhedamimam srinu.

7. In the same manner, the food which is dear to everyone is of three types, and similarly there are three types of sacrifice, austerity and charity. Listen to their distinctions.

आयुःसत्त्वबलारोग्यसुखप्रीतिविवर्धनाः ।
रस्याः स्निग्धाः स्थिरा हृद्या आहाराः सात्त्विकप्रिया: ॥८॥

Aayuh sattvabalaarogyasukhapreetivivardhanaah;
Rasyaah snigdhaah sthiraa hridyaa ahaaraah saattvikapriyaah.

8. The foods that promote life, mental strength, vitalty, health, cheerfulness, and loving nature; which are savoury, nutritious, digestible and agreeable—these are dear to the Satwicas.

कट्वम्ललवणात्युष्णतीक्ष्णरूक्षविदाहिनः ।
आहारा राजसस्येष्टा दुःखशोकामयप्रदाः ॥९॥

Katvamlalavanaatyushnateekshnarookshavidaahinah;
Aahaarah raajasayeshtaa duhkhashokaamayapradaah.

9. The foods that are very bitter, sour, saltish, hot, pungent, dry (tasteless), burning; which produce pain, grief and disease are dear to the Rajasicas.

यातयामं गतरसं पूति पर्युषितं च यत् ।
उच्छिष्टमपि चामेध्यं भोजनं तामसप्रियम्॥

Yaatayaamam gatarasam pooti paryushitam cha yat;
Ucchishtamapi chaamedhyam bhojanam taamasapriyam.

10. The foods that are stale, devoid of taste, foul smelling, rotten, refuse and impure are liked by those who are Tamasicas.

अफलाकाङ्क्षिभिर्यज्ञो विधिदृष्टो य इज्यते ।
यष्टव्यमेवेति मनः समाधाय स सात्त्विकः ॥

Aphalaakaankhsibhiryajno vidhidrishto ya ijyate;
Yashtavyameveti manah samaadhaaya sa saattvikah.

11. The sacrifice that is offered without expectations of fruit, in accordance with the scriptural teachings, with the sense of duty and firm faith, that is Satwic or pure in nature.

अभिसंधाय तु फलं दम्भार्थमपि चैव यत् ।
इज्यते भरतश्रेष्ठ तं यज्ञं विद्धि राजसम् ॥१२॥

Abhisandhaaya tu phalam dambhaarthamapi chaiva yat;
Ijyate bharatashreshtha tam yajnam viddhi raajasam.

12. O Best among the Bharatas (Arjuna), that sacrifice which is offered with the expectations of fruit, for mere show, is to be known as Rajasic or impure.

विधिहीनमसृष्टान्नं   मन्त्रहीनमदक्षिणम् ।
श्रद्धाविरहितं यज्ञं तामसं परिचक्षते ॥१३॥

Vidhiheenamasrishtaannam mantraheenamadakshinam;
Shraddhaavirahitam yajnam taamasam parichakshate.

13. The sacrifice which is contrary to the scriptures, which is offered without the distribution of food, devoid of Mantras and gifts, which is without faith, that is said to be Tamasic or dull.

देवद्विजगुरुप्राज्ञपूजनं   शौचमार्जवम् ।
ब्रह्मचर्यमहिंसा च शारीरं तप उच्यते ॥१४॥

Devadwijagurupraajnapoojanam shauchamaarjavam;
Brahmacharyamahimsaa cha shaareeram tapa uchyate.

14. Service of gods, Brahmins, Guru (spiritual preceptor) and wise men; purity, uprightness, Brahmacharya (sex-restraint), and non-violence— these are called the austerity of the body.

अनुद्वेगकरं वाक्यं सत्यं प्रियहितं च यत् ।
स्वाध्यायाभ्यसनं चैव वाङ्मयं तप उच्यते ॥

Anudwegakaram vaakyam satyam priyahitam cha yat;
Swaadhyaayaabhyasanam chaiva vaangmayam tapa uchyate.

15. That speech which does not cause agitation in others, which is truthful, pleasant and helpful; and repeated study of scriptures— these constitute the austerity of speech.

मनःप्रसादः सौम्यत्वं मौनमात्मविनिग्रहः ।
भावसंशुद्धिरित्येतत्तपो मानसमुच्यते ॥१६॥

Manah prasaadah saumyatwam maunamaatmavinigrahah;
Bhaavasamshuddhirityetattapo maanasamuchyate.

16. Serenity of mind, gentleness, silence, control of senses, elevated feeling of the heart— these are called the austerity of the mind.

श्रद्धया परया तप्तं तपस्तत्त्रिविधं नरैः ।
अफलाकाङ्क्षिभिर्युक्तैः सात्त्विकं परिचक्षते ॥

Shraddhayaa parayaa taptam tapastattrividham naraih;
Aphalaakaankshibhiryuktaih saattvikam parichakshate.

17. These three types of austerity practised with intense faith, without attachment to its reward, is called Satwic or pure.

सत्कारमानपूजार्थं तपो दम्भेन चैव यत् ।
क्रियते तदिह प्रोक्तं राजसं चलमध्रुवम् ॥

Satkaaramaanapoojaartham tapo dambhena chaiva yat;
Kriyate tadiha proktam raajasam chalamadhruvam.

18. The austerity that is practised for the sake of respect, honor and worship, and with hypocrisy is said to be Rajasic or impure.

मूढग्राहेणात्मनो यत्पीडया क्रियते तपः ।
परस्योत्सादनार्थं वा तत्तामसमुदाहृतम् ॥१९॥

Moodhagraahenaatmano yat peedayaa kriyate tapah;
Parasyotsaadanaartham vaa tattaamasamudaahritam.

19. That austerity which is practised with dullness and obstinacy, causing self-torture, and which is for inflicting pain in others is known as Tamasic or dull.

दातव्यमिति यद्दानं दीयतेऽनुपकारिणे ।
देशे काले च पात्रे च तद्दानं सात्त्विकं स्मृतम् ॥

Daatavyamiti yaddaanam deeyate'nupakaarine;
Deshe kaale cha paatre cha taddaanam saattvikam smritam.

20. That gift which is given with the spirit of charity, without expecting anything in return, with the proper consideration of time, place and recipient is Satwic.

यत्तु प्रत्युपकारार्थं फलमुद्दिश्य वा पुनः ।
दीयते च परिक्लिष्टं तद्दानं राजसं स्मृतम् ॥

Yattu pratyupakaaraartham phalamuddishya vaa punah;
Deeyate cha pariklishtam taddaanam raajasam smritam.

21. But the gift that is given with the expectation of a return or with the hope of a future gain, and with a painful feeling, that is declared to be Rajasic.

$$अदेशकाले \quad यद्दानमपात्रेभ्यश्च \quad दीयते \, ।$$
$$असत्कृतमवज्ञातं \quad तत्तामसमुदाहृतम् \, ॥२२॥$$

Adeshakaale yaddaanamapaatrebhyashcha deeyate;
Asatkritamavajnaatam tattaamasamudaahritam.

22. That gift which is given in an improper place at an improper time to an unworthy person, without respect, with insult, that is said to be Tamasic.

$$ॐ तत्सदिति निर्देशो ब्रह्मणस्त्रिविधः स्मृतः \, ।$$
$$ब्राह्मणास्तेन वेदाश्च यज्ञाश्च विहिताः पुरा !'$$

Om Tatsaditi nirdesho brahmanas trividhah smritah;
Braahmanaastena vedaashcha yajnaashcha vihitaah puraa.

23. Om Tat Sat—these are the threefold symbol of Brahman (the Absolute Self). Formerly, the Brahmins, the Vedas and sacrifices were ordained by them.

तस्मादोमित्युदाहृत्य   यज्ञदानतप:क्रियाः ।
प्रवर्तन्ते विधानोक्ता: सततं ब्रह्मवादिनाम् ॥

Tasmaadomityudaahritya yajnadaanatapahkriyaah;
Pravartane vidhaanoktaah satatam brahmavaadinaam.

24. Therefore, the seekers of Brahman perform sacrifice,
gift, austerity and other similar acts enjoined by the
scriptures with the utterance of Om.

तदित्यनभिसंधाय   फलं   यज्ञतप:क्रियाः ।
दानक्रियाश्च विविधाः क्रियन्ते मोक्षकाङ्क्षिभिः॥

Tadityanabhisandhaaya phalam yajnatapahkriyaah;
Daanakriyaashcha vividhaah kriyante mokshakaankhshibhih.

25. Aspirants desirous of liberation perform the acts of
sacrifice, austerity and others with the utterance of Tat
(by remembering God and with the spirit of surrender to
Him who is Tat—the Transcendental Self) without expecting any reward.

सद्भावे साधुभावे च सदित्येतत्प्रयुज्यते ।
प्रशस्ते कर्मणि तथा सच्छब्द: पार्थ युज्यते ॥

Sadbhaave saadhubhaave cha sadityetatprayujyate;
Prashaste karmani tathaa sacchabdah paartha yujyate.

26. O Arjuna, Sat (the True) is used in the sense of reality and of goodness, and also Sat is used for auspicious actions.

यज्ञे तपसि दाने च स्थिति: सदिति चोच्यते ।
कर्म चैव तदर्थीयं सदित्येवाभिधीयते ॥२७॥

Yajne tapasi daane cha sthitih saditi chochyate;
Karma chaiva tadartheeyam sadityevaabhidheeyate.

27. Steadiness in the acts of sacrifice, austerity and gift is also called Sat, and so also actions related to them are known as Sat.

अश्रद्धया हुतं दत्तं तपस्तप्तं कृतं च यत् ।
असदित्युच्यते पार्थ न च तत्प्रेत्य नो इह ॥

Ashraddhayaa hutam dattam tapastaptam kritam cha yat;
Asadityuchyate paartha na cha tatpretya no iha.

28. Those acts of sacrifice, gift and austerity which are performed without faith, are said to be Asat (non-existent), O Arjuna. They are neither useful in this world nor in the other world.

ॐ तत्सदिति श्रीमद्भगवद्गीतासूपनिषत्सु ब्रह्मविद्यायां योगशास्त्रे श्रीकृष्णार्जुनसंवादे श्रद्धात्रयविभाग-
योगो नाम सप्तदशोऽध्यायः ॥ १७ ॥

Om tat sat iti srimad bhagavad gitaasoopanishatsu brahmavidyaayaam yogashaastre sri krishnaarjunasamvaade shraddhaatrayvibhaagayogo naama saptadasho'dhyaayah.

Om Tat Sat.
Thus, in the Upanishad of the Bhagavad Gita,
the knowledge of Supreme Brahman, the scripture of Yoga,
the dialogue between Sri Krishna and Arjuna,
ends the seventeenth chapter entitled,
"The Yoga of Threefold Faith."

अथाष्टादशोऽध्यायः

Atha Ashtaadasho'dhyaayah

Chapter 18

Moksha Sannyaasa Yogah

The Yoga of Liberation through Renunciation

Lord Krishna concludes His teachings in this chapter. Deluded by Maya a person finds himself utterly dependent upon the world. But when he surrenders to God, he discovers his innate freedom and attains Liberation. Integral, whole-hearted surrender is the secret of spiritual evolution and Liberation.

Krishna is symbolic of Vision, Grace and Divinity. Arjuna is symbolic of Action, Self-effort and Jiva (individual Soul). Wherever there is the union of Krishna and Arjuna, Vision and Action, Grace and Self-effort, God and Jiva, there will abide the choicest blessings of life and Supreme Victory in the form of God-realization!

अर्जुन उवाच

संन्यासस्य महाबाहो तत्त्वमिच्छामि वेदितुम् ।
त्यागस्य च हृषीकेश पृथक्केशिनिषूदन ॥१॥

Arjuna uvaacha
Sannyaasasya mahaabaaho tattwamicchaami veditum;
Tyaagasya cha hrisheekesha prithakkeshinishoodana.

1. Arjuna asked: O Great Armed Krishna, the Destroyer of Demon Keshi, I want to know the true nature of Sanyasa (renunciation) and that of Tyaga (relinquishment), O Hrishikesha (the Controller of the senses).

श्रीभगवानुवाच

काम्यानां कर्मणां न्यासं संन्यासं कवयो विदुः ।
सर्वकर्मफलत्यागं प्राहुस्त्यागं विचक्षणाः ॥२॥

Sree Bhagavaan uvaacha
Kaamyaanaam karmanaam nyaasam sannyaasam kavayo viduh;
Sarvakarmaphalatyaagam praahustyaagam vichakshanaah.

2. The Blessed Lord said: The wise say that Sanyasa or renunciation consists in renouncing all actions that are prompted by desire; while Tyaga or relinquishment implies renunciation of the fruits of actions alone.

त्याज्यं दोषवदित्येके कर्म प्राहुर्मनीषिणः ।
यज्ञदानतपःकर्म न त्याज्यमिति चापरे ॥३॥

Tyaajyam doshavadityeke karma praahurmaneeshinah;
Yajnadaanatapahkarma na tyaajyamiti chaapare.

3. Some wise men are of opinion that all actions must be renounced since they are associated with defects; while there are others who declare that actions such as Yajna (sacrifice), Dana (charity) and Tapa (austerity) should not be given up.

निश्चयं श्रृणु मे तत्र त्यागे भरतसत्तम ।
त्यागो हि पुरुषव्याघ्र त्रिविधः संप्रकीर्तितः॥

Nishchayam shrinu me tatra tyaage bharatasattama;
Tyaago hi purushavyaaghra trividhah samprakeertitah.

4. O Best among the Bharatas (Arjuna), listen to my conclusive view regarding relinquishment. Relinquishment or Tyaga, O Tiger among men, are of three types:

यज्ञदानतपःकर्म न त्याज्यं कार्यमेव तत् ।
यज्ञो दानं तपश्चैव पावनानि मनीषिणाम् ॥५॥

Yajnadaanatapahkarma na tyaajyam kaaryameva tat;
Yajno daanam tapashchaiva paavanaani maneeshinaam.

5. The actions in the form of Yajna, Dana and Tapa should not be abandoned; because Yajna, Dana and Tapa promote purity of mind for those who are thoughtful.

एतान्यपि तु कर्माणि सङ्गं त्यक्त्वा फलानि च ।
कर्तव्यानीति मे पार्थ निश्चितं मतमुत्तमम् ॥६॥

Etaanyapi tu karmaani sangam tyaktwaa phalaani cha;
Kartavyaaneeti mè paartha nishchitam matamuttamam.

6. O Partha (Son of Kunti—Arjuna), These actions must be performed by renouncing attachment, and desire for fruits. This is my firm and final view.

नियतस्य तु संन्यासः कर्मणो नोपपद्यते ।
मोहात्तस्य परित्यागस्तामसः परिकीर्तितः ॥७॥

Niyatasya tu sannyaasah karmano nopapadyate,
Mohaattasya parityaagastaamasah parikeertitah.

7. It is not proper for a person to renounce those actions that are his duties (which must be done). If he relinquishes them because of delusion, his relinquishment is then called Tamasic (dominated by dullness and inertia).

दुःखमित्येव यत्कर्म कायक्लेशभयात्त्यजेत् ।
स कृत्वा राजसं त्यागं नैव त्यागफलं लभेत् ॥

Duhkhamityeva yat karma kaayakleshabhayaat tyajet;
Sa kritwaa raajasam tyaagam naiva tyaagaphalam labhet.

8. He who relinquishes his duties because of the fear of physical labor (or discomfort that is involved in performing them) his relinquishment is of Rajasic (dominated by impurity and desire); he does not attain the fruit of his relinquishment.

कार्यमित्येव यत्कर्म नियतं क्रियतेऽर्जुन ।
सङ्गं त्यक्त्वा फलं चैव स त्यागः सात्त्विको मतः

Kaaryamityeva yatkarma niyatam kriyate'rjuna;
Sangam tyaktwaa phalam chaiva sa tyaagah saattviko matah.

9. He who performs his duties, renouncing attachment and desire for fruits) with the understanding that they ought to be performed, his relinquishment is considered Satwic (dominated by purity).

न द्वेष्टचकुशलं कर्म कुशले नानुषज्जते ।
त्यागी सत्त्वसमाविष्टो मेधावी छिन्नसंशयः ॥

Na dweshtyakushalam karma kushale naanushajjate;
Tyaagee sattvasamaavishto medhaavee chchinnasamshayah.

10. Filled with Sattwa or purity, a Satwic relinquisher, having dispelled all doubts by the purity of his intellect, does not hate a disagreeable action, nor does he become attached to an agreeable one.

न हि देहभृता शक्यं त्यक्तुं कर्माण्यशेषतः ।
यस्तु कर्मफलत्यागी स त्यागीत्यभिधीयते ॥

Na hi dehabhritaa shakyam tyaktum karmaanyasheshatah;
Yastu karmaphalatyaagi sa tyaageetyabhidheeyate.

11. It is impossible for an embodied person to renounce all actions; therefore, he who renounces the fruits of

actions is called a Tyagi (a man of relinquishment—a man of true renunciation).

अनिष्टमिष्टं मिश्रं च त्रिविधं कर्मणः फलम् ।
भवत्यत्यागिनां प्रेत्य न तु संन्यासिनां क्वचित्॥

Anishtamishtam mishram cha trividham karmanah phalam;
Bhavatyatyaaginaam pretya na tu sannyaasinaam kwachit.

12. Three types of fruits; pleasant, unpleasant, and mixed; belong to those who have not renounced the fruits of actions, but they do not affect those who have attained renunciation.

पञ्चैतानि महाबाहो कारणानि निबोध मे ।
सांख्ये कृतान्ते प्रोक्तानि सिद्धये सर्वकर्मणाम् ॥

Panchaitaani mahaabaaho kaaranaani nibodha me;
Saamkhye kritaante proktaani siddhaye sarvakarmanaam.

13. O Great Armed Arjuna, learn of Me of the fact that there are five factors implied in the performance of any Karma; this is the view held by the philosophy of

Samkhya (Vedanta) which leads one to the termination of all Karmas.

अधिष्ठानं तथा कर्ता करणं च पृथग्विधम् ।
विविधाश्च पृथक्चेष्टा दैवं चैवात्र पञ्चमम् ॥

Adhishthaanam tathaa kartaa karanam cha prithagvidham;
Vividhaashcha prithakcheshtaa daivam chaivaatra panchamam.

14. These are the five factors: Adhisthana (the field), Karta (actor), Karana (the various instruments), Cheshta (the effort or the functions of vital forces), and Daiva (destiny), being the fifth.

शरीरवाङ्मनोभिर्यत्कर्म आरभते नरः ।
न्याय्यं वा विपरीतं वा पञ्चैते तस्य हेतवः॥१५॥

Shareeravaangmanobhiryat karma praarabhate narah;
Nyaayyam vaa vipareetam vaa panchaite tasya hetavah.

15. Whatever action one may perform by his body, speech and mind, whether righteous or unrighteous, these five are the factors implied in the performance of that action.

तत्रैवं सति कर्तारमात्मानं केवलं तु यः ।
पश्यत्यकृतबुद्धित्वान्न स पश्यति दुर्मतिः ॥

Tatraivam sati kartaaramaatmaanam kevalam tu yah;
Pashyatyakritabuddhitwaanna sa pashyati durmatih.

16. This being so, a dull-witted person attributes actor-
ship to himself alone, and because of his deluded
intellect he does not see rightly.

यस्य नाहंकृतो भावो बुद्धिर्यस्य न लिप्यते ।
हत्वापि स इमाँल्लोकान्न हन्ति न निबध्यते ॥

Yasya naahamkrito bhaavo buddhiryasya na lipyate;
Hatwaapi sa immaanlokaan na hanti na nibadhyate.

17. He who is free of the ego-sense, and whose intellect is
not tainted by the sense of doer-ship (and enjoyership);
such a Sage, even if he were to kill all beings, yet he does
not kill, nor is he bound by such actions.

ज्ञानं ज्ञेयं परिज्ञाता त्रिविधा कर्मचोदना ।
करणं कर्म कर्तेति त्रिविधः कर्मसंग्रहः ॥१८॥

Jnaanam jneyam parijnaataa trividhaa karmachodanaa;
Karanam karma karteti trividhah karmasangrahah.

18. Knowledge, Knowable, and Knower: these are the threefold impulse for action; while instrument (the senses), action, and the doer—these are the threefold basis for action.

ज्ञानं कर्म च कर्ता च त्रिधैव गुणभेदतः ।
प्रोच्यते गुणसंख्याने यथावच्छृणु तान्यपि ॥

Jnaanam karma cha kartaa cha tridhaiva gunabhedatah;
Prochyate gunasankhyaane yathaavacchrinu taanyapi.

19. Now listen of me, the characteristics of knowledge, action, and doer according to the three Gunas, as taught by the Samkhya (Vedanta).

सर्वभूतेषु येनैकं भावमव्ययमीक्षते ।
अविभक्तं विभक्तेषु तज्ज्ञानं विद्धि सात्त्विकम् ॥

Sarvabhooteshu yenaikam bhaavamavyayameekshate;
Avibhaktam vibhakteshu tadjnaanam viddhi saattvikam.

20. The knowledge by which one sees one imperishable and indivisible Being behind the objects that are (apparently) separate from each other, is to be known Satwic or pure.

पृथक्त्वेन तु यज्ज्ञानं नानाभावान्पृथग्विधान् ।
वेत्ति सर्वेषु भूतेषु तज्ज्ञानं विद्धि राजसम् ॥

Prithaktwena tu yajjnaanam naanaabhaavaanprithagvidhaan;
Vetti sarveshu bhooteshu tajjnaanam viddhi raajasam.

21. The knowledge by which one sees multiplicity of beings because of their separateness, that is to be known as Rajasic or impure.

यत्तु कृत्स्नवदेकस्मिन्कार्ये सक्तमहैतुकम् ।
अतत्त्वार्थवदल्पं च तत्तामसमुदाहृतम् ॥२२॥

Yattu kritsnavadekasmin kaarye saktamahaitukam;
Atattwaarthavadalpam cha tattaamasamudaahritam.

22. The knowledge which creates the illusion of perceiving the whole in one single effect, which is without

any rational validity, without any purpose, and without any significance, is called Tamasic.

नियतं   सङ्गरहितमरागद्वेषतः   कृतम् ।
अफलप्रेप्सुना कर्म यत्तत्सात्त्विकमुच्यते॥२३॥

Niyatam sangarahitam araagadweshatah kritam;
Aphalaprepsunaa karma yattatsaattwikamuchyate.

23. The action that is performed with the sense of duty, without expectation of fruit, without dependence, and without attachment and hatred, that action is to be known as Satwic.

यत्तु कामेप्सुना कर्म साहंकारेण वा पुनः ।
क्रियते बहुलायासं तद्राजसमुदाहृतम् ॥२४॥

Yattu kaamepsunaa karma saahankaarena vaa punah;
Kriyate bahulaayaasam tadraajasamudaahritam.

24. The action that is performed with the expectation of fruit, with the sense of egoism (with the sense, "I am the doer."), and with great exertion, that action is called Rajasic.

अनुबन्धं क्षयं हिंसामनवेक्ष्य च पौरुषम् ।
मोहादारभ्यते कर्म यत्तत्तामसमुच्यते ॥२५॥

Anubandham kshayam himsaamanavekshya cha paurusham;
Mohaadaarabhyate karma yattat taamsamuchyate.

25. The action that is undertaken on the basis of delusion, without taking into consideration its (painful) consequences, without any regard to the loss and the injury that is involved in it, and also without any regard to one's capacity is called Tamasic.

मुक्तसङ्गोऽनहंवादी धृत्युत्साहसमन्वितः ।
सिद्ध्यसिद्ध्योर्निर्विकारः कर्ता सात्त्विक उच्यते

Muktasangonahamvaadi dhrityutsaahasamanvitah;
Sidhyasidhyornirvikaarah kartaa saattvika uchyate.

26. He who does not desire the fruits of his actions, who is free of the sense, "I am the doer." is endowed with patience and perseverance, and is ever unaffected by success and failure, he is called a Satwic doer.

रागी कर्मफलप्रेप्सुर्लुब्धो हिंसात्मकोऽशुचिः ।
हर्षशोकान्वितः कर्ता राजसः परिकीर्तितः ॥

Raagee karmaphalaprepsurlubdho himsaatmako'shuchih;
Harshashokaanvitah kartaa raajasah parikeertitah.

27. He who is passionate, desirous of the fruits of action,
greedy, inclined to violence, impure, who is swayed by
elation and grief, such a doer is called Rajasic.

अयुक्तः प्राकृतः स्तब्धः शठो नैष्कृतिकोऽलसः।
विषादी दीर्घसूत्री च कर्ता तामस उच्यते॥२८॥

Ayuktah praakritah stabdhah shatho naishkritikolasah;
Vishaadee deerghasootree cha kartaa taamasa uchyate.

28. He who is careless, vulgar, conceited, arrogant, lazy,
despondent, and procrastinating, such a doer is Tamasic
in nature.

बुद्धेर्भेदं धृतेश्चैव गुणतस्त्रिविधं श्रृणु ।
प्रोच्यमानमशेषेण पृथक्त्वेन धनंजय ॥२९॥

Buddherbhedam dhriteshchaiva gunatastrividham shrinu;
Prochyamaanamasheshena prithaktwena dhananjaya.

29. O Arjuna, now listen to the threefold distinction of intellect as well as of steadfastness according to the three Gunas. I shall explain to you fully and separately.

प्रवृत्ति च निवृत्ति च कार्याकार्ये भयाभये ।
बन्धं मोक्षं च या वेत्ति बुद्धिः सा पार्थ सात्त्विकी।।

Pravrittim cha nivrittim cha karyaakarye bhayaabhaye;
Bandham moksham cha yaa vetti buddhih saa paartha saattvikee.

30. The intellect that knows the distinction between the path of Pravritti (action) and the path of Nirvritti (renunciation), between right action and wrong action, between fear and fearlessness, between bondage and release, that intellect is Satwic in nature.

यया धर्ममधर्मं च कार्यं चाकार्यमेव च ।
अयथावत्प्रजानाति बुद्धिः सा पार्थ राजसी ।।

Yayaa dharmamadharmam cha kaaryam chaakaaryameva cha;
Ayathaavat prajaanaati buddhih saa paartha raajasee.

31. The intellect that creates confusion between what is righteous and what is unrighteous, what is right and what is wrong, that is to be known Rajasic in nature.

अधर्मं धर्ममिति या मन्यते तमसावृता ।
सर्वार्थान्विपरीतांश्च बुद्धिः सा पार्थ तामसी ॥

Adharmam dharmamiti yaa manyate tamasaavritaa;
Sarvaarthaan vipareetaanshcha buddhih saa paartha taamasee.

32. O Arjuna, the intellect which is perverted, which considers evil as good, and sees what is right as wrong, that intellect dominated by darkness is called Tamasic in nature.

धृत्या यया धारयते मनःप्राणेन्द्रियक्रियाः ।
योगेनाव्यभिचारिण्या धृतिः सा पार्थ सात्त्विकी

Dhrityaa yayaa dhaarayate manahpraanendriyakriyaah;
Yogenaavyabhichaarinyaa dhritih saa paartha saattvikee.

33. The steadfastness arising out of Yogic Samadhi by which one controls (acquires mastery over) his mind,

vital forces, and the functions of the senses is known as Satwic.

यया तु धर्मकामार्थान्धृत्या धारयतेऽर्जुन ।
प्रसङ्गेन फलाकाङ्क्षी धृतिः सा पार्थ राजसी ॥

Yayaa tu dharmakaamarthaan dhrityaa dhaarayatearjuna;
Prasangena phalaakaankshee dhritih saa paartha raajasee.

34. The steadfastness with the help of which a person performs actions for the sake of accumulation of merit, fulfillment of desires, and acquisition of wealth, is to be known as Rajasic.

यया स्वप्नं भयं शोकं विषादं मदमेव च ।
न विमुञ्चति दुर्मेधा धृतिः सा पार्थ तामसी ॥

Yayaa swapnam bhayam shokam vishaadam madameva cha;
Na vimunchati durmedhaa dhritih saa paartha taamasee.

35. O Arjuna, the steadfastness with which a dull-witted person, is unable to forsake sleep, fear, sorrow, despondency, and pride is called Tamasic.

सुखं त्विदानीं त्रिविधं शृणु मे भरतर्षभ ।
अभ्यासाद्रमते यत्र दुःखान्तं च निगच्छति ॥

Sukham twidaaneem trividham shrinu me bharatarshabha;
Abhyaasaadramate yatra duhkhaantam cha nigacchati.

36. O best among the Bharatas. now hear from Me the three types of happiness of which Satwic happiness is enjoyed as a result of constant practice, and this leads to the cessation of all miseries.

यत्तदग्रे   विषमिव   परिणामेऽमृतोपमम् ।
तत्सुखं साच्त्विकं प्रोक्तमात्मबुद्धिप्रसादजम् ॥

Yattadagre vishamiva parinaamemritopamam;
Tatsukham saattvikam proktamaatmabuddhiprasaadajam.

37. That which appears like poison in the beginning, but is like nectar in the end, that happiness born of the clear understanding of the Self is called Satwic or pure.

विषयेन्द्रियसंयोगाद्यत्तदग्रेऽमृतोपमम्   ।
परिणामे विषमिव तत्सुखं राजसं स्मृतम्॥३८॥

Vishayendriyasamyogaadyattadagre'mritopamam;
Parinaame vishamiva tatsukham raajasam smritam.

38. The happiness arising out of the contact of senses and their objects, which is like nectar in the beginning but turns out to be poison in the end is called Rajasic or impure.

यदग्रे चानुबन्धे च सुखं मोहनमात्मनः ।
निद्रालस्यप्रमादोत्थं तत्तामसमुदाहृतम्॥३९॥

Yadagre chaanubandhe cha sukham mohanamaatmanah;
Nidraalasyapramaadott'ham tattaamasamudaahritam.

39. But the happiness that keeps the mind deluded from the beginning to the end and which arises from sleep, laziness, and procrastination is called Tamasic or deluded.

न तदस्ति पृथिव्यां वा दिवि देवेषु वा पुनः ।
सत्त्वं प्रकृतिजैर्मुक्तं यदेभिः स्यात्त्रिभिर्गुणैः ॥

Na tadasti prithivyaam vaa divi deveshnu vaa punah;
Sattvam prakritijairmuktam yadebhih syaattribhirgunaih.

40. On this earth (among the mortals) as well as in the heavenly worlds, among the gods, there is no entity that is devoid of the three Gunas (modes) arising out of Prakriti (Nature).

ब्राह्मणक्षत्रियविशां शूद्राणां च परंतप ।
कर्माणि प्रविभक्तानि स्वभावप्रभवैर्गुणैः ॥४१॥

Braahmanakshatriyavishaam shoodraanam cha parantapa;
Karmaani pravibhaktaani swabhaavaprabhavairgunaih.

41. O Scorcher of your foes, according to the Gunas born of their own nature, separate duties are enjoined for the Brahmanas, Kshatriyas, Vaishyas and Shudras.

शमो दमस्तपः शौचं क्षान्तिरार्जवमेव च ।
ज्ञानं विज्ञानमास्तिक्यं ब्रह्मकर्म स्वभावजम् ॥

Shamo damastapas shaucham kshaantiraarjavameva cha;
Jnaanam vijnaanamaastikyam brahmakarma swabhaavajam.

42. Serenity of mind, control of senses, austerity, purity, forbearance, simplicity (or straightforwardness), know-

ledge, wisdom, as well as faith in religion—these are the duties of the Brahmin born of his nature.

शौर्यं तेजो धृतिर्दाक्ष्यं युद्धे चाप्यपलायनम् ।
दानमीश्वरभावश्च क्षात्रं कर्म स्वभावजम् ॥४३॥

Shauryam tejo dhritirdaakshyam yuddhe chaapyapalaayanam;
Daanameeshwarabhaavashcha kshaatram karma swabhaavajam.

43. Heroism, valor, steadfastness, dexterity, not turning away from battle, charity, and lordliness—these are the duties of the Kshatriya born of his nature.

कृषिगौरक्ष्यवाणिज्यं वैश्यकर्म स्वभावजम् ।
परिचर्यात्मकं कर्म शूद्रस्यापि स्वभावजम् ॥

Krishigorakshyavaanijyam vaishyakarma swabhaavajam;
Paricharyaatmakam karma shoodrasyaapi swabhaavajam.

44. Agriculture, cattle-rearing, and trade—these are the duties of the Vaishya born of his nature, while service of others is the duty of the Shudra born of his nature.

स्वे स्वे कर्मण्यभिरतः संसिद्धिं लभते नरः ।
स्वकर्मनिरतः सिद्धिं यथा विन्दति तच्छृणु ॥

Swe swe karmanyabhiratah samsiddhim labhate narah;
Swakarmaniratah siddhim yathaa vindati tacchrinu.

45. Men pursuing their own duties with devotion attain spiritual perfection. Hear from Me the manner in which a person attains spiritual perfection while performing his duty.

यतः प्रवृत्तिर्भूतानां येन सर्वमिदं ततम् ।
स्वकर्मणा तमभ्यर्च्य सिद्धिं विन्दति मानवः ॥

Yatah pravrittirbhootaanaam yena sarvamidam tatam;
Swakarmanaa tamabhyarchya siddhim vindati maanavah.

46. From Whom all these beings have proceeded, and by Whom all this is pervaded, by adoring Him through the performance of one's own duty, one attains spiritual perfection.

श्रेयान्स्वधर्मो त्रिगुणः परधर्मात्स्वनुष्ठितात् ।
स्वभावनियतं कर्म कुर्वन्नाप्नोति किल्बिषम् ॥

Shreyaanswadharmo vigunah paradharmaatswanushthitaat;
Swabhaavaniyatam karma kurvannaapnoti kilbisham.

47. Better is one's own duty though apparently devoid of merit, than other's duty well-performed, because by performing duties born of one's own nature, one does not incur sin.

सहजं कर्म कौन्तेय सदोपमपि न त्यजेत् ।
सर्वारम्भा हि दोषेण धूमेनाग्निरिवावृता:॥४८॥

Sahajam karma kaunteya sadoshamapi na tyajet;
Sarvaarambhaa hi doshena dhoomenaagnirivaavritaah.

48. O Son of Kunti, one should not abandon his natural duty though with defects; because all actions are attended with defects even as fire is with smoke.

असक्तबुद्धि: सर्वत्र जितात्मा विगतस्पृह: ।
नैष्कर्म्यसिद्धिं परमां संन्यासेनाधिगच्छति ॥

Asaktabuddhih sarvatra jitaatmaa vigatasprihah;
Naishkarmyasiddhim paramaam sannyaasenaadhigacchati.

49. He who possesses an intellect that is unattached everywhere, who has controlled his mind, and is free from all desires, he attains perfection through renunciation.

सिद्धिं प्राप्तो यथा ब्रह्म तथाप्नोति निबोध मे ।
समासेनैव कौन्तेय निष्ठा ज्ञानस्य या परा ।।५०।।

Siddhim praapto yathaa brahma tathaapnoti nibodha me;
Samaasenaiva kaunteya nishthaa jnaanasya yaa paraa.

50. O Son of Kunti, having attained perfection, the manner in which he attains Brahman, that you may hear from Me, which is the highest summit of wisdom.

बुद्ध्या विशुद्धया युक्तो धृत्यात्मानं नियम्य च ।
शब्दादीन्विषयांस्त्यक्त्वा रागद्वेषौ व्युदस्य च ।।

Buddhyaa vishuddhayaa yukto dhrityaatmaanam niyamya cha;
Shabdaadeenvishayaanstyaktwaa raagadweshau vyudasya cha.

51. Endowed with pure intellect, firmly controlling the mind and senses, having renounced sound and other objects of the senses, and abandoning love and hatred;

विविक्तसेवी लघ्वाशी यतवाक्कायमानसः ।
ध्यानयोगपरो नित्यं वैराग्यं समुपाश्रितः ॥

Viviktasevee laghwaashee yatavaakkaayamaanasah;
Dhyaanayogaparo nityam vairaagyam samupaashritah.

52. Living in solitude, eating but little; engaged in controlling speech, body and mind, ever devoted to the Yoga of meditation, and taking refuge in dispassion;

अहंकारं बलं दर्पं कामं क्रोधं परिग्रहम् ।
विमुच्य निर्ममः शान्तो ब्रह्मभूयाय कल्पते ॥

Ahamkaaram balam darpam kaamam krodham parigraham;
Vimuchya nirmamah shaanto brahmabhooyaaya kalpate.

53. Having renounced egoism, power, conceit, lust, anger and covetousness, and freed from the sense of "mineness," and peaceful; he becomes fit for becoming one with Brahman.

ब्रह्मभूतः प्रसन्नात्मा न शोचति न काङ्क्षति ।
समः सर्वेषु भूतेषु मद्भक्तिं लभते पराम् ॥५४॥

Brahmabhootah prasannaatmaa na shochati na kaankshati;
Samah sarveshu bhooteshu madbhaktim labhate paraam.

54. Having become one with Brahman, endowed with the purity of mind, he neither grieves (at the loss of objects) nor desires (objects that have not been acquired). Beholding the same Self in all beings, he attains Supreme Devotion to Me.

भक्त्या मामभिजानाति यावान्यश्चास्मि तच्चतः ।
ततो मां तच्चतो ज्ञात्वा विशते तदनन्तरम् ॥

Bhaktyaa maamabhijaanaati yaavanyashchaasmi tattwatah;
Tato maam tattwato jnaatwaa vishate tadanantaram.

55. By Supreme Devotion he knows Me, what and who I am in reality, and having thus known Me fully, he enters into Me.

सर्वकर्माण्यपि सदा कुर्वाणो मद्व्यपाश्रयः ।
मत्प्रसादादवाप्नोति शाश्वतं पदमव्ययम् ॥

Sarvakarmaanyapi sadaa kurvaano madvyapaashrayah;
Matprasaadaadavaapnoti shaashwatam padamavyayam.

56. Having taken refuge in Me, he who performs all his duties at all times, he attains the Eternal and Imperishable Abode by My Grace.

चेतसा सर्वकर्माणि मयि संन्यस्य मत्परः ।
बुद्धियोगमुपाश्रित्य मच्चित्तःसततं भव ॥५७॥

Chetasaa sarvakarmaani mayi sannyasya matparah;
Buddhiyogamupaashritya macchittah satatam bhava.

57. Resigning all actions to Me by the force of understanding, holding Me as the Highest Goal, having taken refuge in the Yoga of steady intellect, do you ever fix your mind on Me.

मच्चित्तः सर्वदुर्गाणि मत्प्रसादात्तरिष्यसि ।
अथ चेत्त्वमहंकारान्न श्रोष्यसि विनङ्क्ष्यसि ॥

Macchittah sarvadurgaani matprasaadaat tarishyasi;
Atha chettwamahankaaraanna shroshyasi vinankshyasi.

58. By fixing your mind on Me, you will cross over all obstacles by My Grace, but if you do not listen to My teachings due to egoism, you will perish.

यदहंकारमाश्रित्य न योत्स्य इति मन्यसे ।
मिथ्यैष व्यवसायस्ते प्रकृतिस्त्वां नियोक्ष्यति ॥

Yadahankaaramaashritya na yotsya iti manyase;
Mithyaisha vyavasaayaste prakritistwaam niyokshyati.

59. Sustained by self-conceit, if you think, "I will not fight," this resolve of yours is vain, because your very nature will compel you to fight.

स्वभावजेन कौन्तेय निबद्धः स्वेन कर्मणा ।
कर्तुं नेच्छसि यन्मोहात्करिष्यस्यवशोऽपि तत् ॥

Swabhaavajena kaunteya nibaddhah swena karmanaa;
Kartum necchasi yanmohaat karishyasyavashopi tat.

60. O Son of Kunti, the action that you do not want to perform due to ignorance, the same you will be constrained to perform, even against your will, bound as you are to your own Karma born of your nature.

ईश्वरः सर्वभूतानां हृद्देशेऽर्जुन तिष्ठति ।
भ्रामयन्सर्वभूतानि यन्त्रारूढानि मायया ॥६१॥

Ishwarah sarvabhootaanaam hriddeshe'rjuna tishthati;
Bhraamayan sarvabhootaani yantraaroodhaani maayayaa.

61. O Arjuna, God who is seated in the heart of all beings, causes all beings to revolve by His Maya, as if they are mounted on a machine.

तमेव शरणं गच्छ सर्वभावेन भारत ।
तत्प्रसादात्परां शान्तिं स्थानं प्राप्स्यसि शाश्वतम्

Tameva sharanam gaccha sarvabhaavena bhaarata;
Tatprasaadaatparaam shantim sthaanam praapsyasi shaashwatam.

62. O Bharata, take refuge in Him alone with all your being. By the Grace of God you will attain supreme peace and supreme abode.

इति ते ज्ञानमाख्यातं गुह्याद्गुह्यतरं मया ।
विमृश्यैतदशेषेण यथेच्छसि तथा कुरु ॥६३॥

Iti te jnaanamaakhyaatam guhyaadguhyataram mayaa;
Vimrishyaitadasheshena yathechchasi tathaa kuru.

63. Thus I have imparted to you the wisdom that is the secret of all secrets, do you reflect upon this fully, and then, do as you like.

सर्वगुह्यतमं भूयः शृणु मे परमं वचः ।
इष्टोऽसि मे दृढमिति ततो वक्ष्यामि ते हितम् ॥

Sarvaguhyatamam bhooyah shrinu me paramam vachah;
Ishtosi me dridhamiti tato vakshyaami te hitam.

64. Again listen to My supreme word, the most secret of all; you are dearly beloved of Me, therefore, I shall speak what is good for you.

मन्मना भव मद्भक्तो मद्याजी मां नमस्कुरु ।
मामेवैष्यसि सत्यं ते प्रतिजाने प्रियोऽसि मे ॥

Manmanaa bhava madbhakto madyaajee maam namaskuru;
Mamevaishyasi satyam te pratijaane priyo'si me.

65. Fix your mind on Me, be devoted to Me, sacrifice to Me, offer adorations to Me; you will indeed attain Me—this I truly promise to you, because you are my dearly beloved.

सर्वधर्मान्परित्यज्य मामेकं शरणं व्रज ।
अहं त्वा सर्वपापेभ्यो मोक्षयिष्यामि मा शुचः ॥

Sarvadharmaan parityajya maamekam sharanam vraja;
Aham twaa sarvapaapebhyo mokshayishyaami maa shuchah.

66. Having renounced all Dharmas (involvement in duties and limitations), take refuge in Me alone. I will verily free you of all sins, do not grieve.

इदं ते नातपस्काय नाभक्ताय कदाचन ।
न चाशुश्रूषवे वाच्यं न च मां योऽभ्यसूयति ॥

Idam te naatapaskaaya naabhaktaaya kadaachana;
Na chaashushrooshave vaachyam na cha maam yobhyasooyati.

67. This teaching of Mine should not be imparted by you to one who does not practise austerity, who is not My devotee, who does not render service (to Me), and who finds fault with Me.

य इमं परमं गुह्यं मद्भक्तेष्वभिधास्यति ।
भक्तिं मयि परां कृत्वा मामेवैष्यत्यसंशयः ॥६८॥

Ya imam paramam guhyam madbhakteshvabhidhaasyati;
Bhaktim mayi paraam kritwaa maamevaishyatyasamshayah.

68. He who will enable My devotees to understand the teachings of this profound scripture, he, the best of My devotees, will doubtless attain Me.

न च तस्मान्मनुष्येषु कश्चिन्मे प्रियकृत्तमः ।
भविता न च मे तस्मादन्यः प्रियतरो भुवि ।६९।

Na cha tasmaanmanushyeshu kashchinme priyakrittamah;
Bhavitaa na cha me tasmaadanyah priyataro bhuvi.

69. Better than Him there is none who could render a dearer service to Me, nor will there be in this world anyone dearer than him.

अध्येष्यते च य इमं धर्म्यं संवादमावयोः ।
ज्ञानयज्ञेन तेनाहमिष्टः स्यामिति मे मतिः।।७०।।

Adhyeshyate cha ya imam dharmyam samvaadamaavayoh;
Jnaanayajnena tenaahamishtah syaamiti me matih.

70. He who will study this dialogue of Ours abounding in Dharma, by him I will be worshipped by the sacrifice of wisdom, such is My view.

श्रद्धावाननसूयश्च शृणुयादपि यो नरः ।
सोऽपि मुक्तः शुभाँल्लोकान्प्राप्नुयात्पुण्यकर्मणाम्

Shraddhaavaananasooyashcha srinuyaadapi yo narah;
So'pi muktah shubhaanlokaanpraapnuyaatpunyakarmanaam.

71. Those who are endowed with faith and free of jealousy, they even on hearing this will become free of sins, and will attain to the higher worlds—those that are attained by men of meritorious deeds.

कच्चिदेतच्छ्रुतं पार्थ त्वयैकाग्रेण चेतसा ।
कच्चिदज्ञानसंमोहः प्रनष्टस्ते धनंजय ॥७२॥

Kacchidetacchrutam paartha twayaikaagrena chetasaa;
Kacchidajnaanasammohah pranashtaste dhananjaya.

72. O Arjuna, have you listened to My teachings with one-pointed concentration. O conqueror of wealth, is your delusion born of ignorance destroyed?

अर्जुन उवाच

नष्टो मोहः स्मृतिर्लब्धा त्वत्प्रसादान्मयाच्युत ।
स्थितोऽस्मि गतसन्देहः करिष्ये वचनं तव ।।७३।।

Arjuna uvaacha
Nashto mohah smritirlabdhaa twatprasaadaanmayaachyuta;
Sthito'smi gatasandehah karishye vachanam tava.

73. Arjuna said: O Invincible Lord, my delusion is gone, I have regained my memory by Your Grace, I am now established (in wisdom), my doubts have fled, I will do as you command.

संजय उवाच

इत्यहं वासुदेवस्य पार्थस्य च महात्मनः ।
संवादमिममश्रौषमद्भुतं रोमहर्षणम् ।।७४।।

Sanjaya uvaacha
Ityaham vaasudevasya paarthasya cha mahaatmanah;
Samvaadamimamashraushamadbhutam romaharshanam.

74. Sanjaya said: Thus have I heard the wondrous dialogue between the Divine Vasudeva and the great-souled Arjuna, which causes my hair to stand on end.

व्यासप्रसादाच्छुतवानेतद्गुह्यमहं   परम् ।
योगं योगेश्वरात्कृष्णात्साक्षात्कथयतः स्वयम् ॥

Vyaasaprasaadaacchrutavaanetadguhyamaham param;
Yogam yogeshwaraat krishnaat saakshaat kathayatah swayam.

75. By the Grace of Sage Vyasa, I have heard this
supremely secret Yoga given by Lord Krishna— the Lord
of Yoga Himself (to Arjuna).

राजन्संस्मृत्य संस्मृत्य संवादमिममद्भुतम् ।
केशवार्जुनयोः पुण्यं हृष्यामि च मुहुर्मुहुः ॥७६॥

Raajan samsmritya samsmritya samvaadamimamadbhutam;
Keshavaarjunayoh punyam hrishyaami cha muhurmuhuh.

76. O King, remembering again and again the wondrous
and purifying dialogue between Lord Krishna and Arjuna,
I experience repeated thrill of joy.

तच्च संस्मृत्य संस्मृत्य रूपमत्यद्भुतं हरेः ।
विस्मयो मे महान्राजन्हृष्यामि च पुनः पुनः ॥

Taccha samsmritya samsmritya roopamatyadbhutam hareh;
Vismayo me mahaan raajan hrishyaami cha punah punah.

77. O King, remembering again and again that supremely wondrous form of Hari (Lord Krishna), great is my
astonishment, and I rejoice again and again.

यत्र योगेश्वरः कृष्णो यत्र पार्थो धनुर्धरः ।
तत्र श्रीर्विजयो भूतिर्ध्रुवा नीतिर्मतिर्मम ॥७८॥

Yatra Yogeshwarah krishno yatra paartho dhanurdharah;
Tatra shreervijayo bhootirdhruvaa neetirmatirmama.

78. Wherever there is Krishna, the Lord of Yoga, and
wherever there is Partha (Arjuna), the wielder of the bow,
there will indeed abide, prosperity, victory, glory and
righteousness; this is my firm conviction.

ॐ तत्सदिति श्रीमद्भगवद्गीतासूपनिषत्सु ब्रह्मविद्यायां
योगशास्त्रे श्रीकृष्णार्जुनसंवादे मोक्षसंन्यासयोगो
नामाष्टादशोऽध्यायः ॥ १८ ॥

*Hari om tat sat iti srimad bhagavad gitaasoopanishatsu
brahmavidyaayaam yogashaastre sri krishnaarjunasamvaade
mokshasannyaasyogo naama ashtaadasho'dhyaayah.*

Om Tat Sat.
Thus, in the Upanishad of the Bhagavad Gita,
the knowledge of Supreme Brahman, the scripture of Yoga,
the dialogue between Sri Krishna and Arjuna,
ends the eighteenth chapter entitled,
"The Yoga of Liberation through Renunciation."

Om Shantih Shantih Shantih

Swami Jyotirmayananda

About Swami Jyotirmayananda
and his Ashram

Swami Jyotirmayananda is well-recognized as the foremost proponent of Integral Yoga, a way of life and thought that synthesizes the various aspects of the ancient Yoga tradition into a comprehensive plan of personality integration.

Swami Jyotirmayananda has brought inspiration to thousands world-wide, yet still maintains an intimate setting at his main Ashram in Miami. A priviledged few have the honor of actually studying and working under the direct guidance of Swamiji.

Both the Yoga Research Foundation and the main Ashram lie in the southwest section of Miami, two minutes from the University of Miami and 15 minutes from the Miami International Airport. The Yoga Research Foundation is located in a commercial area, easily accessible from anywhere in the county. In addition to the lecture hall, the Foundation also houses a bookshop, offices, warehouse, press, computer and publication facilities.

The main Ashram is on a two and a half acre plot surrounded by trees and exotic plants, reminiscent of a forest hermitage such as those used by the ancient Sages. Adjoining are subsidiary Ashrams that house student/residents and Foundation guests. The grounds are picturesque, with tall green eucaliptus trees swaying with freedom in the winds, mango blooms spreading their aroma of sublimity, birds singing a song of eternal joy, and a lake of lotus blooms reflecting the expansion of the Heavens. Surpassing them all, however, is the holy presence of Sage Swami Jyotirmayananda that fills the atmosphere with a silent message powerful enough to change the very destiny of mankind.

In such an environment, the soul is nurtured and nourished, allowing for a total education and evolution of one's Inner Self. With a Work/Study Scholarship, students are able to attend all classes conducted by Swamiji tuition-free. In return, students devote their talents and expertise to the Foundation's noble mission. Such opportunity is open to anybody who is devoted to the ideals of truth, non-violence and purity. If interested, write for more information.

More YRF Publications of Related Interest

by Swami Jyotirmayananda

Integral Yoga — A Primer Course $2.85
Yoga Can Change Your Life..........................4.99
Concentration and Meditation (cloth)...................9.50
Yoga Guide 2.99
Yoga Essays for Self Improvement 4.99
The Yoga of Divine Love—Narada Bhakti Sutras........4.99
Integral Yoga Today...............................2.50
The Mystery of the Soul (Katha Upanishad)............2.99
The Way to Liberation (Mahabharata), 2 Vols..........4.99
Yoga Exercises for Health and Happiness..............4.99
Death and Reincarnation (cloth)......................9.50
Raja Yoga — Study of Mind (cloth).....................9.50
Mantra, Kirtana, Yantra and Tantra 3.99
Mysticism of Hindu Gods and Goddesses 3.99
Beauty and Health through Yoga Relaxation 1.99
Yoga Quotations 3.99
Yoga Mystic Poems 2.99
Yoga Mystic Songs for Meditation, 7 Vols.
   by Swami Lalitananda.............................2.99
Yoga in Life — by Swami Lalitananda 2.99
Yoga Mystic Stories................................3.99
Yoga Stories and Parables 3.99
Raja Yoga Sutras..................................2.99
Yoga Wisdom of the Upanishads 4.99
Yoga Secrets of Psychic Powers 4.99
Jnana Yoga (Yoga Secrets of Wisdom) 1.99

Vedanta in Brief..3.99
Yoga Vasistha, 3 Vols.................................4.99
Yoga of Sex-sublimation, Truth and Non-violence......3.99
Applied Yoga (cloth)...................................9.50
Yoga of Perfection (Srimad Bhagavad Gita)............3.99
Yoga of Enlightenment (Gita—Chapter 18) 4.99
Waking, Dream and Deep Sleep.........................2.99

International Yoga Guide (monthly magazine), single issue... 1.50
Annual subscription to the International Yoga Guide... 15.00
Bound annual volume of the International Yoga Guide... 15.00

Cassette tapes available on all aspects of Yoga and Vedanta:
Exercises, Meditation, Raja, Bhakti and Jnana Yogas. Cassettes also available on practical topics, i.e., What is Love?,
How to Control the Mind, How to Remove Depression, Inspirational Music, etc. Home study course also available.

Daily classes held in Hatha Yoga, Bhakti Yoga, Meditation,
Yoga Vasistha, Bhagavad Gita, Upanishads, Panchadashi.
Work-study scholarships also available.

YOGA RESEARCH FOUNDATION
6111 SW 74th Avenue
Miami, Florida 33143
Tel: (305) 666-2006